The Future of the American Labor Movement

Coming at a time of profound change in the global conditions under which American organized labor exists, *The Future of the American Labor Movement* describes and analyzes labor's strategic alternatives. The analysis is broadly cast, taking into account ideas that range from the current European Social Dialogue to the methods of the nineteenth-century American Knights of Labor. There are a number of intriguing strategies, including worker ownership and labor capital strategies, that have potential for reviving the labor movement in the United States. This book demonstrates the necessity for a number of diverse strategies to be pursued simultaneously. For this to work, one has to think in terms of a broad *movement* of labor, consisting of diverse parts, held together by a clear idea of its purpose and a new structure. The treatment includes an introduction by Lynn Williams, former president of the United Steelworkers of America, and an interview with John Sweeney, president of the AFL-CIO.

Hoyt N. Wheeler is Professor of Management and Chair of the Management Department in the Moore School of Business at the University of South Carolina. He is a former president of the Industrial Relations Research Association and editor of its magazine *Perspectives on Work*. Professor Wheeler has served as a member of the faculties of the University of Minnesota and the University of Wyoming and has been a Visiting Professor and Visiting Scholar at the University of Paris I, Sorbonne. His teaching experience includes teaching graduate and undergraduate classes and noncredit labor education classes and programs, and he has won teaching awards at both the University of Minnesota and the University of South Carolina.

Professor Wheeler's publications include *Industrial Conflict: An Integrative Theory*, which was selected by *Choice* magazine as one of the Outstanding Academic Books of 1986; *Workplace Justice: Employment Justice in International Perspective* (coeditor); and articles in such journals as *Industrial Relations, Industrial and Labor Relations Review, Labor Studies Journal, British Journal of Industrial Relations, Personnel Psychology, Labor Law Journal*, and *The Annals of the American Academy of Political and Social Science*. He is a coauthor of the chapter on the United States in Bamber and Lansbury's widely translated text *International and Comparative Employment Relations*. Hoyt Wheeler is an attorney, having been a partner in the Charleston, West Virginia, law firm of Kay, Casto and Chaney, specializing in labor law. He is also a long-time arbitrator and a member of the National Academy of Arbitrators. He is active in the International Industrial Relations Association, serving as Rapporteur for its 1989 World Congress in Brussels, and is founding Co-Chair of its Study Group on Employee Rights and Industrial Justice.

The Future of the American Labor Movement

HOYT N. WHEELER

University of South Carolina

PUBLISHED BY THE PRESS SYNDICATE OF THE UNIVERSITY OF CAMBRIDGE
The Pitt Building, Trumpington Street, Cambridge, United Kingdom

CAMBRIDGE UNIVERSITY PRESS
The Edinburgh Building, Cambridge CB2 2RU, UK
40 West 20th Street, New York, NY 10011-4211, USA
477 Williamstown Road, Port Melbourne, VIC 3207, Australia
Ruiz de Alarcón 13, 28014 Madrid, Spain
Dock House, The Waterfront, Cape Town 8001, South Africa

http://www.cambridge.org

First published 2002

Printed in the United Kingdom at the University Press, Cambridge

Typeface Times Ten 9.75/12 pt.   *System* QuarkXPress [BTS]

A catalog record for this book is available from the British Library.

Library of Congress Cataloging in Publication Data Available

ISBN   0 521 81533 9   hardback
ISBN   0 521 89354 2   paperback

To Elizabeth Anne Dawson Scrivener Wheeler ("Liz"),
et le deuxième printemps.

If the reader discovers any reasoning in conflict with his own, let him not resort to abusive epithets in order to disprove what is said in these pages; rather . . . show wherein the error exists, that others may profit thereby.

Terence V. Powderly, Grand Master Workman, Noble Order of the Knights of Labor, 1889.

Contents

vii

Foreword

This is a point in the history of the American labor movement, and of labor movements throughout the world, when realities are changing rapidly – even cataclysmically. It has been said of such times that:

> ideas, economic and otherwise, grow out of ... experience. When one stage of society meshes smoothly into the next ... ideas are reshaped in a gradual and orderly fashion. In the case of a cataclysmic historical change ... events leap ahead and ideas lag behind (Bernstein 1960: 262).

At present, events have indeed leapt ahead of ideas regarding the labor movement. For labor to cope with new and powerful economic and social forces, it is necessary for its ideas to catch up. It is important that this happen, given that the labor movement is at the very heart of American democracy.

This book is an attempt to facilitate the American labor movement's catchup by identifying and analyzing ideas that offer some hope for it. As there is nothing new under the sun, almost none of the ideas put forward here are original in the sense that no one has ever thought of them before. Instead, they consist of a revival of old ideas, new combinations of ideas, changed emphases, and a restructuring of the ways that strategies are put together. Also, there is an attempt to figure out what is central to a labor movement and to suggest a new structure for it.

To the extent that this is a successful enterprise, its success is owed to the contributions of a large number of trade unionists and scholars. In Europe, in 1994, a round of European interviews began in Paris with Jerry Zellhoefer, European Representative, AFL-CIO; John Evans, General Secretary, Trade Union Advisory Council, Organization for Economic Cooperation and Development (OECD); and Dr. Ulrich Briefs, University of Bremen, Germany. In Antwerp, Belgium, there was an interview with Ferre Wyckmans, Adjunct General Secretary, LBC-NVK; and in Utrecht, the Netherlands, with Jan Peter van den Toren, Research Officer, CNV. In Brussels, it was David Foden, Research Officer, European Trade Union

Institute; Peter Coldrick, General Secretary, European Trade Union Confederation; and Jeff Bridgford, Director, European Trade Union College; and
attendance of a meeting of the Trade Union Regional Network and a discussion with its Executive Secretary, Joe Mitchell (Joe Mitchell contributed
ideas on other occasions as well). In London, there were interviews with
Gavin Laird, General Secretary, Amalgamated Engineering and Electrical
Union; and Mike Smith, Head of Press and Information, Trades Union Congress. In Geneva, the interviewees were Leon Lynch, Director of International Affairs, United Steelworkers of America; Jack Calamatta, Deputy
General Secretary, General Workers Union, Malta; Angelo Gennari,
Research Director, CISL, Italy; Peter Unterweger, Head of Automotive
Department, International Metalworkers Federation; Mona Hemmer, Inter-
national Secretary, AKAVA, Finland; Heli Puura, Jurist, SAK, Finland; Amaia
Betelu, International Representative, ELA, Basque Country, Spain; Tom Etty,
International Department, FNV, the Netherlands; Simon Steyne, Inter-
national Officer, Trades Union Congress (TUC), United Kingdom; Rene
Pizzaferri, International Officer, CGT-L, Luxembourg; Rosalynn Noonan,
Workers' Adviser, New Zealand Confederation of Trade Unions (NZCTU)
National Executive, New Zealand; and Dwight Justice, International Con-
federation of Free Trade Unions (ICFTU).

There were also a number of interviews in the United States. In
Washington, in 1997, at the AFL-CIO there were discussions with Bob Welsh,
Executive Assistant to the President; Jonathan Hiatt, General Counsel; Nancy
Mills, Acting Director, Center for Workplace Democracy; and Ron Blackwell,
Director of Corporate Affairs. In Washington, in 1997, there were also inter-
views with Gregory A. Humphrey, Executive Assistant to the President and
the Secretary Treasurer, American Federation of Teachers; Tom Woodruff,
Director of Organizing, Service Employees International Union; Frank
Hurt, President, and David B. Durkee, Executive Vice President, Bakery,
Confectionery, Tobacco Workers and Grain Millers International Union;
Ken Edwards, Research Director, International Brotherhood of Electrical
Workers; Evelyn Temple, Assistant to the President, and John Dunlop,
Director of Collective Bargaining/Compensation, National Education
Association; M. E. Nichols, Vice President, Communication Workers of
America; Bill Luddy, Administrative Assistant to the President, and Denny
Scott, Head, Industrial Department, United Brotherhood of Carpenters and
Joiners of America; and Richard M. Bank, Special Counsel to the General
President, and Paul Boldin, Research Director, International Brotherhood of
Teamsters, Chauffeurs, Warehousemen and Helpers of America.

In 1999 the following officials of the United Steelworkers of America were
interviewed in Pittsburgh: Richard Davis, Vice President for Administration;
Roy Murray, Director, Collective Bargaining Services Department; and Kim
Siegfried, Special Assistant to the Secretary Treasurer. Also in 1999, there was
a discussion with Charles Taylor, then State Coordinator, Carolina Alliance

for Fair Employment (CAFE), and in 2000 with Steve Henry, attorney, another of its founders. Last, and far from least, was a 2001 interview with AFL-CIO President John J. Sweeney.

I would like to thank M. E. Sharpe, Inc., publishers of *WorkingUSA* for publishing my paper on the Trade Union Regional Network (Wheeler 1999), and for permission to include material from it in this book (reprinted by permission from M. E. Sharpe, Inc., Armonk, NY 10514); and to thank the *Journal of the Law and Economics of Employee Ownership* for permission to use two figures developed by Chris Mackin and Fred Freundlich. I would also like to express my appreciation to Dean Jacques Rojot of the University of Paris I, Sorbonne, Werner Sengenberger of the International Institute of Labor Studies of the International Labour Organization, and Joe Ullman of the Riegel and Emory Center for Human Resources Research at the Moore School of Business at the University of South Carolina for their support and the financial support of their organizations. Professor Rojot and Professor John Addison of the Department of Economics, Moore School of Business, University of South Carolina, and my son, Jeffrey Wheeler of the National Labor Relations Board, were kind enough to read parts of this book and provide me with a number of very helpful comments. Priyanka Gupta, while a student in the University of South Carolina Master of Human Resources program, furnished valuable research assistance.

I am especially grateful for, and honored by, the introduction to this book written by Lynn Williams. Lynn is one of the true statesmen of the American labor movement whose vision, eloquence, and dedication have contributed immeasurably to there being a labor movement whose future can be studied.

Hoyt N. Wheeler
Columbia, South Carolina
September 1, 2001

Introduction

Lynn R. Williams, former President,
United Steelworkers of America

There is no subject of more compelling interest and concern to those who care about working people and their unions, than to consider the future of the American labor movement. In this volume Professor Wheeler presents us with a most thoughtful and comprehensive review and analysis of how the present difficult circumstances came to be, including an intriguing look at some historical precedents and an innovative, inclusive, and wide-ranging set of ideas and proposals about how a positive future might and indeed will unfold.

There can be no doubt that recent decades have been difficult for the American labor movement. The statistics are familiar, presented most frequently in terms of the decline in union density, that is, in the reduced percentage of eligible workers represented by unions, from a peak of 32.5 percent in 1953 to the present percentage of approximately 13.5 percent. Of course there are an array of subordinate statistics in and around these overall numbers showing the percentage of representation to be much higher in the public than the private sector; the enormous growth in the service sector outstripping in sheer volume labor's many effective organizing efforts with and among service workers; the decline of manufacturing and, therefore, much of labor's base; and the relative lack of unionization in the new economy.

Labor's fundamental explanation for these circumstances is management's vicious and unremitting hostility to the labor movement. This is expressed in word and deed by most private-sector employers when their workers attempt to organize a union, aided and abetted by egregiously inadequate labor laws, which have been destructively interpreted and applied to labor, during most of the last fifty years. One of the worst of many negative developments was an early court interpretation that permitted employers to permanently replace strikers with scabs, thereby undercutting the effectiveness of much strike action and in so doing denying American workers the most fundamental democratic right of all, the right to withdraw their labor. Although this was an early decision, it was not until the Reagan union-busting years of the eighties that this interpretation came into general use.

The impact of these and related developments has been to make the legally mandated unit-by-unit organizing approach exceedingly difficult. This is true particularly as employers have been permitted – ironically in the name of free speech – to keep their employees hostage for antiunion captive-audience meetings and one-on-one antiunion supervisory interviews and subject them to constant harassment when they attempt to exercise their "right" to organize. Fear of breaking what behavioral laws there are provides little constraint to employers' antiunion activities. The only remedies against employers are civil in nature and penalties are nonexistent. Justice is delayed so that, in many instances, the organizing effort has long been chilled by illegal employer interventions by the time any attempt at achieving justice has come to a conclusion.

There is both considerable research and considerable commonsense evidence for this explanation of the affairs that I have sketched out. Whenever the employer's ability to express hostility is constrained by contravening political power in the public sector, by neutrality clauses in collective agreements in the private sector, or by a tougher set of laws and practices constraining hostile acts by the employer (e.g., as by the National Mediation Board's administration of such matters in the transportation sector), the success rate of union-organizing campaigns is much higher. The percentage of union density within the jurisdiction of the National Mediation Board, for example, is much closer to the international norms for such representation that exist in most developed industrial democracies.

One of the great disappointments of the last half-century has been the utter failure of the business establishment to support or even, with rare exceptions, to give expression to the importance of a free, strong labor movement as a foundation stone of democracy. There was a time and place in the last century, in Europe immediately after World War II, when farsighted leaders, including some American business, government, and political leaders, were instrumental not only in insisting that the labor movement be rebuilt immediately as a bulwark against Nazism, but also in inventing new institutions, such as the iron and steel community and its codetermination, among whose purposes was to guarantee labor a place at the tables of power in economic decision making. This is an idea and approach that has persevered across Europe ever since. The American labor movement, however, in its organizing efforts has faced unremitting hostility at home, whatever American representatives may have done at an earlier time in Europe. Also when establishing North American satellites many European companies have employed American antiunion tactics even when codetermination works perfectly well in their company in their home country.

In this book, Professor Wheeler conducts a thorough, detailed, wide-ranging investigation and discussion both about how the present circumstances came to be and about what should, can, and must be done to change them. He examines the "enabling conditions" that make it possible for a labor movement to develop. Four of these conditions have to do with the workers' perceptions of themselves, their work, their fellow workers, and the role of collective bargaining; the others have to do with the level of employer opposition and the level of government support. It seems clear that no broadly representative labor movement, in terms of the percentage of the eligible workforce it represents, exists in the world without either the support of effective laws, as in Europe or as in America before the laws' deterioration, or a societal understanding of the movement's importance, as in Great Britain before the Thatcher government and its attack on their traditional social contract.

A most interesting aspect of the book is the taxonomy of union styles or types that are used both to enrich our understanding of the labor movement and also as an analytic tool for thinking about how to proceed into the future. In this, Professor Wheeler moves far beyond the traditional social versus business unionism dichotomy. They include Pure and Simple Unionism, by which is meant unionism that is straightforwardly preoccupied with direct union action in the collective bargaining arena as the principal mechanism for pursuing its members' interests. He discusses Cooperationist Unionism, which includes the worker-participation activities of the last twenty years, with some concern that such activities make it more difficult to maintain labor's broader social vision. He includes Militant Radical Unionism with its zeal to build a new society, as exemplified by the Industrial Workers of the World (IWW), rather than be embroiled in the existing society as collective bargaining inevitably requires. There is also, among others and one of the most important, Social Democratic Unionism, which attempts to achieve many of the unions' objectives through political and government action but involves itself in collective bargaining as well. The author uses this taxonomy as an excellent tool for analysis and an aid to understanding, not as a means of rigid categorization. Different unions and labor movements exemplify different categories, syntheses, and combinations.

The role of globalization is not neglected in the analysis. The author sees it, in combination with the technological advances, as creating a world of customization that has destroyed America's traditional mass production advantage, resulting in stagnant or declining wages for our production workers but relatively high wages for those who enjoy a skill match with the high-tech jobs of the new economy. For the labor movement, these developments, along with the rise of the service sector, the increases in immigration, and the changing role of women in the workplace, have all represented challenges to traditional organizing and bargaining methods and to living successfully with a law structured in earlier and different times.

These worldwide changes have also seen the introduction of lean production systems from Japan, autonomous work groups from Sweden, and other worker-involvement high-performance systems. As mentioned previously, one of the concerns is whether these really are compatible with strong, democratic trade unionism. They certainly have a potential to structure workers away from labor's broader concerns into a more enterprise-based way of considering the world, but that is not the only possible or necessary result. They are indeed powerful tools that can be very helpful in maintaining a productive manufacturing base in America and that can be focused on the more general needs of an industry, a region, or the country, not simply on the needs of one enterprise. They also have the advantage of helping unionists to become much more fully informed and aware of all that is happening around them, which can in turn result in the exercise of greater power and solidarity, flowing from a deeper base of knowledge and understanding.

Although Professor Wheeler discusses the European movement as little involved in Cooperationist approaches and moving slightly away from the Social Democratic mode to something more akin to the categorization of Pure and Simple – meaning in this context a greater focus on direct collective-bargaining solutions – there is also the possibility that the fundamentals of a Cooperationist system have been in place for so long, in the form of codetermination mechanisms, that they are simply part of the atmosphere, part of the way in which the labor movement functions as it moves on to incorporate other approaches as well.

Praiseworthy note is made of the enormous variety of strategies, tactics, and approaches with which the American labor movement is involved, both as a result of its own programs and of the ideas that sympathizers and other activists around it propose or in which they become engaged. Thus there are discussions of the home-care campaign in Los Angeles; the importance of work and family issues; the necessity for more imaginative approaches to white-collar organizing; associational unionism and the need to accommodate the needs and concerns of professionals; and the AFL-CIO's Voice@Work program, which focuses on the violations of the right to organize in our society. I don't mean this to be an exhaustive list, only to indicate the variety of the subject matter. I don't think there is anything happening, or in the contemplation stage, that is not given consideration by our author.

Along the way, two key approaches are presented as being less utilized than seems to be the case to me. One is the corporate or comprehensive campaign idea, which the author suggests is not being used as much as it was. My sense, possibly distorted by the experience of my own union, is that the corporate campaign does not have as high a profile as before, precisely because it has become a much more normal element in the way in which the labor movement carries out its responsibilities. Certainly in the Steelworkers, in the AFL-CIO, and, I believe, in many other affiliates, the process of conducting corporate campaigns has been institutionalized so that it is an essential element in coping with any critical and difficult collective-bargaining situation.

Similarly, Professor Wheeler is somewhat dubious about the extent to which an international strategy is becoming significant in our collective bargaining. Again, the reality is difficult to determine with any precision. Obviously, with internationally diversified companies a great deal of collective bargaining occurs without reference to what the company's activities may be in other countries. However, there is a great deal more international information sharing than ever before, for example through databases maintained by international trade secretariats, and a great deal more communication through both formal channels and informal, person-to-person contact facilitated by today's technologies. Certainly, again referring to experiences with my union, the international circumstances and potential for influence are routinely examined in any difficult collective-bargaining situation.

This book includes some very interesting and pertinent historical material, particularly with regard to the goals and style of the Knights of Labor. It is fascinating to contemplate the reach of the Knights around the developed world in their all too brief period of dramatic growth and support. One of the principal mechanisms was their assemblies, which provided a gathering place for collective political and social action, not simply for trade unionists but for like-minded individuals and groups across the community. It is proposed that the AFL-CIO might well assume a role as the instigating and umbrella organization for a modern version of this approach, particularly given the proliferation of political, environmental, safety and health, and other nongovernmental organizations (NGOs) with whom labor has many shared concerns.

Such an approach would also provide access to the various worker-rights groups to whom the author pays considerable attention. There are a multitude of these groups, such as the Carolina Alliance for Fair Employment (CAFE) organization in the Southeast that Professor Wheeler emphasizes, particularly in areas where organizing is especially difficult, which struggle to help workers have some voice and some impact. Frequently their role has been to support organizing campaigns in which unions are involved; sometimes they provide the only voice that is available and can enable the workers to survive the antiunion activities of the employers.

Another of the author's key concerns is to consider various ways by which the hostility of employers can be minimized. Considerable hope, in this regard, is expressed regarding the growth of employee ownership. Worker-owners, in union settings in which democratic worker-owner rights such as pass-through voting and Board of Director membership have been established, can clearly ensure there is no antiunion bias. Also presented are ways by which the issue of employer hostility might be finessed, such as using a Cooperationist approach, or a focus on economic development, as a means of affirming that unions are part of the solution, not of the problem. I remain concerned that such approaches, although helpful, are not enough. What American workers must endure in seeking representation is simply unconscionable. I don't believe the labor movement or its friends can rest until a way is found for workers in America who wish to bargain collectively to have free and unimpeded access to the exercise of that fundamental right. In no way, of course, does this excuse the labor movement from pursuing all the changes, reforms, strategies, and tactics that it must on its own behalf. It is simply that our society must pay much greater attention to what is decent, fair, and consistent with the democratic values that we espouse.

The discussion of Social Democratic Unionism, particularly in relation to developments in Europe, has important implications for the future. European unions are seen to be emphasizing direct-action Pure and Simple trade-union approaches to a greater extent than before, mentioning in that regard the metalworkers' achievement of a reduced thirty-five-hour workweek through collective bargaining rather than by legislative action. Concurrently, however, one of the most dynamic elements on the European scene is the mandating of works councils across borders. This is the single strongest push in the direction of international collective bargaining, or, more accurately, international collective action concerning workers' rights and representation that is being undertaken anywhere throughout the world. This development was very much the result of initiatives taken by the European Commission under the leadership of Jacques Delors, certainly with trade-union advocacy, encouragement, and support.

Attention is given to the increasing importance of regional developments, using as particular examples the Trade Union Regional Network (TURN) in Europe, with its emphasis on economic development and worker training, and the development of the Heartland Project in the United States, a union-sponsored fund for investment and economic development. One of the interesting aspects of TURN has been that it functions through the direct networking of local unions across Europe, not through the national organizations. One of the regrettable developments is that support funding from the European Commission ran out in 1996. Despite this fact TURN continues to function.

The importance of labor intellectuals in contributing to a positive change in labors' circumstances is also considered. The role of intellectuals in making labors' case and providing articulate and effective support for working people and their needs is indeed an honorable one. One of the most encouraging developments through these difficult years has been the amount of energy and talent that is coming into the movement from students, recruited often by the AFL-CIO's Organizing Institute, as they join in labors' struggles.

A critically important focus of the prescription for the future is that the labor movement should have its commitment to democracy in all its facets – dignity, voice, freedom, equality – at the center of its program.

My hope is that in this introduction I have communicated some sense of the breadth and the depth of Professor Wheeler's work. He demonstrates on every page a profound understanding of the American labor movement, its roots, its significance, and its concerns, along with a sympathetic, informed, and positive commitment to its future. We can all learn a great deal from the insights that have been the result of the diligence of his scholarship and the breadth of his experience.

ONE

A Future for the American Labor Movement?

That so long as man shall live and have his being, so long as there shall dwell in the human heart a desire for something better and nobler, so long as there is in the human mind the germ of the belief in human justice and human liberty, so long as there is in the whole makeup of man a desire to be a brother to his fellow-man, so long will there be a labor movement.

Samuel Gompers, President, American Federation of Labor, 1904

As we begin the twenty-first century, many of the institutions of Western society are undergoing dramatic change. The labor movement in the United States has been especially affected by powerful economic and social forces. The threshold question in thinking about this is whether there is a future for the labor movement in advanced postindustrial societies. Is the very idea of a labor movement a viable one for the twenty-first century? This is an important question, given the contributions of trade unions and their allies to the development and maintenance of democracy, both in America's workplace and in its political system.

Even in this time of great change, the labor movement remains, in essence, what it has always been – a set of organizations and individuals that function to serve the rights and interests of workers. So long as the phenomenon of employment exists it would seem that there would be a social need, and worker demand, for organized instruments of economic and social power for those who are employed by others. Collective action by workers in defense of their interests is a natural and necessary response to the tensions of employment (Gompers 1919; Barbash 1984). This being the case, the questions then become the degree of power that the labor movement will have and the forms that it will take. However, as we shall see, even the basic premise that it will continue to exist is currently being called into question.

1

WHERE ARE WE, HOW DID WE GET THERE,
AND WHERE ARE WE GOING?

It is clear that the American labor movement is in trouble. In 2000, the percentage of the labor force unionized ("union density") in the United States was 13.5 percent. In private industry, it stood at 9 percent, roughly what it was prior to the great surge of unionization in the 1930s. Among government employees American unions are doing much better, with 37.5 percent of them being union members in 2000 (Bureau of Labor Statistics 2001). The reasons for this difference are not entirely clear, but it is likely that this is at least in part attributable to the lower level of management resistance to unions in the public sector.

In 2000, total union membership declined by 219,000, after going up by 300,000 in 1999 (Bureau of National Affairs 2000c, 2001a; Bureau of Labor Statistics 2001). Total union membership at the beginning of 2001 stood at 16.3 million (Bureau of Labor Statistics 2001). Organized labor's decline in density has been rather steady since 1953, when the proportion of the labor force unionized stood at 32.5 percent (Troy and Sheflin 1985). Despite often heroic efforts on the part of dedicated American trade unionists over the years, the decline in union density has not been arrested.

Although American unionists have recently paid a great deal of attention to organizing new members, the results of these efforts have been mixed. On the one hand, in 1999 they managed to organize 74,000 home health-care workers in California, and have had some other significant victories in the last few years. On the other hand, in 2000 they were involved in only 2,849 representation elections, compared to 3,114 in 1999 and 3,229 in 1998. Their win rate did increase slightly from 51.3 percent in 1999 to 52.1 percent in 2000 (Bureau of National Affairs 2001b). These secret ballot elections, conducted by the National Labor Relations Board (NLRB), in which workers choose whether or not they want a union, have historically been the chief avenue for gaining new members. However, in recent years, there has been a great deal of organizing outside of the NLRB processes. Accordingly, their successes in organizing are not entirely captured by looking at election results.

Union performance has improved in decertification elections, in which workers vote on whether to get rid of their union. There were fewer in 1999 than in 1998 (373 compared to 475), and fewer in the first six months of 2000 compared to the same period in 1999 (188 compared to 199) (Bureau of National Affairs 2000e). Also, the union win rate increased between 1998 and 1999 (about 36 percent compared to about 30 percent in 1998) (Bureau of National Affairs 2000c).

In the last three years there has been some increase in union organizing activity in union-resistant regions of the country. This has included the author's home state of South Carolina, which is the second lowest in union density (about 3.5 percent). Yet, as elsewhere, this has not resulted in a significant increase in union density (Thomas 2000).

Are we to conclude from this experience that organized labor is doomed to disappear, or to permanently represent only a tiny proportion of the American workforce, as some writers suggest? Why did unions decline? Is this a temporary setback from which they will recover, or a permanent shift away from collective organizations of workers? Will the American labor movement assume new forms as we move into a new century? What are the strategies and tactics that might enhance its chances for future success?

Causes of Union Decline

There are numerous explanations for how American labor came to its present low state. According to some, there has been a failure on the part of unions to expend sufficient resources on organizing new members. Some scholarly studies have identified particular tactics that seem to be more effective than others (Bronfenbrenner and Juravich 1997). Presumably, then, their failure to organize in part may be attributable to not expending sufficient effort and using the wrong tactics.

Another possible cause of union decline is increased employer opposition, along with labor laws that facilitate it (Freeman 1988). Although, as William Gould, former chair of the NLRB has argued, "the law can be a convenient scapegoat" (1993: 47), the American legal system has clearly permitted employers to vigorously oppose unions, and they have done this with devastating effects upon the labor movement. Based upon some very compelling testimony from workers and union organizers, the Federal Commission on the Future of Labor-Management Relations, or Dunlop Commission, found that the law is woefully lacking in protections for workers who wish to organize (Commission on the Future of Labor-Management Relations 1994). An international organization, Human Rights Watch, recently declared that the American legal system is so deficient as to violate the basic human rights of workers to organize and bargain collectively (Bureau of National Affairs 2000d). Indeed, one could argue that looking at union and worker actions to explain the lowering of union density in the United States is an exercise in blaming the victim. An organized attack on labor, mounted by a powerful antiunion movement in the business community and tolerated by the law, is perhaps the most parsimonious explanation of this phenomenon.

An interesting analysis by Michael Goldfield (1987) argues that labor's decline is rooted in weaknesses that arose during its years of power (mid-1930s to mid-1950s). These include the regionalization of unions that led to national political weakness, destruction of rank-and-file democracy, bureaucratization of unions, the elimination of radical oppositions in unions, and unions becoming subordinate to the Democratic Party in politics.

Clearly, any explanation of union decline would have to include the economic environment. The transition of the American economy from being dominated by relatively highly unionized manufacturing employment to one dominated by lightly unionized service employment is important (Troy 1990, 1999). The increased diversity of the workforce has no doubt lessened the solidarity that is necessary for collective action. Also of obvious importance is the increased competitiveness of both domestic and global product markets, and the related transfer of production to overseas locations and to the nonunion southern and western regions of the United States (Edwards 1986). These factors will be discussed in more detail in Chapter 2. The crucial question, of course, is whether these conditions, which do not appear to be likely to change in the near future, will permanently consign organized labor to only marginal significance in the American economy and society, or leave room for the growth of a renewed and enlarged labor movement.

The Future

There is, of course, considerable disagreement about the future of the American labor movement. The arguments sound pretty much the same as they did in earlier eras. There are arguments by management groups that unions are obsolete and serve no function in a modern economy. Each generation of managers and their apologists predictably comes to the conclusion that there was some time in the distant past when unions might have been useful, but that they have been rendered useless by current conditions and enlightened managers. There are counterarguments from unionists that the employment relationship by definition requires adversarial representation of an independent worker interest in order to avoid exploitation of workers by capitalists and their representatives. These arguments, and others, make for an interesting and lively literature on the general subject of the future of unions.

The View that Unions are Dead

Perhaps the best-reasoned statement of the view that unions have virtually no favorable prospects appears in a recent book by a long-time student of trends in unionization, Leo Troy (1999). Troy argues that the collective system of worker representation has in fact already been replaced by an "individual system of employee representation" (p. 195). According to him, this is the result of a "structural transformation of the labor market" (p. 196). This occurred because of (1) the passage of the Taft-Hartley Act in 1947, which gave workers the right not to belong to a union; (2) the rise of service employment; and (3) growing domestic and global competition. These conditions not only reinforced the longstanding employer aversion to unions, but also affected worker preferences. According to Troy, the end result is that unions are in a "twilight zone" from which they are not likely to emerge. They will stay at a union density of about 9 percent as we enter the twenty-first century and will not do better than this in the foreseeable future. He sees union efforts to change this as a "hopeless task" (p. 199).

Troy believes that the individual representation system will continue to be the dominant one because it is the one preferred by both managers and employees. He cites numerous surveys of employee sentiments that show a large majority of nonunion workers saying that they would not vote for a union. NLRB election results also support this conclusion. As he argues, a number of studies show that unions are associated with lower profitability, making management opposition to unions economically rational. There is also an explicit management philosophy that validates and makes sense of the nonunion preferences of managers. Modern human-resource management provides the mechanisms that make this work, and employee handbooks provide a system of governance.

Troy explains how the individual representation system works by focusing on the role of the supervisor in it. He argues that the individual representation system can and does include complaint procedures that provide "fair dealing and due process" (p. 118). He judges the same to be true for discipline procedures. He concludes that this system is superior in many respects to the collective representation system of unions.

There is a "third way" of nonunion forms of collective representation (Kaufman and Taras 1999) that is rejected by Troy. Kaufman (2000) argues that nonunion forms of employee representation were mistakenly outlawed by the Wagner Act in 1935. He and others have argued that collective mechanisms other than unions can effectively serve the interests of workers. In recent years there has been something of a movement toward organizations that resemble the old employer-dominated "company" unions of the 1920s and 1930s. These organizations currently suffer from the legal impediment of violating Section 8 (a) (2) of the National Labor Relations Act (NLRA). However, Republican members of Congress have made efforts to obtain passage of legislation such as the Team Act that would open the door for company unions. When the president is a Republican their chances of success are increased. If the Team Act were to pass, the option of sham unions would be available to employers. This form of union substitution would pose a threat to the future of unions if, as was the case historically, it were to be used as a union avoidance device.

A ground for pessimism that must be taken into account is the extreme degree to which American management is willing to resist unions. It is generally believed that there was a post–World War II understanding, a "labor accord," between unions and major corporations that unions would be tolerated by management. When the conditions that induced employers to participate in collective bargaining ended, there came a decline in their willingness to bargain with unions (Edwards and Podgursky 1986). Unions had come to have a negative effect on profitability because they needed to provide benefits and services that workers valued, but found it difficult to do this without putting unionized employers at a disadvantage relative to nonunion competitors (Hirsch 1991). This effect may have been exacerbated by the increased bargaining strength of unions in the highly capital-intensive, automated world of the modern factory, particularly those utilizing just-in-time inventory. In this setting the costs of strikes to employers are especially high (Poole 1981).

One is compelled to conclude that there is reason for unions to be concerned about the accuracy of the doomsayers' predictions for organized labor's future. Troy claims, paraphrasing a well-known political expression, that "It's the numbers, stupid" (Troy 1999: 199). The quantitative evidence shows that there is indeed a very steep mountain for unions to climb in order to regain the strength that they had at their height. As Troy argues, in order to regain their peak density of over 30 percent, they would need to hold on to their present membership and organize another twenty-five million new members. He asks whether anything similar to this result is likely to happen in the foreseeable future.

The View that the Unions will Rise Again

There has been no lack of writers willing to argue that unions will once again rise to a position of power and influence in American life. They base this conclusion on a wide variety of arguments.

Longstanding Arguments. To start with, it is clear that the situation of being in a weak position is not a new one for organized labor. Union declines have often prompted scholars to address the question of whether unions were dead. In the nineteenth century Richard T. Ely observed:

A reaction appears to have set in, and it is probable that for some time the power of organized labor will decrease; but a change will again come, and the unions and various associations will once more report an increasing membership. The progress of the labor movement may be compared to the incoming tide. Each wave advances a little further than the previous one; and he is the merest tyro in social science, and an ignoramus in the history of his country, who imagines that a permanent decline has overtaken organized labor (Ely 1886: 90).

Writing a century later, historian David Montgomery (1987) agrees with Ely. According to Montgomery, the story of American labor has never been one of either a "progressive ascent from oppression to securely established rights," or of being "irretrievably snuffed out by the consolidation of modern capitalism" (p. 7). Instead, its growth has been interrupted just when it seemed to be on the verge of permanent victory, and it has revived just when it seemed about to be overwhelmed by its enemies. According to him:

The taproot of its resilience has been the workers' daily experience and the solidarities nurtured by that experience, which have at best encompassed a lush variety of beliefs, loyalties, and activities within a common commitment to democratic direction of the country's economic and political life (p. 8).

Ely explains the ebb and flow of union membership as resulting from workers deserting unions during hard times, but then, when circumstances are more favorable, pouring back into the unions (Ely 1886). Montgomery (1980) argues that the social relations of production, while often changing over the last 150 years, have remained within boundaries that delineate "industrial capitalism" (p. 486). During this epoch, both technical knowledge and the power to make decisions have been systematically and increasingly monopolized by managers. Also, the decisions by management regarding production have remained based on the corporation's need for profit, not what is best for the community. Workers have had no choice but to submit to this arrangement as a price for being paid their wages.

Yet, we may now be in a unique time. Some observers believe that we are experiencing a sea change in the world of work that has changed workers' daily experiences; one that is comparable in magnitude to the shifting of the Western economies from farm to factory in the early twentieth century (Leone 1993; Thurow 1996). These forces are described in some detail in Chapter 2. They include the rise of the service sector; a highly disturbed global economy; and broad advances in technology, communications, and transportation.

With respect to this "postmodern" situation, a British scholar, John Kelly (1998), has delivered a penetrating critique of writings by economists and others who argue that there has been a shift in both the world and national economies and societies that necessarily dooms the labor movement. Kelly maintains that, "Contrary to postmodernist claims that the classical labour movement is in terminal decline, long wave theory suggests that it is more likely to be on the threshold of resurgence" (1998: 1). His prediction is that "the long period of employer and state counter-mobilization will not last. As the next long economic upswing gathers momentum then so too should the organization and mobilization of workers across the capitalist world" (p. 130).

Current Arguments. Not surprisingly, labor and its friends believe the current setbacks to be temporary, as Richard Ely and David Montgomery have argued was the case in the past. Douglas Fraser, former president of the United Automobile Workers (UAW), says,

In every single democracy in the world you will find a vibrant, vital labor movement. The reason is that in a democratic society, where you have a system of checks and balances, a labor movement is absolutely indispensable. . . . There will always be unions as long as there are bosses (quoted in Shostak 1991: 1).

Like Douglas Fraser, Shostak (1994) founds his hopes upon the necessity for society to have a counterweight to businesses' preference for following the market without regard to human costs. Tom Geoghegan, author of the challenging book, *Which Side Are You On? Trying to Be for Labor When It's Flat on Its Back* (1991), puts the case this way:

For twenty years we have tried to do without unions. And we can't. We can cry. We can curse. We can try out New Paradigms. And read books by New Democrats. But in the end it will do no good (Geoghegan 1994: 30).

Is there hope that the sea will indeed change so that it is once again favorable to unions? David Bonior, a Democratic congressman friendly to labor, says:

If you can show them [workers] that they can have the power to control their lives, that they can have a larger voice, and that, working together, people can make a difference, then that's it – end of story. You will unleash a power greater than any you could ever imagine. The labor movement can fulfill that role (Bonior 1997: 94).

John Sweeney, former president of the Service Employees International Union (SEIU) and now president of the AFL-CIO, exudes feelings of confidence and optimism about the labor movement's future. He is justifiably proud of his union's successes in organizing, and also recruiting successes across the American labor movement since he came to lead the federation. His theme of unions as "organizing organizations" has taken root, and is reflected in the actions of many unions. Nevertheless, he recognizes that, even in a year when labor is able to organize several hundreds of thousands of new workers, it can still fall behind the growth in the labor force (Swoboda 1997). Another prominent labor leader, Stephen Yokich, president of the UAW, argues that the current "shut up and settle for less" attitude of management will not be tolerated by workers, who will organize as a response to it (Yokich 1998).

Popular newspaper columnist David Broder has written optimistically about labor's future. He sees a ray of hope for unions in a significant victory among 74,000 home health-care workers in Los Angeles in 1999, and in the creative style of union leaders involved in this campaign – what he calls a "new unionism" that was involved in that victory. According to him, that success was based upon a new commitment to organization, outreach to immigrants, and alliances with a Republican governor and a Roman Catholic cardinal (Broder 2000).

Official documents of the American labor movement provide some important insights into the thinking of labor leaders about the future of the movement. One of the more interesting ones produced in recent years is *The New American Workplace: A Labor Perspective*, produced by the AFL-CIO Committee on the Evolution of Work and approved by the Executive Council of the AFL-CIO in 1994. This forward-looking report claims a place for labor in the new participative workplace, saying,

> The moment has come for unions to insist upon the right of workers to participate in shaping the work system under which they labor and to participate in the decisions that affect their working lives. Unions have an equally important role to play in assuring that workplace change plants strong roots. Unions provide a check on managers and owners who waver in their commitment to the new work order or who seek to revert to old ways (AFL-CIO 1994: 14).

In a report by the SEIU Committee on the Future, *Directions for a 21ˢᵗ Century Union* (SEIU undated), John Sweeney's home union declares that in order to succeed the union must "offer a compelling vision of change . . . project that vision forcefully and creatively . . . give workers a reason to join us in our struggles . . . [and] show workers that together, through their union, they can improve their own lives and help build a more just and equitable world" (p. 30).

These broad visions of the labor movement's functions are quite compelling. However, they may at least implicitly run afoul of the historical experience of unions in American society. That experience would seem to indicate that labor should tend to its knitting – deliver the bread and butter that workers want.

The basic logic of unions as collective-bargaining institutions remains a very powerful rationale for traditional American unionism. As Sidney and Beatrice Webb described it long ago, this logic has to do with substituting the stronger collective will of a number of workers for the weakness of the individual worker (Webb and Webb 1911). Both the work of the SEIU Committee on the Future and a relatively recent (1992) comprehensive survey of trade unionist and worker preferences show that they want from their union "a good contract; enforcement of the contract; and, the ability to keep their job long enough to collect on the contract" (Wilson Center for Public Research 1992: 2). Clearly, as indicated by David Montgomery's observations on the history of the American labor movement, the future of the labor movement must be rooted in the daily experiences and needs of workers. Reflecting these experiences and needs is what gives it enduring value.

Selig Perlman (1949) argued that unions should base their behavior on the psychology of workers (what he called "scarcity consciousness"), rather than the ideas of "intellectuals" about what workers *should* want. Perlman's "scarcity consciousness" may or may not reflect the psychology of modern workers. However, his fundamental insight – that unions must reflect the needs and be an organic creation by workers – is one of which labor needs to be constantly mindful.

Although the American legal system has largely failed to "encourage the practice and procedure of collective bargaining," one of the stated purposes of the NLRA, it is capable of responding somewhat to the needs of unions.

Since the appointment of members to the NLRB by President Clinton, there have been some improvements in the law from the perspective of unions. This has mainly occurred through changes in the effectiveness of the processes of the law during this period. More recently, however, there have been some breakthroughs in the substance of the law. Perhaps the most important of these is a recent NLRB decision (*M. C. Sturgis Inc.* 2000) holding that "supplied," that is temporary, workers can vote in the same election unit as permanent employees without this requiring the consent of both the temp agency and its client. This could significantly increase the chances of unions organizing these workers.

In sum, we see some general agreement in the literature about the situation in which the American labor movement finds itself. As to how it got there, there is less agreement. As to its prospects, we find pessimism among some scholars, as well as among organized labor's historic enemies. To the contrary, we find optimism among labor's officials and union-friendly scholars.

There are really two main questions about the future of the American labor movement. The first is whether it will be strong or weak. The second is what forms it will take. It seems to this writer that these questions are interrelated. That is, whether it will be strong or weak depends upon whether there are forms that, if adopted, would lead to a strong labor movement. It also depends on the likelihood that the labor movement will adopt those forms and strategies that have the potential to lead it to a position of strength.

One approach to the question of what forms it will take is to identify, analyze, and evaluate current union strategies. It is believed that the fundamentally pragmatic nature of American unions (Taft 1964) will lead them to adopt the forms and strategies that prove to work out in practice. It is expected, then, that those forms and strategies that meet this test will continue to be utilized, and the future American labor movement will be shaped accordingly.

This presupposes that the American labor movement will experiment with various approaches in the first place. This is not very difficult to conclude. Even a casual observation of their behavior in the past decade or so indicates pretty clearly that American unions (as well as those in Western Europe) are quite innovative and will try out nearly anything that has a chance of being successful. This is aided considerably by the end of the Cold War and its attendant biases, which had caused traditional American unions to avoid anything that might have the slightest chance of forcing them to carry what has been called the "burden of socialism."

In the chapters that follow, labor movement strategies and tactics in both the United States and Western Europe will be identified, analyzed, and evaluated with reference to their potential for strengthening the American labor movement. At the end of the day, it is believed that we will find some promising avenues to a successful future for American labor.

However, before we look at the strategies and forms of the American labor movement it is necessary to consider the current environment of U.S. industrial relations. This environment poses both problems and opportunities for labor. Any analysis and evaluation of present or future strategies and forms must take environmental factors into account. This is a particularly compelling requirement in a time of great change in the environment. One of the fundamental questions with which this book must grapple is whether the ground upon which labor movements are built has changed so greatly that certain, or even all, forms of a labor movement have been rendered obsolete. Trade unions have conventionally, and correctly, been viewed as being primarily a protective response to environmental realities and management policies that are largely beyond their control (Barbash 1984). As Montgomery (1980) argues, it is the conditions of work and the workplace experience of workers that have allowed unions to rise again and again from the ashes of apparent defeat. But what if those conditions have changed so much that unions are no longer an appropriate response to workers' experience or, as is more likely, to make certain forms and strategies obsolete and others newly promising?

The phenomena observed and analyzed in this book are at several levels. First, there is the level of the current general economic, political, and social environment over which labor movements have little or no control. Forces such as globalization that are part of this environment generate tensions and contradictions to which trade unions and their allies must respond. Second, there are specific conditions, such as government support for unions, that enable the existence of a strong labor movement, over which labor may have some influence. Just like the forces in the general environment, these do not directly determine the strength of a labor movement. Unlike general environmental conditions they are susceptible to union power. Therefore it makes sense for union strategies and tactics to aim at changing these conditions to make them more favorable to unions. They influence the chances of more direct actions being successful. Third, there are the actions by labor, for example energetically organizing new members, that are under their control and also directly produce a stronger labor movement.

In the balance of this chapter, we will take a brief look at the general environmental conditions (these will be discussed in some depth in Chapter 2). This will be followed by a description of the enabling conditions. The enabling conditions constitute the first of two analytical frameworks that will be utilized to understand, analyze, and evaluate various labor movement forms, strategies, and tactics. Last, the second of these analytical frameworks – ideal types of unions – will be described.

A GLANCE AT THE CURRENT ENVIRONMENT

As was true at the beginning of the twentieth century, early in the twenty-first century the environment of employment relations is in a state of considerable change. In the United States we have witnessed the rise of competitive pressures on business to heights that are unprecedented in the twentieth century. International competition, deregulation, and the demands of the stock market for ever-increasing profits have all caused managers to cut labor costs, increase flexibility, and seek new ways to provide quality products at low prices (Capelli et al. 1997).

One effect of the new competitiveness is the focus on product quality and the resultant development of new forms of work organization. This is the well-publicized movement to teams and other participative mechanisms – what has been called the "new human resource technologies." What they have in common is that they attempt to extract from the employee the largest possible amount of knowledge, commitment, and energy, and in the process give individual employees increased influence over the processes of work (Appelbaum and Batt 1994; Cappelli et al. 1997).

The drive for flexibility and cost cutting has led to an increased casualization of labor. Involuntary part-time work has been on the increase. There has been an increase in temporary work. Contracting out work to owner-operators (independent contractors) instead of having it done within the employment relationship has also been on the rise (Commission on the Future of Labor-Management Relations 1994). Rather than cut wages for existing employees, firms cut their wage bill by contracting out work to other employers who pay low wages (Klaas and Ullman 1995). If capitalists organizing workers into armies for purposes of production created the conditions for these workers to organize for their own purposes (Marx and Engels 1848), the dispersal of these armies may have destroyed those conditions.

Another phenomenon that is of considerable importance for unions is the increasing diversity of the workforce. Workforce participation by women continues to rise. The workforce is increasingly non-White, with Hispanic workers growing as a proportion of the workforce. The proportion of foreign-born workers is high by recent historical standards and is expected to grow. The difficulty of building solidarity among such a diverse group of workers is apparent.

The New Deal model of industrial unionism was born and prospered under some very special conditions: (1) oligopoly in many product markets, with limited competition; (2) routinized work within narrow and unchanging job classifications; (3) full-time, permanent jobs (Osterman 1994); and (4) a relatively homogeneous workforce – largely male, semiskilled or unskilled, and with an historically high proportion of native-born workers. These conditions have largely evaporated.

Whatever particular causes one selects as accounting for the decline of American unions over the last several decades – employer hostility; changing industrial and geographic mix; unions failing to expend resources on organizing, etc. (Edwards 1986; Goldfield 1987; Freeman 1988; Troy 1990) – it would seem that part of the problem may be that the very ground upon which unions are based, the daily experiences of workers (Montgomery 1987), has shifted and a new set of circumstances has come into being.

To add to the problems of labor, particularly in organizing new members, the new, competitive, global economy has produced an American economy of both high employment and low inflation. What has been called the "great American job machine" has become the envy of the world. This experience supports the ideology of unregulated labor markets, which is popularly viewed as having helped to produce this result. As trade unions by definition attempt to moderate the effects of pure, unregulated markets, they contradict this ideology and may be seen as threatening this beneficial result. It may take a failure of this system such as the Great Depression to produce an intellectual environment conducive to collective worker organization. However, even without a system failure, there would seem to be ample room for criticizing the results and challenging the ideology.

In spite of the fact that the American economy is in a period of unparalleled growth, creating jobs and wealth at a virtually unprecedented rate, there is a "Great Divide" between the winners and losers in the new economy (Reich 2000). The economic expansion, for all its successes, has clearly left behind the working poor. Along with more wealthy persons than ever before, there has been an increase in the numbers (about five million people) and percentage (about 3 percent) of Americans whose incomes are below the poverty line (Bureau of National Affairs 2000a). Workers in such occupations as janitor, nursing-home worker, home health-care aide, and hospital orderly are making less in real terms than they were fifteen years ago (Reich 2000). Especially vulnerable are part-time and contingent workers. Part-time workers earn approximately half the total compensation of full-time workers. Average total compensation for unionized workers remains significantly greater than for nonunionized workers – $25.88 per hour compared to $19.07 per hour (Bureau of National Affairs 2000b). At least on its face, all of this would seem to suggest both a problem and a solution. The problem is an economically deprived economic class. At least one obvious solution is unionization.

Given these circumstances, which we will consider in greater depth in Chapter 2, what form of labor movement stands the greatest chance of success? That is, what form is most likely to create or support the conditions necessary for the survival and prospering of a labor movement? What form is most compatible with these environmental conditions?

FRAMEWORKS FOR ANALYSIS

This book will utilize two frameworks for understanding, analyzing, and evaluating union strategies and tactics. The first is a set of conditions that are believed to facilitate the existence of a strong labor movement – termed *enabling conditions*. As noted previously, these conditions are to some degree susceptible to union influence and are therefore useful targets for union strategy and tactics. The second framework is a taxonomy of ideal union types.

The set of enabling conditions is for testing the usefulness of the strategies and tactics, it being believed that strategies and tactics that contribute to the existence of these conditions are more likely to lead to a stronger labor movement than those that do not. Focusing on this set of indirect influences on labor-movement strengths provides a different and more complex perspective than limiting one's inquiry to the much-studied (see Wheeler and McClendon 1991) union actions to directly increase union membership. The taxonomy of ideal union types is intended to provide an understanding of the fundamental nature of various union strategies and tactics. This should also assist in our analysis.

The Enabling Conditions

What are the conditions subject to labor's influence that enable the existence of a strong labor movement? To begin with, we must ask what we are talking about when we speak of a labor movement. We can then systematically inquire as to what conditions enable it to be successful.

It is important to recognize that a labor movement consists of more than just labor unions. A labor movement can be defined as a set of institutions and persons that performs the function of advancing the interests of workers. In modern economies a worker is usually defined as a person who meets the common-law definition of *employee* (or the older term, *servant*). That is, someone else – an *employer* (or the older term, *master*) – has the right to control the manner in which the employee performs his or her work. In exchange, the employee is compensated financially (Commons 1968). This role differs from that of nonemployees who are paid to do work, primarily in that nonemployee "independent contractors" retain control of how their work is to be done. The idea of a labor movement is founded on the assumption that persons who occupy the role of worker have interests in common that are separate from, and may be at odds with, those of persons who act in other roles.

Labor movements have various components. Although in the United States it is customary to take only labor unions into account, even here there are other parts of a labor movement that are worth considering. These components include informal rank-and-file worker groups; worker organizations other than unions (both extraunion organizations such as the Carolina Alliance for Fair Employment [CAFE] and intraunion ones such as the Teamsters for a Democratic Union); political parties and politicians; and labor intellectuals. What counts is whether *some* component of a labor movement is capable of creating sufficient levels of the enabling conditions. As will be argued in Chapter 9, it would help if these components were organized in some systematic fashion.

For a labor movement, as we have defined it, to prosper in a society it must include these enabling conditions: (1) *workers perceptions that the work role*

*is important to their lives; (2) solidarity among workers; (3) workers percep-
tions that there are distinctive worker interests; (4) the benefits of collective
action at least equaling the costs; (5) employer opposition being held within
tolerable boundaries; and (6) government support, or at least tolerance* (see
Barbash 1984; Wheeler 1985).

For any movement to come into being and endure, the phenomena upon
which it focuses must be salient to its potential members. If work is not an
important activity in a society it is unlikely that human beings in the role of
worker will take the trouble to organize a movement around its concerns.
Workers should be more susceptible to unionization to the degree that they
see the work role as central to their lives.

Labor movements are fundamentally social and collective in nature. They
depend upon workers being willing to take risks and make sacrifices for the
common good of members of some group with which they identify. Persons
without feelings of affection or brotherhood for one another make poor candidates for participants in any social movement. Because it is work concerns
to which labor movements relate, the human beings in that role must have
feelings of some common bonds relating to work in order to form and
participate in a social movement of this type. Solidarity, it should be noted,
has two faces. There is the inward-looking face toward one's brothers and
sisters – "us." There is also the outward-looking face toward an outgroup of
supervisors, managers, or owners – "them" (see McClendon, Wheeler, and
Weikle 1998).

The necessity for a perception of distinctive worker interests flows naturally from the requirement of solidarity. It must be possible to identify the
"us" and the "them." That is, there must be salient differences between these
groups for a movement of one of them to make any sense.

Assuming some degree of rationality in human behavior, it is important
for workers to believe that the costs of collective action do not exceed its
benefits. It is believed that humans are predisposed toward collective action
and find it intrinsically fulfilling and satisfying. This is rooted in the basic in-
clinations of human beings as social animals (Midgley 1978). Therefore, it is
not necessary for collective action to produce a more favorable result than
individual action. However, if it has significantly greater costs or fewer
benefits, it cannot be expected to appeal to most of us.

Affecting the costs and benefits of collective action very significantly are
the attitudes of the owners of capital and their agents (professional managers)
toward it. Especially under modern conditions, capital is extremely powerful.
Therefore, a labor movement that cannot somehow gain at least a grudging
acceptance on the part of capital is likely to be doomed to failure.

Government is another major player in the industrial relations system. Its
support, or at least tolerance, would seem to be necessary for the survival of
a labor movement (Masters 1997). This is especially true where capital has
great power, as it does in all modern postindustrial societies. Government is

the only source of power in a union's environment that has the muscle to effectively aid it in its struggle with the forces of capital. It is a necessary ally.

For the most part, the enabling condition approach, and the conditions themselves, can be solidly grounded in industrial relations theory. Although this writer's own theoretical approach, labeled as the "integrative theory of industrial conflict" (Wheeler 1985; Wheeler and McClendon 1991), deals primarily with the processes by which workers form and join unions, this framework is of utility in thinking about enabling conditions. It starts out with deprivation leading to three possible paths to individuals supporting a union. If the deprivation is caused by the employer taking away existing rights or interests, the employee may move to an immediate readiness to take some action against the employer. If the deprivation arises from a gap coming to be perceived between the worker's achievements and expectations, and the worker is blocked (frustrated) in the attempt to close this gap, the worker will be ready to take action. With or without a deprivation, a worker may rationally calculate that it would be beneficial to take collective action, and thereby become ready to act.

In the Wheeler formulation, whether this action takes the form of unionization or other collective action depends on the presence of certain facilitating conditions and the absence of certain inhibiting conditions. The facilitating conditions are love, hope, and saliency. That is, they include solidarity among workers and a lack of identification with the employer; perceptions that the collective action will be instrumental in achieving the worker's expectations; and the idea of this collective action being made salient by leaders or particular events. The inhibiting conditions include a fear of punishment for taking collective action and a belief that unions are wrong. This theory has been tested empirically (Wheeler, McClendon, and Weikle 1994; Weikle, Wheeler, and McClendon 1998; McClendon, Wheeler, and Weikle 1998) with some success.

Some theorizing by John Kelly (1998) posits a useful framework for analyzing the environment in terms of its favorableness to unions. It is based upon mobilization theory and long-wave theory. Kelly posits deprivation, deriving from exploitation, as leading to collective worker action whenever the conditions are ripe. Although significantly differing in some fundamentals, Kelly's rethinking of industrial relations is similar in a number of respects to the Wheeler integrative theory of industrial conflict. The chief difference is that the Wheeler theory of industrial conflict has its "starter" in a particular view of human nature (which Kelly would no doubt reject), while Kelly's is founded on a Marxist analysis of exploitation of workers under capitalism. Both theories identify deprivation as a condition that may lead workers to form collective organizations, although they differ as to the source of the deprivation. Both consider worker deprivation to be a common condition.

In support of our enabling conditions, both the mobilization theory as articulated by Kelly (1998) and the integrative theory model of Wheeler

(1985) posit solidarity among workers and the workers perceptions that their interests are different from those of employers – the necessary "us" and "them." Both involve calculations of the costs and benefits of collective action. Both emphasize the importance of the employer's policies and actions to the occurrence of collective action by workers. Both recognize the importance of the role of government.

For the purposes of this book, the crucial point made by Kelly in his mobilization theory analysis is that exploitation is constantly present, and that differences in worker militancy and collective action can be explained in large part by differences in the various kinds of resources that they can mobilize to respond to this exploitation. These resources include worker perceptions of solidarity versus with their employers; the instrumentality of union organizing; oppression (or lack of it) by employers; and government repression or support.

The framework utilized in this book takes the view that *a labor movement is likely to be strong where the enabling conditions are favorable.* To the extent that a particular form of labor movement contributes to or reinforces these conditions, it improves its chances of success. Of course, some of these conditions are more readily amenable to labor's influence than others. While, for example, affecting employer opposition might be readily achieved by donning the mantle of more cooperative unionism, it might be well nigh impossible to affect strongly held worker perceptions that work is not central to their lives. However, it is believed that, unlike general environmental conditions, all of these conditions are at least to some degree susceptible to labor's influence.

Taxonomy of Ideal Types of Unions

One approach to considering a set of alternative strategies for the labor movement is to think in terms of ideal types of unionism. While this involves a high degree of simplification, it permits us to observe distinctive strategic thrusts more clearly than do more realistic, and therefore more complex, depictions of labor organization and structure.

The Logic of Ideal Types. The classification scheme utilized here is constructed on a functional basis. That is, it types union strategies by looking at the functions performed rather than on the more usual basis–structure (craft, industrial, etc.). This follows Hoxie (1921) in looking at "fairly distinct alternative forms of union action" that can serve "as guides to the essential character" of the organizations studied (p. 45). These types represent fundamentally different logics of unionism. Breaking them down into types is a statement that unions "from the practical standpoint cannot be interpreted, evaluated, and judged as a simple consistent whole, or as a succession of more or less accidental and temporary variations from a single normal type" (Hoxie 1921: 54).

The reasoning underlying Richard Hyman's much more recent (1996) classification of European trade unions is similar to Hoxie's. Hyman (1996) created categories called trade union "identities" (p. 63) that classify ideal types of unions on the basis of the key function and focus of union strategies. In a 2001 analysis of European trade unions, Hyman (2001) uses a somewhat different set of ideal types, "each of which is associated with a distinctive ideological orientation" (p. 1). Hyman (2001) agrees with Hoxie that there is no single agreed-upon definition of trade unions, arguing that "the meaning of trade unionism has historically been bitterly contested and today ... is a subject of doubt and disputation" (p. 165).

The Ideal Types. The ideal types of American unions identified in this book are: Pure and Simple Unionism, Militant Radical Unionism, Cooperationist Unionism, Social Democratic Unionism, and Reformist Unionism. Hoxie's types are labeled: "Business Unionism," "Uplift Unionism," "Revolutionary Unionism," and "Predatory Unionism" (1921: xvii). In 1996, Hyman adopts the categories of: "Guild," "Friendly Society," "Company Union," "Social Partner," and "Social Movement" (p. 70). In 2001, Hyman identifies three types of European unions: "business unionism," "social-democratic unionism," and "anti-capitalist opposition" (pp. 2–3).

As Hyman explains his 2001 version of ideal types: "first, unions are interest organizations with predominantly labour market functions; ... second, vehicles for raising workers' status in society more generally and hence advancing social justice; ... third, 'schools of war' in a struggle between labour and capital" (pp. 1–2). The first of these describes "business unionism," the second "trade unionism as a vehicle for social integration" that has as a "priority ... gradual improvement in social welfare and social cohesion"; and the third "a form of anti-capitalist opposition" with "a priority for militancy and socio-political mobilization ... to advance class interests" (pp. 2–3). These obviously match up pretty well with our categories of Pure and Simple Unionism, Social Democratic Unionism, and Militant Radical Unionism (the last two being more important in Europe than in the United States).

Hyman considers his three ideal types to make up a triangle, with the focus of each type being on a different point of this geometric representation of labor strategies. He sees the focus of business unionism as being the market, social democratic unionism as focusing on society, and anticapitalist opposition unions as focusing on class. Hyman argues that "a body resting on a single point is unstable" (p. 4). Accordingly, ideal types in their pure forms (confined to a single point) are quite rare, if they exist at all. According to Hyman, "in most cases, actually existing unions have tended to incline towards an often contradictory admixture of the three ideal types" (p. 4).

As with Hoxie's functional types, the ideal types used in this book "do not represent exactly and exclusively the ideas and activities of any particular union organization or group" (Hoxie 1921: 45). Instead, they are a mecha-

nism to assist us in recognizing various broad approaches that differ significantly. As Hyman says, "Ideal types are not the same as empirical instances;
no trade union movement can fully assume any of the identities outlined.
What is at issue is a question of priorities and strategic choices . . ." (Hyman
1996: 72). For example, a union that is predominately Pure and Simple would
be classified as such. If such a union adopted a Cooperationist strategy
such as labor-management "partnership" its leaders should recognize that it
is pursuing a different logic that may be in conflict with its basic strategic
orientation.

Pure and Simple Unionism. One ideal type is unions as they historically have
been in the United States. These organizations aim to serve the economic and
human dignity needs of their members that arise from work. Their concern
is chiefly with the welfare of their members rather than of the working class
or society as a whole. They have a strategic orientation that is fundamentally
economic, relying upon collective bargaining backed by strike power to
achieve their goals. The goals are largely bread and butter. Political action
is engaged in, but has as its principal aim the strengthening of collective
bargaining. These unions are "organic" worker organizations, deriving their
direction from the expressed desires of their members who tend to be mainly
oriented toward job-related outcomes. The underlying theory is one of advocacy of employee interests. These are believed to be fundamentally opposed
to employer interests, leading to a mainly adversarial posture. There is an
acceptance of the capitalist system and of a range of authority and discretion
for management within the firm. The term *pure and simple unionism* was
apparently coined by Samuel Gompers, the father of the American labor
movement. He argued that such unions were the "natural organizations of
workers" (Gompers 1919: 3).

In the typology posited by Robert Hoxie (1921) this would be "Business
Unionism." Another common label is "Bread and Butter Unionism," used
because of the emphasis on the practical needs of its members. Under
Hyman's ideal types these would be classified as "Guilds" (1996) or "business" (2001) unions, which are "interest organizations with predominantly
labor market functions" (2000: 1).

Examples of this type of union include nearly all current American
unions – UAW, Teamsters, United Food and Commercial Workers, Service
Employees International Union, etc., although most of them would tend to
view themselves somewhat more broadly. Examples of Pure and Simple
strategies include collective bargaining and striking against particular
employers for the purpose of improving pay, benefits, or job security. Also
included are strategies and tactics explicitly aimed at the survival and welfare
of the union as a going concern – as a business. Obviously, many things that
unions do have effects on the welfare of the organization. What makes Pure
and Simple union strategies distinctive is their focus on the financial and

membership base for the survival and growth of the union as an institution or business.

Pure and Simple unions may also have the characteristics of Hyman's (1996) Friendly Societies, providing mutual insurance for their members. Hyman (2001) cites the providing of inexpensive holidays and insurance, as well as financial services and advice by British unions in the 1990s as examples of a return to the early forms of craft unionism (p. 108), that is Pure and Simple.

Militant Radical Unionism. Another future is that of a form of unionism that is a militant movement for radical protest against existing economic and political institutions. At its core is a cry of the heart against the evils of the system. It aims at drastic change in the society as a whole, and sees ameliorative actions by unions to achieve better conditions of work as being useless at best. The strategy is to bring down exploitative and oppressive structures so that better ones can be erected. This is to be achieved by social protest, political action, and general strikes. Organizationally it might involve one big union uniting all workers or highly fragmented groups of workers acting independently and spontaneously. The philosophical base might be in anarchism or Marxism. In the more spontaneous forms, there might not be any particular philosophical base.

The prime example of this form of unionism in the United States is the Industrial Workers of the World (IWW). However, this type of labor movement is not necessarily limited to the IWW model or even anarchist or Marxist movements. It can exist wherever workers rise in protest to oppressive conditions, whether or not a broad philosophy is involved. The old machine-smashing British Luddites are an example of this.

This is a labor movement that is essentially protest. It rejects, or at least does not consider as a salient alternative, a continuing routinized relationship with employers such as exists under collective bargaining. Instead it aims to lash out at employers, either simply out of anger or with the idea of eliminating the employer altogether and changing society. In Hoxie's (1921) typology, this would be Revolutionary Unionism, encompassing both its revolutionary and socialist forms. This fits Hyman's (2001) category of anti-capitalist opposition unionism. He describes these as " 'schools for war' in a struggle between labor and capital," that are "a form of anti-capitalist opposition" with "a priority for militancy and socio-political mobilization . . . to advance class interests" (p. 2).

There are few examples of Militant Radical Unionism in the United States and Western Europe at present. "Wildcat" strikes (strikes not authorized by the union) in the United States and other countries are often a cry of the heart. These have occurred from time to time in coal mining in West Virginia in the United States, and in this same industry in the United Kingdom and other countries. Some of the spontaneous strikes that are characteristic of

French labor relations may be examples of this. The rhetoric of Western European unions has often sounded Militant Radical, but their actions have seldom matched their words on this.

Cooperationist Unionism. Another form of worker organization is one that adopts a unitarist perspective with respect to management. Its aim is to co-operate with management to achieve greater efficiency and quality of per-formance and products. Its method is to participate in management, using problem-solving techniques. It emphasizes communication and mutual under-standing. The fundamental logic of action is not one of exercising power, but of working with management for the common good of workers, managers, and shareholders. It denies any basic opposition of interests between workers and managers, and does not accept any natural or necessary division of authority and functions between managers and other employees. Quality circles, autonomous work groups, employee committees, peer committees to review grievances, and participation in company decision-making processes at various levels are typical structures. Loyalty is primarily to the firm rather than to an outside labor movement or a social or economic class.

Examples of Cooperationist Unionism range from historic American employee-representation plans (company unions) to modern employee committees in nonunion firms in the United States. The Solidarity unions of Central America and Japanese Enterprise Unions have some characteristics of this category. Hoxie (1921) would probably label these, at least in their most extreme form, as Dependent Unions. Hyman (1996) would classify Cooperationist Unions as Company Unions, which he describes as focusing on management and functioning as a "productivity coalition" with manage-ment (p. 70).

Examples of Cooperationist strategies also include labor-management "partnerships" in the United States and the United Kingdom (Hyman 2001), although these generally retain something of Pure and Simple Unionism as well. Also under this heading would fall the reorientation of such unions as the British Amalgamated Engineering and Electrical Union (AEEU) toward more harmony and cooperation with management. Another example is the Dutch trade union emphasis on a "coalition" model rather than a "con-frontation" model of labor relations.

Social Democratic Unionism. Indigenous to Western Europe is a type of unionism that combines the pragmatism of Pure and Simple Unionism with some of the vision, rhetoric, and ideology of Militant Radical Unionism. Social Democratic Unionism has its roots in both European confessional (Roman Catholic) unionism and nineteenth-century socialist unionism (Hyman 2001). Its aim is the welfare of the working class. Its methods include collective bargaining, politics, and cooperation/participation. Bargaining tends to be multiemployer and national. Law, influenced by political power, is a key instrument for achieving favorable conditions of work and life. The benefits of collective bargaining come to be spread beyond union members and the firms involved in bargaining through extension laws. Participative mechanisms are established by law and are avenues for the exercise of power to serve the interests of workers as well as to improve the performance of the firm. A form of corporatism, or concertation, exists at the national level, in which trade union federations join with employer federations and government to make general economic and social policy. Examples would include most of the unions of Western Europe.

Social Democratic strategies include unions acting in the society as a representative of all workers, not just their members. Becoming a "partner" in the economy is a Social Democratic strategy that parallels the Cooperationist strategy of partnering with management. Participating in the administration of social benefits, such as unemployment compensation, is another example of a Social Democratic strategy. Under Hyman's 1996 classification scheme, this would be Social Partner unionism, which would have government as its focus and political exchange as its function (p. 70). Hyman's later (2001) categorization labels this as Social Democratic (p. 3).

Reformist Unionism. Another type of unionism that combines some of the characteristics of Pure and Simple Unionism and Militant Radical Unionism, but has its own special character, is Reformist Unionism. Its aim is improving the lives of all of those human beings who produce goods and services, insuring that they receive the full fruits of their labor. This is not limited to union members, or even to members of a class. It utilizes collective bargaining, but is averse to the strike as an instrument in the process. It accepts a unitarist perspective, but only in conjunction with worker ownership in worker cooperatives. It organizes geographically as well as firm by firm and includes, and forms coalitions with, various other groups that have progressive goals. It operates as a mutual benefit society. It relies heavily on education and politics, and expressly aims at a better society. Reformist Unionism "stresses mutual insurance, and drifts easily into political action and the advocacy of cooperative enterprises, profit-sharing, and other idealistic plans for social regeneration" (Hoxie 1921: 47).

The prime example of Reformist Unionism, drawn from American labor history, is the Knights of Labor. In Hoxie's (1921) typology, this would be Uplift Unionism. Hoxie (1921) notes that it may be the case that Pure and Simple unions (*business unions* is his term) will sometimes be found to also "have the uplift in mind, and an idealistic viewpoint" (p. 47). Other examples consist of union advocacy of employee ownership, both in the forms of employee stock ownership and in cooperatives. Hyman's 1996 taxonomy would probably classify these strategies as Social Movement Unionism, which would have mass support as their focus, and campaigning as their key function (p. 70).

Setting out ideal types of unions aims to serve two principal purposes. First, it may help to organize our thinking about labor strategies. Second, it may call our attention to the fact that there are different fundamental assumptions and logics underlying strategies that derive from different ideal types.

PLAN OF THE BOOK

The general intention of this book is to set out and analyze a set of union strategies that might be interesting or useful to trade unionists and scholars of the American labor movement. Although it is not intended primarily as a text, a scientific treatise, or the author's personal reflections, it is a combination of these things and perhaps something more. The idea is to look at the environment in which American trade unions operate, survey its strategies and tactics, and then examine in some depth two strategies associated with two ideal union types that are not commonly considered to be part of the American labor movement's arsenal of weapons – Reformist Unionism and Social Democratic Unionism. From this rather unconventional perspective it is hoped that some fresh ideas will make their way into the labor movement. Given its current state, merely doing the same things and hoping for different results is unlikely to produce a stronger and livelier movement. Now is an especially appropriate time for some thinking outside the usual American box.

What's more, the answers to labor's problems are likely to be neither simple nor easy. The revival of American labor to tip the balance of power in their favor to even a slight degree

will require not only restoring unions but drastically transforming them. It will require not only recruiting new allies but creating a new political culture. It will require not only a more cohesive national strategy but also the formation of a meaningful global labor movement (Moberg 1999: 21).

This study focuses on the private (nongovernmental) sector of the American economy, mainly because this is where the problems for the American labor movement chiefly lie. This is not to say that there is not considerable room for building the labor movement among government employees. It is rather that the situation in the private sector is so grave.

The book is structured in the following manner. In Chapter 2 we will look in some depth at the current industrial relations environment and its impact on American unions. In Chapter 3 comes an overview of the current strategies and tactics used by the various organizations that make up the American labor movement. This is followed by Chapters 4, 5, and 6, which describe and analyze in some depth three strategic approaches that are fundamentally Reformist in nature. Chapter 4 covers the Knights of Labor of the nineteenth century. Chapter 5 deals with modern employee-rights organizations. Chapter 6 is about employee ownership.

Chapter 7 reviews the strategies of the historically Social Democratic trade unions of Western Europe. This is not a comprehensive description of European labor movements. Instead, it is an attempt to identify and discuss some of their strategies that might be of some interest to American labor unionists and scholars.

Chapter 8 focuses on one particular strategy that is fundamentally Social Democratic – unions facilitating economic development. Chapter 9 sets out general conclusions about the future of the American labor movement. And finally, the Appendix contains a verbatim account of an interview with John J. Sweeney, President of the AFL-CIO.

TWO

Industrial Relations in a Time of Change

Globalization is not the only thing influencing events in the world today, but to the extent that there is a North Star and a worldwide shaping force, it is this system.

Thomas L. Freidman, The Lexis and the Olive Tree, 2000

In order to predict the future of the American labor movement, it is necessary to have a firm grasp on the environmental conditions under which it is likely to be operating. If, as argued in Chapter 1, the environment in which the American labor movement operates is believed to be undergoing rapid and dramatic changes, exactly what is the nature of these changes? What are their expected consequences?

THE FORCES MOTIVATING CHANGE

Change in the American workplace has been motivated by a powerful conjunction of forces and circumstances. These have included globalization and the resulting increased competition (both domestic and international), technological change, the shift from manufacturing to services, workforce developments, and an increased receptiveness to change on the part of managers, workers, and unions.

Globalization is a system that has powerful implications for all aspects of American society. It has been compellingly argued that "Globalization is not just some economic fad, and it is not just a passing trend. It is an international system – the dominant international system . . ." (Friedman 2000: 7). Globalization has been defined as "the inexorable integration of markets, nation-states and technologies to a degree never witnessed before" (Friedman 2000: 9).

Globalization is characterized by free-market capitalism that places enormous competitive pressure on all firms that become part of the global

25

economy. Multinational companies try to sell globally. To do this, a multinational company is pressured to produce globally by "slicing up its production chain and outsourcing each segment to the country that can do it the cheapest and most efficiently" (Thurow 1996; Friedman 2000: 133).

The "sharply rising competition in world and domestic markets" (Appelbaum and Batt 1994: 3) has been rightly identified by industrial relations scholars (see Capelli et al. 1997) as a major force for change. It has been cogently argued that business as usual no longer works. There are two main reasons why this is so. First, firms in the newly industrialized countries are able to compete in price-conscious markets, paying wages that are much lower than those paid in the United States. Second, because of the diversity and customization made possible by computer-based technology, the cost advantages of American-style mass production have been lost, and there is increased domestic and international competition in quality-conscious markets (Appelbaum and Batt 1994: 3). Even the distinction between domestic and foreign competition may be obsolete, as there may no longer be such a thing as an American economy, given that it is so intertwined with those of other countries (Naisbitt and Aburdene 1990).

In addition, in the 1980s it became obvious that simply doing the same old things a bit better might not be sufficient for American firms to match the competition. Japanese firms were manufacturing better quality goods more cheaply offshore. They were also moving into the United States and doing the same thing, thereby proving that automobiles, televisions, and other products could be successfully made in the United States using their management techniques (Lawler 1992).

One consequence of these forces is management adopting new forms of work, including the ones used by the Japanese. The authors of *Workplace 2000* (Boyett and Conn 1991) argue that American business has come to recognize that it can no longer operate on Theory X command and control management principles because it can no longer afford Theory X employees. This is because (1) firms can't afford the army of supervisors that such employees require; (2) Theory X work no longer exists; (3) the old tradeoff of obedience (even subservience) for job security is no longer feasible; (4) a higher level of performance is required under modern conditions; and (5) the three key strategies for success – quality, customer service, and product innovation – cannot be achieved without employee involvement (Boyett and Conn 1991).

In consequence of revolutions in information technology, some futurists claim that a major shift is taking place in the location of work. Workers at the end of the nineteenth century were largely either farmers or home-based tradesmen. By 1970, this had changed to the point where only 6 percent of workers were self-employed or worked out of their homes. Sixty to 70 percent of workers traveled to a central location to work. It is argued that at the beginning of the twenty-first century, with more than half of the workforce consisting of "information workers," we are returning to a situation where most work can be done at home. A predictable outcome of this situation is for firms to reorganize in such a manner as to outsource to home workers/contingent employees everything that is not necessary to their core competencies (Bureau of National Affairs 1999).

Labor Market Forces for Change

In addition to the pressures of competition, there are a number of related phenomena occurring in the labor market that seem to be encouraging change in the American workplace. These include the creation of an increasing number and proportion of skilled jobs, declining or stagnant real wages, long hours of work, and the growth in involuntary part-time and temporary employment.

Changes in technology are generally believed to have, on balance, raised skill requirements for workers. This means that firms more fully utilizing the skills and brainpower of their employees have a competitive advantage (Boyett and Conn 1991; Commission on the Future of Labor-Management Relations 1994; Thurow 1996). The new industrial composition of employment has also led to greater demand for more highly skilled workers who are able to assume multiple responsibilities, and fewer high-paying jobs for manual workers (Commission on the Future of Labor-Management Relations 1994; Thurow 1996).

As is shown by the amount of involuntary part-time employment and temporary employment discussed in the following text, underemployment is a rather serious problem. On the other hand, the American economy has shown a capacity to produce jobs – "the great American job machine" – that is the envy of the industrialized world. There is, however, legitimate concern over the quality of these jobs.

Real hourly compensation for American workers has been essentially stagnant for the last 20 years, and has declined for male workers. This experience is unprecedented in the United States' experience of the last 75 years. Real hourly pay in the 1980s and 1990s increased at rates well below their historic pattern (Commission on the Future of Labor-Management Relations 1994; Mishel, Bernstein, and Schmitt 1999). By some measures, workers in France, Germany, Japan, and Sweden have hourly earnings that are greater than those of American workers (Ross, Bamber, and Whitehouse 1998). In 1996, hourly compensation for manufacturing production workers was higher in nearly all of the continental Western European countries (Portugal, Spain, and Italy being the exceptions) than it was in the United States (Mishel, Bernstein, and Schmitt 1999).

There has developed an economic bifurcation of the American labor force. Low-wage workers are worse off than comparable workers in other advanced countries, while high-wage workers are better off than workers anywhere else in the world. This difference is becoming increasingly pronounced

(Commission on the Future of Labor-Management Relations 1994; Mishel, Bernstein, and Schmitt 1999). We have reduced the differences in pay relating to race and gender, but substantial differences remain (Commission on the Future of Labor-Management Relations 1994; Mishel, Bernstein and Schmitt 1999). Poverty actually increased during the recent economic boom (Bureau of National Affairs 2000c).

American workers put in more hours of work per year than workers in any other industrialized country except Portugal (Mishel, Bernstein, and Schmitt 1999). This is largely because of the greater length of vacations of European workers. Europeans typically receive four- to five-week vacations beginning in their first year of employment. This advantage of European workers is a "relatively new phenomenon" (Commission on the Future of Labor-Management Relations 1994: 19). In 1999, 53 percent of American married-couple families had both the husband and the wife employed (Bureau of National Affairs 2000b). Couples with small children and single parents are spending "considerably more" hours working than they did around mid-century (U. S. Department of Labor 2000: 5).

Finally, there has been in the United States, as in other advanced countries, an increase in involuntary contingent employment. The percentage of the workforce consisting of part-time employees has remained about the same during the 1980s and 1990s. It actually dropped between February 1995 and February 1999 from 18.6 percent to 16.7 percent (General Accounting Office 2000). However, the proportion of these workers who are working part-time *involuntarily* had increased until in 1992 6.5 million of the 20.6 million part-timers were involuntarily in that class. These workers are paid less than half of the compensation of full-time workers, have higher turnover, are disproportionately young and female, and are less likely to be covered by a pension or health insurance plan (Bureau of National Affairs 2000a). Many are not covered by the Employee Retirement Income Security Act (ERISA), the Family and Medical Leave Act (FMLA), and unemployment compensation (Commission on the Future of Labor-Management Relations 1994; General Accounting Office 2000).

One estimate of the number of temporary employees showed their numbers as more than tripling between 1979 and 1992 to 2.5 million (Commission on the Future of Labor-Management Relations 1994). A more complete measure showed about 7.2 million temporary employees in 1995, making up 5.9 percent of the labor force. However, although their numbers had increased somewhat to 7.4 million by 1999, their percentage of the labor force dropped slightly to 5.7 percent (General Accounting Office 2000). Some estimates predict that the proportion of contingent workers will be 15 percent by 2010 (Bureau of National Affairs 1999). Just like part-timers, they are disproportionately young, female, black, and low wage (Commission on the Future of Labor-Management Relations 1994).

Although it is clear that "temping" is attractive for at least some workers because it fits their lifestyle or because it may lead to a permanent job, temporary employment is not without its disadvantages. One of these is a much lower probability of having employee benefits such as health insurance or a pension. Also, just like part-timers, they are also much less likely to be covered by various pieces of protective labor legislation (Bureau of National Affairs 2000d). There is also the phenomenon of the "permatemp." Such employees are in fact long-term employees, as permanently attached to their employer as persons who are classified as permanent employees. The chief distinction between them and other employees, other than their typically being considered employees of temp agencies, is that they do not receive the same benefits and pay. A highly publicized case of this type of employment involves Microsoft Corporation (Jorgensen and Riemer 2000) that resulted in a multimillion-dollar court settlement in December 2000.

An organization that adopts a strategy of having a core of permanent employees, surrounded by a peripheral group of contingent workers, has been described as "amoeba-like." In such an organization the nucleus of, say, one-fifth of employees stays with the firm, with a very fluid set of temps, consultants, and project teams expanding and contracting (Bureau of National Affairs 1999). Whether this creates a tolerable work situation for a human being on the periphery is a matter open to dispute.

The forces motivating change include both such product market forces as increased international and domestic competition and such labor market forces as increased demand for skilled workers, high underemployment, and less favorable conditions of work (high hours, low pay, insecure employment). These do indeed seem to pose a strong set of conditions in favor of some kind of change in the American workplace.

The Rise of the Service Sector

The American economy has come to be predominantly a service economy. The proportion of the labor force employed in the service sector has risen steadily over several decades. In 1999 the service-producing sector employed about 80 percent of the employed non-farm workforce (ftp://ftp.bls.gov/pub/specialrequests/ee/cesua50.txt). It has been persuasively argued (Herzenberg, Alic, and Wial 1998) that the transition of the economy from manufacturing to services in large part accounts for the declining real wages, rising inequality, declining job security, and low productivity growth that have been experienced by the American economy since the 1970s.

Although services are extraordinarily diverse, there are some characteristics that distinguish them from goods. For one thing, they ordinarily cannot be "produced in advance, shipped, and then stored until a customer comes along" (Herzenberg, Alic, and Wial 1998: 22). Also, most products of service are intangible. In the words of Herzenberg, Alic, and Wial (1998) they cannot be dropped on your foot. Even the results of service activity that are tangible, such as a movie or a legal brief, acquire value almost entirely from the skills and knowledge that go into them.

One of the implications of service employment for the employment relationship is that jobs become less linked to a particular employer. Also, many employees find themselves isolated in small establishments where the pay is low. Jobs that are specific to a particular firm, and internal labor markets, have broken down. There is no institutionalized way for workers to move easily to another firm (Herzenberg, Alic, and Wial 1998). There has been an increase in outsourcing and networking. This has redistributed power, along with the proportion of a firm's wage bill, from low-skill to high-skill workers. The pressures for internal equity that minimize inequalities within a firm disappear when the low-skill work is subcontracted to another employer. As previously noted, firms tend to cut wage bills by contracting out work to a low-wage employer rather than cutting wages of their own employees (Klaas and Ullman 1995). According to Herzenberg, Alic, and Wial (1998), this creates a need for employment rights and obligations to be, rather than firm-specific, based upon "business networks, industries, or geographical areas" (p. 122).

A CONTEXTUAL FACTOR: THE CHANGING AMERICAN LABOR FORCE

As if things were not complicated enough in this world of changing conditions of product and labor demand forces, American employers and unions have to deal with these in the context of a labor force that is becoming increasingly diverse. The American workforce has come to contain more females and minorities than ever before, is getting significantly older, and will have increasing proportions of immigrants.

The New American Workforce

Women increased their labor force participation rate to 57.9 percent in 1993 from 33.9 percent in 1950 (Commission on the Future of Labor-Management Relations 1994). It is projected that the labor force will be 47.5 percent female by 2008, compared to 45 percent in 1989 (Bureau of Labor Statistics 2000). Approximately two-thirds of the labor force entrants in the decade 1993–2003 will be women (Craver 1993).

The labor force is increasingly non-White, and this trend will continue at least to 2008. Between 1954 and 1994 the percentage of the workforce that was non-White increased from 10 to 15.2 percent (Commission on the Future of Labor-Management Relations 1994). By 2008 it is expected to reach 18.1 percent (Bureau of Labor Statistics 2000). The White non-Hispanic population percentage will decline from 75 percent in 1992 to 53 percent in 2050. The Hispanic population will grow rapidly and replace Blacks as the largest minority group in 2013 (Ahlburg 1993: 162–3). It is expected to rise from 7.4 percent in 1988 to 12.7 percent in 2008 (Bureau of Labor Statistics 2000). The category of Asian and other (which is mainly Asian) will increase from 3 percent of the labor force in 1988 to 5.7 percent in 2008. Blacks will increase modestly from 10.9 percent of the labor force in 1988 to 12.4 percent in 2008 (Bureau of Labor Statistics 2000).

The average and median ages of the workforce are increasing (Commission on the Future of Labor-Management Relations 1994; Leonard 1989). By 2005 the median age is predicted to be at 40.5, about where it was in 1962 before it declined as a result of the baby boom. Between 1998 and 2008 workers in the prime working age (25–54) work group are projected to increase by only 5.5 percent while workers 55 and over will increase 47.9 percent. Pension and health benefits will become more important and the feasibility of financing early retirement more questionable (Commission on the Future of Labor-Management Relations 1994).

Immigration has increased. The proportion of foreign-born workers in 1994 was 9 percent (up from 4.7 percent in 1960). Immigrants are increasingly from developing countries, with relatively low education and skill levels (Commission on the Future of Labor-Management Relations 1994).

WHAT ARE THE CHANGES IN WORK?

Brought about, at least in part, by the forces just described, a "transformed workplace" may have developed in the United States. The transformed workplace has been described in various ways. A broad vision of it is rather ecstatically expressed in *Workplace 2000* (Boyett and Conn 1991) as being a place where the relationship between American managers and workers will be permanently altered, with the line of demarcation between them becoming increasingly blurred. According to these writers, the traditional adversaries will become partners, and the lion will lie down with the lamb. Authoritarian management will die out because it doesn't work anymore (Boyett and Conn 1991: 83). Rigid hierarchies will disappear, along with the "ceremonial trappings of power." The goal of management will be harmony and unity, and making workers feel "intimately connected" to the enterprise, "even if in reality that connection is transitory" (Boyett and Conn 1991: 109). This idyllic situation is described as the "enchanted workplace" (Boyett and Conn 1991: 114).

It does indeed appear that a number of companies have "humanized" their production facilities, providing employees with a considerable degree of autonomy on the job and enabling employees to influence the way in which their work is structured (Fisher, Schoenfeldt, and Shaw 1991: 435). The Commission on the Future of Labor-Management Relations (Dunlop Commission) identified a wide variety of forms that these arrangements have taken, including:

quality circles, employee participation teams, total quality management teams, team-based work structures with a variety of responsibilities, safety and health committees, gain sharing plans, joint labor-management training programs, information sharing forums, joint task forces for a variety of problems, employee ownership programs, and worker representation on corporate boards of directors (Commission on the Future of Labor-Management Relations 1994: 29–30).

The authors of *The New American Workplace* (Appelbaum and Batt 1994) observe that all of these forms that, taken together, are said to make up "transformed or high-performance" work systems share some common features:

the use of flexible technologies; some form of workers participation or teamwork; substantial worker education and training; the flexible deployment of workers; a commitment to employment security; a narrowing of the gap between workers and managers, as evidenced by education levels and worker involvement in managerial decision making; quality consciousness; and an active role for unions and representative employee committees in achieving performance gains in the production process (Appelbaum and Batt 1994: 57).

The rationale for these systems is mainly one of "employee involvement," which has been defined as "a participative process to use the entire capacity of workers, designed to encourage employee commitment to organizational success" (see also, Boyett and Conn 1991; Cotton 1993: 3). This is sometimes justified from one or more of the following perspectives. From a *cognitive* perspective, it is argued that workers who are more involved will have more information and will be able to use it for the benefit of the organization. From a *motivational* perspective, workers who feel a greater sense of control over their work, job satisfaction, and perceptions of equity will increase their effort. From another perspective, the increase of employee *discretionary* behavior will lead to perceptions of being trusted by management that employees will then reciprocate by being willing to act beyond the call of duty, thereby "reducing the amount of control necessary and allowing innovation and management of unanticipated circumstances" (Watson 1993: 10). Last, a *rewards* perspective argues that these processes provide rewards that will give employees incentives to be more productive (Watson 1993: 10). Also, it has been argued that the goal of such programs is simply "to empower groups of employees to identify and solve performance problems in their own area of expertise" (Fisher, Schoenfeldt, and Shaw 1991: 435).

Even the advocates of the "enchanted" or "high-touch" workplace recognize that it can have its downside. Except where employees have representation in the very highest councils of the organization, they are asked to be committed to goals of someone else's making. A few very highly skilled employees may be able to handle this by selecting organizations for which to work that have goals that they find congenial. However, for many employees this can become "high touch coercion" (Boyett and Conn 1991: 114–15).

Participation chiefly means taking responsibility, and really having no place to hide when things go wrong (Boyett and Conn 1991). There will also be the situation described, but apparently not recognized as being anomalous, by the authors of *Workplace 2000*, that there will be a great deal of job insecurity at the same time that employees are being asked to see themselves as part of a "family" and to go beyond the call of duty at work, and where "membership, purposefulness, belonging, and meaning" are to be provided (Boyett and Conn 1991: 3). The transformed workplace may provide a "family," but perhaps a very dysfunctional one from the standpoint of employee members who are expendable at the will of the more powerful members.

Increasing Use of Traditional Approaches

Two strategies for the reform of mass production became increasingly popular in the 1970s and 1980s. One is what has been called the "American human resource model." The other is an attempt to make the mass production more efficient by cutting costs (Appelbaum and Batt 1994: 8–9).

The American human-resource model is seen by the authors of *The New American Workplace* as relying chiefly upon the theories of organizational behavior. This model attempts to improve productivity by increasing employee satisfaction and perceptions of equity, and by utilizing more effective communication and better incentives for performance (Appelbaum and Batt 1994). It takes a unitary view of the employment relationship, seeing employees as having the same interests as managers and shareholders. This perspective holds that employees are valued resources of the organization and, as such, deserving of development and nurture. It has much in common with strategies utilizing employee involvement, and is termed "enlightened management" (Appelbaum and Batt 1994: 9). However, unlike employee involvement, it does not aim to challenge the basic "logic of mass production" (Appelbaum and Batt 1994: 9).

Some companies have attempted to make mass production efficient by "cutting labor costs, out-sourcing work, and relying increasingly on high turnover and a contingent work force of part-time, temporary, and leased workers" (Appelbaum and Batt 1994: 9). We will probably see more of this in the future, as companies become flatter and leaner (Capelli et al. 1997). "Downsizing has made this flatter workplace a reality in most companies even today" (Boyett and Conn 1991: 2).

Lean Production

Perhaps the most popular of the new strategies among managers, both in the United States and in other advanced countries, is the Japanese lean-production model. While it involves elements of employee involvement, it is a great deal more than that. Because of its importance, it will be described in some detail.

Lean production is a "coherent, composite management concept geared to avoiding waste in the inputs and outputs of production" (Sengenberger 1993: 3). It aims at continual progress as to both quality and quantity. "It merges flexibility and quality which are the strength of the craft system, with speed and low unit labour costs, which are the advantages of high volume production" (Sengenberger 1993: 3).

One of the best descriptions of the Japanese system is in *The New American Workplace* (Appelbaum and Batt 1994). According to these authors this system is founded on the notion that "impediments to the smooth flow of materials . . . cause delays and imbalances in production against which firms must hold inventory buffers or work in progress. In lean production, engineers use a variety of techniques to reduce these impediments" (Appelbaum and Batt 1994: 33). These techniques include involving workers in the solving of problems to simplify processes and reduce defects. This leads to continuous incremental improvements – *kaizen*. Close links are forged between innovation and production, and there is a good deal of contact between engineers and production workers (Appelbaum and Batt 1994).

The lean-production system is fragile as well as lean. It requires committed and capable workers who will respond quickly and flexibly to problems as they arise. Pay, training, and employment security are geared to attracting and holding "a multiskilled workforce with a high level of commitment to the firm and the ability to solve problems" (Appelbaum and Batt 1994: 34). Teams assume a great deal of responsibility for maintenance, safety, and quality control. However, the teams are not autonomous. Foremen remain important. Workers have involvement in decisions but upper-level managers ultimately have the authority to make the decisions. The system of production, with statistical controls, just-in-time inventories, cycle-time analysis, and process simplification, leads to continuous improvement, in "small steps" (Appelbaum and Batt 1994: 35).

In lean production, according to Sengenberger, "Everybody is expected to contribute to the firm's success. Everybody is seen as a qualified problem resolver, and subjected to 'creative tension,' which in consequence breaks up a good deal of the separation of conception and execution of work – between 'head' work and 'hand' work" (1993: 5).

It is said that the "key technological features" of the Japanese system yield the following results: just-in-time production, small-lot production (allows quick and effective feedback on quality problems), and human control. Human control has the following aspects: "Giving wisdom to the machine" (steadily enhancing a machine's effectiveness by incremental improvements); visible control of production (workers watch for visible signs of problems); self-management of the work process (high degree of responsibility for specifying and modifying methods of doing work at their work stations); saving labor output (constantly striving for new labor-saving techniques); self inspection; building quality into the process; and constant effort for improvement (Shimada 1993: 29–30). This system requires workers who are skilled, motivated, and adaptable. Having such workers is achieved by recruiting trainable and flexible applicants and training them in multiple skills; having a job structure that has a few broad classifications and uses job rotation; and creating rewards that include bonuses and promotions (Shimada 1993: 31). Also, there is participation through information sharing among problem-solving groups, collective bargaining, and joint consultation with unions. "All of the major Japanese automobile companies are unionized, and these enterprise unions play a critical role in the Japanese production system" (Shimada 1993: 32).

One of the more insightful descriptions of lean production is provided by a European manager of a Japanese plant, Peter D. Wickens (1993). According to him, to achieve quality in the long term it is necessary to have two contradictory elements at the same time – a committed workforce and managerial control of the processes of production. With only a committed workforce short-term quality may be obtained, but ultimately the techniques necessary for this may lead to employees doing what each of them individually deems best – "almost anarchy." On the other hand, if you have only control of the processes of production you lose "any feeling of ownership," leading to a lack of motivation and, ultimately, alienation. He terms this the "paradox of production" and argues that the object is to resolve this paradox.

Assuming that the worker doing a job knows more than anyone else about how to do it better, the question is how to open the door to that knowledge so that it is used productively instead of not at all, or even against the company. According to Wickens, "The key to opening that door of knowledge is to give responsibility for that standard operation to the production people" (1993: 47). While these employees must work within certain guidelines, they are responsible for the task and for improving it. This applies to ease of working as well as to productivity, quality, and safety. He says that, "In order to resolve our paradox of production we must, therefore, give ownership of change to the people doing the job via the process the Japanese call **kaizen** and which we use now both as a noun and a verb . . . at its basic level it is simply a person saying to his boss, 'why don't we move this jig from here to there?' The boss replies 'that looks a good idea, why don't you tie in with the other shift, make sure they're happy with it and if there are no problems come in on Saturday and do it'" (Wickens 1993: 46–7).

To make this work, Wickens says that you cannot treat workers as second-class citizens. According to him:

. . . at a visible level we have no reserved car parking spaces but we do have a single dining room and we all wear the same blue uniforms; going deeper, the holidays, sickness benefit, medical insurance, pension are the same; deeper still we have everyone on annual salaries with merit progression, performance appraisal and objectives for everyone. No one clocks on or off but we do not stop pay for lateness or absenteeism. Once you start down this route there is no logical stopping place (1993: 47).

One aspect of Japanese lean production that has been especially popular among American managers is the quality circle. It has been called "somewhat of a fad" (Lawler 1992: 123). These are voluntary, and generally include employees from a particular area of a plant. They are told to focus on improving quality. They sometimes look at issues of productivity and cost reduction. Typically, employees are not rewarded for participation in quality circles. Quality circles are usually mandated top down from higher management. They have no formal authority except to make suggestions, and are a parallel organization that has no effect on the traditional power relationships in the firm. It has been said that they do not make substantial changes in organizations and "do not represent a major move toward involving employees psychologically or financially in their organizations" (Lawler 1992: 123–9).

Autonomous Work Groups (Swedish Sociotechnical System)

The Swedish Sociotechnical System (STS) approach to work design "is aimed at creating work situations in which teams instead of individuals have a whole and meaningful piece of work to do, receive feedback about the work, and have considerable autonomy in how they accomplish the work" (Lawler 1992: 88). The STS approach involves teams that are "formal, functional work groups," not quality circles or ad hoc groups formed for a particular purpose. For flexibility, teams have "far reaching, high degrees of competence, and team members engage in a variety of tasks" (Appelbaum and Batt 1994: 30), but not every team member does every task. Wage premiums encourage ongoing training, and new employee training is substantial. Group gainsharing is used. In Sweden, "The state regulates layoffs and plant closings, and tight labor markets and full-employment policies, rather than no-layoff clauses in union contracts, successfully provided employment security until the recession of the early 1990s" (Appelbaum and Batt 1994: 30). Under this approach, teams

are designed so that the task for which the team is responsible constitutes a whole and meaningful piece of work. The literature on the sociotechnical approach . . . emphasizes that the team should at least be responsible for the total transformation of a product of a service. Sometimes this transformation is called a **state change**, and it can be conceptualized as changing a raw material to a usable product that is in a different condition and has identifiable customers (Lawler 1992: 89–90).

It is believed that in order for teams to have feelings of responsibility for their work it is necessary for them to "make important decisions about how the work is done and [they] must feel in control of the work process" (Lawler 1992: 92). Teams vary as to the degree to which they have authority, as reflected in their names – "self-managing work teams, autonomous work groups, shared management teams, semiautonomous teams" (Lawler 1992: 92). According to Lawler:

Highly autonomous or self-managing work teams make virtually all decisions that are required to run a small business. For example, they hire and fire people, determine pay rates, set and maintain quality standards, specify work methods, manage inventory, deal directly with customers and suppliers, and so on. They are very close to being a small business or mini-enterprise (1992: 92).

Some of these teams do increase the power of employees substantially, particularly when they "are given a considerable amount of supervisory decision-making authority . . . work teams can often make scheduling, capital investment, and other types of decisions that affect multiple individuals and move teams toward a total business experience in a mini-enterprise environment" (Lawler 1992: 96). The supervisor moves into the role of a coordinator, having frequent contact with the group, and being held responsible for the overall performance of the group, but is not directly involved in their activities (Boyett and Conn 1991: 248). This separation of responsibility and authority on the part of the supervisor may be a crucial weakness in this approach.

The best known U.S. example is Saturn Corporation. Saturn has instituted labor/management committees and self-managed work teams. Problem-solving teams and online comanagement by the union have been added since the plant's inception. In negotiations in the labor/management cooperation model,

one primary outcome of the negotiations is consensus on how decision making will be conducted throughout the contract period. Therefore, the negotiations in the labor/management cooperation model concern the process of **how** decisions will be made, rather than trying to anticipate all possible future situations and resolving **what** their outcomes are during the negotiation period. The labor/management cooperation model focus on the process of decision making results in both a decrease in the pressure of the negotiation process, and additional flexibility in operation of the organization once the contract is in place (Watson 1993: 8).

Similar to the STS are the various Quality of Working Life (QWL) programs that became popular in unionized firms in the 1970s. Such a program can be defined as "a joint labor-management program designed to increase employee involvement and to help both the worker and the organization" (Cotton 1993: 34). "Broad-ranging committees" that engaged in union and worker participation in decision making at multiple levels of the organization were adopted at Ford, AT&T, and Miller Brewing Company, among others (Commission on the Future of Labor-Management Relations 1994).

PREVALENCE AND SIGNIFICANCE OF CHANGES

How prevalent are the changes described previously? Are they affecting a small or a large proportion of firms or employees? Furthermore, how important are they? Are they achieving the results for which they are intended? Will they live or die? These are the questions that will be addressed in this section. The attempt to answer them is broken into two unequal parts. The first, which will be quite brief, relates to traditional practices such as conventional human resources strategies, downsizing, and contingent employment. The second has to do with the more innovative ones that, in one way or another, include employee involvement in the management of the enterprise.

Traditional Practices: Human Resources, Downsizing, Contingent Employment

As to prevalence, it appears that the American human resource model, downsizing, and contingent employment are all quite widespread. The more enlightened human resources view of management has been gaining acceptance for some time and is generally subscribed to by most managers (Kochan, Katz, and McKersie 1986; Appelbaum and Batt 1994). Also, downsizing has become almost wildly popular (Cascio 1993).

Practices Including Employee Involvement: In General

How widespread is change? After a good deal of uncertainty for a number of years as to the degree to which new and innovative practices are widespread, it appears that it may be possible to finally approach an answer to this question. This is because of several recent studies, and the findings of the Dunlop Commission whose special charge it was to analyze and encourage these practices.

From their review of the evidence presented to them, the Dunlop Commission concludes that a "substantial majority" of large firms uses some form of employee participation and that a number of small firms use informal modes of participation. They estimated that between one-fifth and one-third of the workforce were covered by some form of participation. However, it is their view that a relatively small proportion of employers had established what could be called a "high performance workplace" (Commission on the Future of Labor-Management Relations 1994: 36).

The Dunlop Commission bases its view on a number of studies. One of the more interesting ones is by Paul Osterman (1994). His estimate is that about 35 percent of private-sector establishments with fifty or more employees had "made substantial use of flexible work organization" (Osterman 1994: 186). As Osterman says, his findings are similar to those of an earlier study of Fortune 1000 companies, reported in 1990.

In addition, the Dunlop Commission cites 1990 surveys of Fortune 1000 firms that found that 86 percent had some experience with employee involvement (this was up from 70 percent in 1987). Twenty percent of these firms reported having participatory processes covering more than 50 percent of their employees (Commission on the Future of Labor-Management Relations 1994). A 1993 survey of fifty-one large firms found that between 80 and 91 percent of them had committees dealing with either health and safety, productivity, or quality. Approximately 25 percent of their employees were participating in some form of team. A survey of mainly large manufacturing firms reported that 31 percent of their employees were involved in some form of decision making (Commission on the Future of Labor-Management Relations 1994). Also, a survey of Fortune 1000 companies found that 47 percent of them both used work teams and believed that their use of teams would greatly increase (Lawler 1992).

It appears that few organizations have performed "major transformations" and where they have occurred this has often been under "unique circumstances" (Appelbaum and Batt 1994: 8). Many successful cases involve a company in an economic crisis where the firm has both a risk-taking leadership and the necessary resources to undertake a costly conversion to participative structures and sustain possible short-term losses to profitability. These are rather rare circumstances.

How significant are the changes? In order to judge the importance of these changes it is necessary to reach some conclusions about how successful they have been and, in general, what their consequences are. Both the Dunlop Commission (Commission on the Future of Labor-Management Relations 1994) and a number of writers have arrived at some conclusions about employee involvement strategies in general.

The Dunlop Commission found as follows:

While most of those testifying about their efforts reported their programs resulted in improved productivity, quality, or some other indicators of economic performance, the empirical studies on this issue completed to date show mixed results. Some of these efforts fail to survive long enough to produce significant economic gains. Studies that have attempted to isolate the individual effects of single programs such as quality circles or teams tend to find small or insignificant effects on performance (p. 45).

The largest positive effects on economic performance have been found in studies that measure the combined effects of workplace reforms (i.e., where participation is combined with changes in employment practices, manufacturing policies and management structures and decision-making procedures) (p. 46).

Similar conclusions have been reached by several writers (Arthur and Dworkin 1991; Bettenhausen 1991; Appelbaum and Batt 1994), although some have disagreed (Craver 1993). A 1994 survey study in Michigan did find evidence supporting the positive effects of participatory programs and group-based incentive pay on firm-level performance (Cooke 1994).

The programs that are most successful may be those that involve actual decision making by employees (Lawler 1992). The most effective forms of employee involvement appear to be autonomous work teams and gain-sharing. Next come QWL, job enrichment, and employee ownership. Last come quality circles and representative participation. One author (Cotton 1993) concludes that (1) involvement must be focused on the employee's everyday work rather than organizational policy as a whole, (2) employees need to have some degree of control or power to make decisions, (3) the system must allow for changes to be instigated by the worker, and (4) the system must require a major change in the work life of the employee (e.g., from individual to team focus). The Dunlop Commission found that programs that were integrated with the human resource policies of the firm and, in unionized settings, involved the union as a joint partner were the most likely to survive (Commission on the Future of Labor-Management Relations 1994).

Some studies using data gathered in the mid- to late 1990s cast doubt on the effectiveness of the new "high performance" systems. One such study (Capelli and Neumark 2001) found strong evidence of increased labor costs and little or no positive effects on firm performance. Another study (Godard 2001) found positive effects on worker attitudes of moderate levels of alternative work practices, but weak or negative effects at higher levels. Lean forms of work organization and team autonomy and responsibility for a good product had negative effects. However, team-based work and information sharing had positive effects on worker attitudes.

Lean Production

There seems to be general agreement in the literature that the Japanese system of lean production works. That is, it is capable of producing high-quality products at low cost. Furthermore, it can do this in the United States and other advanced countries as well as in Japan. In a widely touted book, *The Machine that Changed the World* (Womack, Jones, and Roos 1990), the authors argue that this system has permanently changed the world competitive environment. It has been claimed, with some justice, that "the Japanese lean system is rapidly making the traditional Ford mass production system and the newer, parallel, team-based systems of Volvo obsolete" (Rehder 1992: 57). Japanese transplants in the United States have "established unprecedented standards of quality, productivity, and for the most part, lower absenteeism, lower turnovers, and less contentious employee/management relations" (Rehder 1992: 58).

The European manager quoted previously in this chapter has the following explanation of the reasons that he believes the Japanese system to be a superior solution to the paradox of production:

We have not sought to go down the Swedish route. Having been to Volvo, Udde-valla and calculated how long it takes them to undertake the final assembly of a car, I conclude that while it is an interesting social experiment there is no way they can make money. The Swedes . . . lose "control of the process", hence quality of build suffers and significant rectification areas have been incorporated into the physical structure of Uddevalla. They still suffer high labour turnover and with the very long job cycle, training then becomes a major problem. Having been told by Volvo that "If we can't build cars this way in Sweden we can't build cars in Sweden", I am not surprised at Volvo's recent decision to close both Kalmar and Uddevalla (Wickens 1993: 49).

Lean production has been characterized as a "sophisticated cost-cutting philosophy" (Cooke 1993: 81). As such, it has created a competitive situation in which Western firms have had to cut costs one-third to one-half below those incurred in traditional mass production. This may be the fatal weakness of the Swedish model, given the market reality that in the long term the customer will prefer the low-cost model over the high-cost model, quality being equal (Cooke 1993). This reality has struck home for many German manufacturers, given their high costs. Their ability to move in this direction is helped by the fact that in Germany there is a long-established chain of middle-sized suppliers on whom some of the cost-cutting burden can be placed (Cooke 1993).

It does appear that world markets have demanded of the American auto industry that it develop new forms of work organization. The old Fordist ways have shown their inability to compete with the products of a system that is based on shop-floor teamwork, high intensity of work, and cooperative enterprise unionism. New United Motors Manufacturing, Inc. (NUMMI), the General Motors-Toyota joint venture in the United States, has demonstrated that world-class productivity and quality can be produced under this system in the United States. It also appears that many workers like teams and the opportunity to participate, as well as a clean and efficient environment where they are treated with respect. It has been argued that few workers miss "the old drill-sergeant bosses and the tension of constant labor-management antagonism" that existed previously (Turner 1991: 61).

There is, however, clearly a downside, what might even be called a darker side, to lean production. First, worker involvement is tightly restricted. This can be disappointing to workers who have been led to believe that they will be decision makers in a flat organization, when the reality is quite different (Rehder 1992). The fact that the jobs are rare good-paying positions makes workers quite anxious to keep them, leading to a system of work that can be "a highly threatening form of social manipulation and intimidation" (Rehder 1992: 59).

The situation at NUMMI has been described as one where outsourcing leads to fewer jobs being present at the plant, training opportunities being in fact quite limited, and a "wide cleft" remaining between skilled and unskilled workers. Cycle time is very short (about one minute) and there is considerable pressure to meet high standards while at the same time working intensely and quickly. Buffer time is gone, and everyone works "60 seconds in every minute." There is also great pressure to avoid absenteeism, leading to some workers coming to work when they are sick and the forcing out of frequently ill workers (Turner 1991).

One criticism of the Japanese system is its fragility. It depends on just-in-time deliveries, an interruption of which can cause problems. More importantly, it relies heavily on a system of high-stress work that has led to high labor turnover and absenteeism even at its birthplace – Toyota motor works in Japan (Sengenberger 1993). Also, it is dependent upon cooperative relations, which may be impossible to achieve under a regime of downsizing (Sengenberger 1993).

In addition, there are explanations of the success of the Japanese system that have little to do with employee involvement. Extraordinarily long hours of work – averaging 2,300 per year in Japan, "massive outsourcing of final assembly," rapidly declining wages as one moves down the supplier chain, high utilization of capacity, better use of automation, having a more manufacturable product, having government policies that are supportive, the use of joint research projects, lower pressures for short-term profit, and "more engineers and fewer accountants" are given by a trade union federation official as explanations for the success of the Japanese system (Unterweger 1993).

As to employee relations, the Japanese system is accused of really being management by stress. It is maintained by some observers that worker discretion is not so great as is commonly supposed. At Mazda's U.S. plant, improvements in the process – *kaizen* – are permissible only with supervisory permission, and tasks and their sequencing are set out in great detail. There is also the practice of deliberately setting production goals higher than can be achieved by the number of employees in a department, and then raising the goals when the original ones are met (Unterweger 1993; Sengenberger 1993).

The system's use of suppliers has been criticized as a "master-slave" rather than a partnership relationship. It is said that suppliers are "squeezed like lemons" to innovate and produce at lower cost (Cooke 1993: 87).

Lean production exists in both union and non-union settings. In non-union settings management is obviously freer to act as it pleases, giving it more flexibility to establish and adjust these systems. However, the disadvantage of non-union settings has been argued to lie in the maldistribution of power, under which

truth, sincerity and commitment suffer. Production is a cooperative effort: cooperation can be compelled, but its quality suffers when it becomes obedience. If companies really want workers to "buy into" new production concepts, they would be well advised to encourage representative workers' organizations (Unterweger 1993: 66–7).

This may mean that these systems are more durable in unionized settings (Unterweger 1993).

As noted previously, quality circles are an aspect of lean production that became quite popular in the United States. Experience with quality circles has generally shown that they are capable of producing some short-term results, but that the advantages tend to be short-lived (Griffin 1988; Steel and Lloyd 1988; Adam 1991; Cotton 1993). Quality circles can lead to an increased interest in participative systems, but if management is not truly ready to move in this direction they can alienate and disappoint workers who are interested in participation. Perhaps the real weakness of quality circles is that they are a parallel system that builds in inefficiencies and costs (Lawler 1992).

Quality circles are the most visible and easiest to implement feature of the Japanese system. This is probably what led to their widespread adoption in the West. However, it may be that this part of the Japanese system cannot survive on its own, and may not have been the best part of the Japanese system to borrow (Hill 1991).

In sum, it appears that the Japanese lean-production system, at least when adopted in its entirety, does deliver the goods in terms of quality and cost. There is reason to suspect that there are substantial human costs involved, but these are at least partly offset by the human benefits of participation, at least as compared to traditional Fordist mass production. Whether it is sustainable in Western societies is a question that remains to be answered. Also, it may be possible to achieve the same results with systems that are more congenial to Western values. We now turn to a system that many claim to do this.

Autonomous Work Groups

The system of autonomous work groups has been described as a radical approach to employee involvement, but it may have been the fastest-growing approach in the 1980s and 1990s (Cotton 1993). Research has generally showed it to be associated with improved employee attitudes and the attitude-related behaviors of absenteeism and turnover. Its relationship with productivity measures has been less consistent. Productivity improvements appear to occur through (1) lowering costs by eliminating supervision and (2) improving work methods through employee suggestions (Cotton 1993). Overall, the research results have been described as being "relatively positive" (Cotton 1993: 199).

Compared to the lean-production system, autonomous work-group systems such as those used by Volvo at Uddevalla do seem to be more successful at increasing workers' empowerment, quality of work life, and opportunities to realize their true mental potential, and do this without excessive work stress. This system has been described as truly involving the workers' minds with their jobs. The Japanese lean system has real "technical, organizational, political, economic, environmental and social constraints," and is arguably at odds with political and social forces in the West, and even in Japan. It is Japanese lean production, not autonomous work groups, that one finds associated in Japan with the term *karoshi* – death by overwork (Lawler 1992: 68).

One of the more interesting aspects of the STS that devised autonomous work groups is that this system was discovered, not invented. In 1951, Eric Trist was studying the effects of new machinery and the "modern" system of developing specialized jobs in a mine when they found that the "old-fashioned" processes of the miners worked better in terms of both productivity and satisfaction. What they found the more productive miners doing amounted to their having self-directed teams and rotating jobs (Trist and Bamforth 1951). Also, this system is quite similar to the system of internal subcontracting that was used in the American iron and steel industry in the nineteenth century. Consequently, perhaps one can argue that, rather than being a radical innovation, this is a relatively normal and natural way for human beings to organize work. If so, it may be that, although this system departs substantially from the Fordist way of doing things, it may not be so difficult to institute as some writers (e.g., Cotton 1993) suggest.

The related strategy of QWL has been successful in improving labor-management relations, and may be a necessary condition for having employee participation in a unionized setting. There is some evidence of positive effects on quality and productivity (Cotton 1993). There is the well-known Mishel and Voos (1992) study that finds that participative structures are more successful in unionized settings. This conclusion has been confirmed by Cooke (1994).

Overall, there does appear to be both evidence and logic in favor of the utilization of autonomous work groups. However, it is very troubling that doubt remains as to whether they can be sufficiently cost effective to compete in other than upper-scale luxury markets. Volvo's plants at Uddevalla and Kalmar have closed. Saturn has yet to show that it can be consistently profitable over time, and it is not spreading as a practice in the American automobile industry, or even within General Motors, the company that started and owns it. Although these processes may be more socially desirable than Japanese lean production, their future is not particularly bright unless they can demonstrate an ability to be cost competitive and profitable.

CONCLUSIONS ON THE TRANSFORMED WORKPLACE

Looking back at the questions raised at the outset of this chapter, it is possible to reach several tentative conclusions. First, and most obvious, the essence of most of the changes that are occurring appears to be employee involvement in the management of the enterprise. A necessary component of this is a blurring of the lines between rank-and-file workers on the one hand and managers on the other. The purpose of managers in doing this seems to be increasing both the motivation and the opportunity of ordinary workers to contribute to the quality of products, cost savings in the process, and the profitability of the enterprise. The democratization of the workplace may be an effect of this process, desired by some but at best irrelevant to others.

The second question – whether these changes work – is a more difficult one. Of course, it must be decided by what criteria this is to be judged. An obvious set of criteria consists of the purposes for which these changes were instituted by the people who had the power to do so – managers. They hope to achieve quality, cost savings, and profitability. On balance, it appears that the Japanese lean-production system does this. It remains to be seen whether this is the case with autonomous work groups using the STS approach. If one adopts the standpoints of employees or society at large, the question is even more difficult to answer. Employees clearly gain from the job security and high wages possible under Japanese lean production, and may like the participation that they have under it. On the other hand, the work pressures are intense and the opportunities for participation are really quite limited. American society benefits from the wealth created, but may be damaged by the physical and psychological effects of management by stress. Both employees and American social values would appear to be served by autonomous work groups, but this system must be economically viable to survive.

As to why these systems work, to the extent that they do, it seems to me that employee involvement probably operates in several ways to affect quality and productivity. The cognitive argument that workers gain information that enables them to be more productive and the view that involvement gives them an opportunity for this have some appeal. It may be that employees do respond to being trusted by going beyond the call of duty in their work. It is probably the case that individual employees differ in their taste for participation, and therefore, in its effects upon them. The impression one forms from the literature is that involvement alone is probably not enough to cause an employee to make a greater contribution to quality and productivity. Rather, it takes either the stick of management by stress or the carrot of ownership (discussed in Chapter 6) or gainsharing, in addition to the opportunities to contribute that involvement provides. It may well be that the presence of a union removes an important impediment to productivity-increasing behavior by making it less likely that the worker or his or her fellows will suffer unwanted consequences, such as job loss, from contributing to productive efficiency.

These systems are likely to endure to the extent that they are compatible with productive efficiency and the production of goods and services that can compete in the marketplace, both as to quality and as to cost. It seems that they can be humanized sufficiently to be tolerable to workers, and yet meet enterprise needs. It is uncertain whether this is true for Japanese lean production in the long run, but it may well be.

There do appear to be multiple paths to achieving quality and productivity using some form of employee involvement. It is probably true that the STS's autonomous work groups are more consistent with the needs and interests of both workers and American society if this system can meet the bottom-line criterion of productive efficiency.

As to the more traditional practices – human resources, downsizing, and the use of contingent employees – the picture is not much clearer. The human-resource practices will probably continue to evolve in the same general directions that they have in the past, adjusting to employee involvement by developing new strategies for such functions as staffing and compensation. They will serve these functions reasonably well, but will probably not account for any dramatic transformations in the workplace.

Downsizing and the increasing use of contingent employees seem to have no end in sight. The popularity of downsizing on Wall Street probably guarantees its use, at least until investor thinking changes. Contingent employment, a worldwide phenomenon, will probably continue to grow as well. One should not dismiss the possibility that these practices will, at least in the medium term, be more important than the more appealing practices of employee involvement. Indeed, they may ultimately do in employee involvement. Clearly there are industries and situations where traditional employment relations will remain the norm, and any adjustments will be for the purpose of cost cutting.

IMPLICATIONS FOR THE LABOR MOVEMENT

All of the changes discussed in this chapter have some impact on the American labor movement. In addition to taking them into account in discussing various particular strategies elsewhere in this book, it might be useful to briefly summarize their effects here.

The forces of both international and domestic competition, in addition to driving employers to adopt the various changes in the employment relationship described in this chapter, cause employers to be highly cost conscious. This means that they have a strong incentive to avoid unions where there are none, and to bargain very hard where unions are present (Masters 1997). Unions are generally able to negotiate higher wages, and therefore impose higher wage costs, than would be present in their absence. Even worse, from a competitive standpoint, is the possibility of a strike. Although strikes are very rare indeed these days, fear of them runs high in capital-intensive industries, particularly if they rely on just-in-time Japanese-style methods. In the prevailing free-market ideology, unions are seen as inhibiting efficiency, growth, and profitability. Ascendant capital argues plausibly that labor is part of the problem, not part of the solution to achieving prosperity.

The increasing diversity of the workforce gives rise to some special problems for unions. It negatively impacts the solidarity necessary for collective action. It is more difficult for workers to act together if they are very different persons in terms of ethnic background, sex, and age. However, this barrier was overcome by unions organizing basic industries in the 1930s. Some of the organizing tactics used then, such as the Steelworkers Organizing Committee (SWOC) linking the various national-origin clubs that existed in the mill towns, might be revived. It appears that the organizing of Latino workers in California and changes in policies toward immigrants that are discussed in Chapter 3 indicate an ability of unions to organize this wave of immigrants just as they organized earlier waves.

As to the traditional approaches to employment relations that have flowed from the forces described here, human resource strategies do threaten the unions' reason to exist. If management is benevolent and kind, one could argue that unions are unnecessary. This is the same argument that was made for what was known as "personnel welfarism," which was in fashion and used as a union substitution device prior to the Great Depression of the 1930s. In the words of the old union organizing song . . . "Boom Went the Boom" when the Depression hit and personnel welfarism was shown to be a slender reed for workers to lean upon. So long as economic times remain good, human-resource strategies may impede the growth of unionism.

Downsizing, even in the absence of the promises of "enlightened" human-resource management practices that give rise to high worker expectations, creates opportunities for unions. Workers generally tend to have some expectation of security of continued employment. When this is unmet, this expectations/achievements gap is highly likely to lead to feelings of deprivation. At least if other remedies fail, workers will be inclined to turn to unions.

The increasing casualization of work, on the surface at least, makes life very difficult for unions. Part-time and temporary employees are historically difficult to organize. Yet their needs are great. This is an area where some real innovations are required.

The newer participative approaches also call for union innovation and creativity. Lean production is an effective means of producing high-quality products at low cost. It is probably useless to oppose it in principle. So unions need to work out ways to cope with it. It appears from the experience at NUMMI and other unionized facilities employing lean-production techniques that a union can still serve a highly useful purpose in representing worker interests. The reality of lean production, unlike its idealized image, leaves considerable room for bargaining and worker representation.

Autonomous work groups fit rather nicely into a broad perspective of worker representation. They constitute a means for worker control over their working lives. Therefore, they are very consistent with the goals of a labor movement. The forms are different, but worker interests remain fundamentally the same. However, here as in other participative approaches, the system

blurs the line between labor and management. Unions accustomed to thinking in terms of well-defined roles of worker and manager can become confused and deeply troubled by these new models. Functioning in such a system
clearly requires moving beyond the traditional attitudes and practices of Pure
and Simple Unionism.

In the following chapters we will look at various forms, strategies, and
tactics of worker organizations. These will be viewed in terms of the ideal
types of unions that they represent and tested against the conditions that are
believed to enable the existence of a strong labor movement. Throughout
this analysis the environmental conditions previously set out must be kept in
mind. They set constraints upon and provide opportunities for action. They
also influence the outcomes of strategies in both predictable and unpredictable ways.

THREE

A Survey of American Union Strategies

The ground-work principle of America's labor movement has been to recognize that first things must come first. The primary essential in our mission has been the protection of the wage-worker, now; to increase his wages; to cut hours off the long workday, which was killing him; to improve the safety and the sanitary conditions of the work-shop; to free him from the tyrannies, petty or otherwise, which served to make his existence a slavery. These, in the nature of things, I repeat, were and are the primary objects of trade unionism.
Samuel Gompers, President, American Federation of Labor, 1911

For over two centuries the American labor movement has demonstrated an impressive degree of creativity and flexibility in dealing with its many problems. Among national labor movements, American labor has often led the way in trying out new ideas and strategies, and there is extensive literature documenting this. The writings about American labor union behaviors that are aimed at ensuring their survival can be conveniently broken down into two categories: (1) descriptions of, and prescriptions for, broad *strategic* directions for American labor; and (2) descriptions of, and prescriptions for, specific *tactical* responses to the challenges that they face.

AMERICAN UNION STRATEGIES FOR SURVIVAL

Although American unions have taken a variety of forms, the predominant one throughout their history has been that of Pure and Simple Unionism. This type of unionism has come in many guises. However, it has a constant core – looking out for the practical, bread-and-butter needs of workers that arise from work. We will first consider the more typical strategies that are essentially Pure and Simple. From these we will move to examples of some other strategies that, while less typical of American trade unions, are nevertheless important to their future.

49

Pure and Simple Unionism

Craft Unionism. The classic example of Pure and Simple Unionism is American craft unionism. It was the first form of unionism to come into existence in the United States. Shoemakers, printers, and other skilled tradesmen were the earliest trade unionists. This form of unionism has historically been the hardiest, surviving even in the most difficult times. This is partly because the natural bonds of common interest, friendship, and mutual respect among members of a craft make for very intensive solidarity.

The powerful surge of industrial unionism in the 1930s eclipsed craft unionism, shielding it from the view of the general public. However, it continued to have considerable strength in a number of industries, construction being the most important. This old and enduring form of unionism may deserve new attention as industrial unions have faded in strength (see Shostak 1991).

It is still true that a common craft provides a basis for solidarity. Skilled craft workers have a greater ability to organize than do unskilled workers. They have both stronger individual bargaining power and the organizational skills to operate a successful, businesslike organization. In the building trades the union hiring hall has long been an effective method for providing employment to a group of workers that move from employer to employer. This model is one that has been copied by temporary employment agencies. Could unions perform this function for temporary workers of many kinds, and do this more cheaply and better than private agencies? Some unions, including the International Union of Operating Engineers (IUOE), have attempted to do this.

A further advantage of the craft form of organization is its ability to provide a stream of trained, competent workers to employers. In the building trades, and in some other fields as well, individual employers have no incentive to train workers who may soon move on to work for someone else. The long-term interests of employers as a group require a trained workforce. Yet the interests of individual employers militate against this coming about. A good solution to this dilemma is a union of workers who train one another and spread the costs of training across the industry. The United Brotherhood of Carpenters and Joiners (Carpenters) recognizes this rationale, and is utilizing it in an attempt to encourage employers to move away from their traditional aversion to the union (Luddy 1997).

Craft unionism was historically "crucial to the survival of unionism among many groups of workers," showing "a vitality and durability that have gone unrecognized" (Cobble 1991: 7). According to Cobble (1991),

The emphasis on building solidarity through craft identity, on upgrading the status of the trade by monitoring entrance standards and workplace job performance, and on providing benefits and services that would travel with workers from jobsite to jobsite all created sources of loyalty among workers that allowed unions to sustain themselves and exert power over multiple small worksites (p. 7).

So, perhaps one promising direction for American unions is back to the future, harkening back to the classic American trade union – a guildlike organization of craft workers.

Occupational Unionism. In her book on unions of waitresses (1991), Sue Cobble coins the term *occupational unionism* to distinguish these unions from the worksite-based unionism of mass-production workers. As described by her, waitress unions of this type had a great deal in common with craft unions. In a paper on unions of low-wage workers in services, Howard Wial (1993) speaks of geographical/occupational unionism. He distinguishes this not only from industrial unions that are worksite-based, but also from craft unions on the grounds that these workers do not have true craft skills.

Among waitresses, "Occupational unionism emphasized the occupational identity of the worker and tied union power to control over those within the occupation" (Cobble 1991: 137). It relied on the hiring hall and the closed shop. The union hiring hall offered free services to workers and employers. The union "exercised control over the labor supply in the industry, offered employers a vital service, and provided members employment security and flexibility in a highly transitory, unstable sector of the economy" (Cobble 1991: 139). The union spread available work among its members, thereby avoiding layoffs. It screened members with some care, and invested in training programs for them. Members were expected to comply with craft standards while on the job, and would be disciplined by the union for such offences as absenteeism. The union policed the sobriety and honesty of its members. Supervisors belonged to the union and were obligated to operate in a fair manner. In addition to the advantages of this system to workers, it gave employers a supply of responsible workers and encouraged patronage of union restaurants.

What Wial (1993) describes as the emerging model of union structure that is being used in organizing low-wage workers, "is one in which workers are organized geographically along loose occupational lines" (p. 23). It combines elements of different types of unions. Similar to waitress unionism, it borrows heavily from craft unionism, utilizing areawide multiemployer bargaining, portability of benefits, and involvement of the union in referring workers to employers and training them. Similar to amalgamated and federated craft unionism, it involves a "loose grouping of related occupations as a basis for organizing" (p. 23). From general geographical unionism, it borrows the notion of having a geographically based local union as the basic unit of organization.

The vision of unionism expressed by Wial's geographical/occupational unionism sees the union as "both an economic pressure group and a social movement" (Wial 1993: 24). As an economic actor it uses collective bargaining to raise wages and improve working conditions. It attempts to remove wages from competition in the labor market. "As a social movement, it expresses members' sense of collective identity and promotes members' vision of social and economic justice" (p. 24). This type of unionism is complex in that it requires a structure that is compatible with both its economic and social facets. It involves acting together with other social activist groups such as those advocating immigrants' rights (Masters 1997).

Wial's chief model for geographical/occupational unionism is Justice for Janitors, a Service Employees International Union (SEIU) program. Justice for Janitors organizes all janitors in a geographical area into a single local union. It then proceeds to persuade all the employers in the area to have a uniform set of economic terms of employment for janitors. A similar strategy is utilized by the Hotel and Restaurant Employees Union (HERE) for hotel workers, and District 1199 of the Health Care Employees Union in nursing homes.

Wial (undated) argues that current National Labor Relations Board (NLRB) law does not permit the kind of bargaining unit that is necessary for this type of unionism. What is needed is the establishment of multiemployer units, sometimes across industries. This would permit network-based bargaining by unions that are structured to conform to modern interfirm relations and to the real structure of the labor market. This is very similar to the historic patterns of organizing and bargaining in the apparel industry, which has always been characterized by multiple small employers concentrated in a geographical area. Special exceptions have been made in the National Labor Relations Act (NLRA) for this industry, and also for construction, which has similar characteristics. Wial notes that at Saturn the United Automobile Workers (UAW) local union is expanding to include firms that have relations with Saturn. Here, network-based bargaining may be emerging from a single-employer relationship in which the union has organized the firm that dominates the network. He recommends changing American labor law to broadly allow, even encourage, network-based bargaining.

In their book on the new economy, Wial and coauthors propose, in addition to various other policy changes, a set of ideas that would "foster the growth of worker associations on a multiemployer basis" (Herzenberg, Alic, and Wial 1997: 150). They envision these organizations as not only engaging in collective bargaining for higher wages and better quality jobs, but also acting to establish career paths that are multiemployer in scope and work to create "economies of depth" (p. 150). The "economies of depth" would consist of education and training to make workers at once more productive and more marketable.

It is recognized that the expansion of multiemployer collective bargaining would require some changes in the NLRA. This might include permitting employees of different employers to bargain jointly with the employers if a majority of workers at each employer voted to do so. Employers would not be permitted to withdraw from these units whenever they wish. This would require a broad grant of authority to the NLRB to certify "broad occupational, sectoral or network-based bargaining units" (Hertzenberg, Alic, and Wial 1998: 163). Legalization of prehire agreements, such as those used in the construction industry, would be another possible instrument for the development of multiemployer units. Under a prehire agreement an employer agrees that a particular union will represent employees hired for a future project, unless the employees vote otherwise. Abolition of the strictures against secondary boycotts would also facilitate multiemployer organizing and bargaining.

Occupational unionism can be understood as a more general case of unionism than craft unionism. It is essentially craft unionism without craft skills. Yet, in low-wage work, simple skills such as showing up for work and understanding the logic behind rules against absenteeism and tardiness, as well as the necessity for safe practices, particularly in handling hazardous chemicals, may be best taught and delivered by an occupational union. This form of unionism may be especially appropriate where there are grounds for solidarity such as race and ethnicity that are capable of taking the place of the bonds of craft. It has worked well for the SEIU in its Justice for Janitors campaign. Whether it is a generally useful model for low-wage workers under current law is questionable. Yet, it suggests a type of unionism that may be appropriate for a particular industrial reality – a multiplicity of small employers among whom employees circulate on a regular basis. That this form is appealing in its application to low-wage workers, but perhaps not so much for others, suggests that, in order to survive in a complex economy, the labor movement must be sufficiently complex to match up with the variety of situations with which it is confronted. What must be avoided is a "one size fits all" mentality where one form that works in a particular setting is seen as a magic bullet to solve labor's problems in all situations.

Industrial Unions. Industrial unions comprise, along with craft unions, the two American "primary union types" (Barbash 1984: 52). This has been said to represent a difference between an exclusive (craft) and inclusive (industrial) approach to membership (Barbash 1984). Industrial unions claim jurisdiction of workers in an entire industry or group of industries (Estey 1981). Unlike craft unions, industrial unions have as their "characteristic environment a factory worksite, capital-intensive employment, high or middle-range technology, complex industrial organization, and national and international product markets" (Barbash 1984: 53). Industrial unions, perhaps because they are more involved in the core of the economy, are more likely to be involved in a broad range of political programs that have to do with the economy as a whole (Barbash 1984).

Industrial unions also have a special history. The militant radical Industrial Workers of the World (IWW), the "Wobblies," of the early twentieth century embraced industrial unionism. They saw the craft unions as elitist and overly narrow in their goals. The industrial unions that followed them, for example, Autoworkers, Steelworkers, Rubberworkers, Textile Workers, and Mineworkers, started out as more idealistic and political than the craft unions. Indeed, they often behaved more like social unions than bread-and-butter ones. Although they have since evolved into unions that can best be described as Pure and Simple unions, the major industrial unions have always retained some of the social movement goals of their early years. They have generally been more interested in the welfare of a working class than have the craft unions. Also, they have often been especially active in the international arena.

Industrial unions rose to prominence in the 1930s. Through their federation, the Congress of Industrial Organizations (CIO), they led the unionization of mass production industry. This happened because they had a form of organization that made sense for the industrial reality of the day, which did not lend itself readily to craft organization. It also happened because the industrial union leaders, such as John L. Lewis and Phillip Murray, had the will to organize the millions of unskilled and semiskilled workers that labored in America's factories. A number of the organizers were militant radical Communists, who seriously challenged the leaders for control of these unions. It is these struggles that account for much of the bitterness of traditional Pure and Simple unionists toward Communists.

Modern industrial unions are mainly collective-bargaining organizations. Yet, they retain something of the social movement flavor of their ancestral roots. Also, they have gone well beyond their original industrial jurisdictions to become what the British call "general unions." That is, they organize workers wherever the opportunity arises without regard to the industry in which they are employed. Much the same thing has happened to traditional craft unions such as the Teamsters, Electrical Workers, and Operating Engineers, who now represent a wide variety of workers. This has allowed these unions to grow, but has created problems of solidarity among members who have little in common. It is a real challenge for a union to develop expertise in the affairs of workers across many different industries and occupations.

Reform of Existing Unions. A suggestion that one frequently sees in the literature, and recently in statements of union leaders, is that unions would be successful if they would only clean house and do a better job of being unions. Undemocratic practices and dishonesty are evils that have long bedeviled American labor. They have often stripped it of its credibility and of public support. In addition, American unions have also often been accused of losing their idealism; being insufficiently aware of the need for changes in their structure and approach; and of a number of other weaknesses, real or imagined.

Criticism of labor in these regards has come from labor's friends as well as from its enemies. Arthur Shostak (1992) writes that unions need to require staffers to go to the field, have exemplary relations with their own staff unions, have line officers stand for election by secret mail ballot, have their publications include contributions from critics of incumbent officers, elect officers to work for change, and bring ideas from overseas into collective bargaining. William Gould, who was vigorously attacked by Congressional Republicans for allegedly being too pro-union while he was chair of the NLRB, argues that unions "must rid themselves of their lethargy and radically restructure their organizations along the lines of early industrial unions" (1993: 263).

Sol Barkin, a long-time labor activist and scholar, argues that American unions have historically failed to speak to how they contribute to economic growth and development, "leaving themselves open to the charge that they would cause loss of jobs" (Stabile 1993: 201). According to him, unions have lost their idealism and have failed to acquire technical expertise comparable to that of management on important issues. Barkin argues that unions must transform themselves in "a drastic overhaul of spirit and structure" (p. 206). Included among these reforms are: (1) more centralization of power in the AFL-CIO national office; (2) putting into effect innovative programs that "cultivate among workers a faith in a continuously improved life"; (3) being "strictly democratic"; (4) having a political stance and image "tinged with social ideals" so as not to appear to be a narrow interest group; and (5) bringing in intellectuals to help formulate new propaganda (p. 206).

There have long been movements for democracy and reform inside the labor movement. The Teamsters for a Democratic Union (TDU) is a group of reformers within what has historically been among the most corrupt of American unions. Although the reforms that they advocate may be in jeopardy with the election of James Hoffa, Jr. (who they opposed) to the leadership of the union, they are nevertheless still a force with which to be reckoned. The Miners for Democracy, a political movement within the United Mineworkers of America (UMWA), led a cleaning up and democratization of that union. There have been similar movements within a number of other unions, including the New Dimensions movement within the UAW, which has opposed the workplace cooperation favored by the national leadership.

A national organization of this type that provides support to the various intraunion democracy organizations is the Association for Union Democracy (AUD). The AUD originated with the publication of a newsletter, *Union Democracy in Action*, by Socialist Party leader Norman Thomas and Herman Benson in 1959. Thomas and Benson had at that time organized a Citizens Committee to call for an investigation of the murders of two reform leaders of the Painters Union in the San Francisco Bay area. After the successful conclusion of this work, the Citizens Committee decided to form the AUD. The AUD reached its thirtieth birthday as an organization in 1999. During its long life it has been a courageous gadfly, insisting on honesty in the labor movement and supporting individuals and groups within unions who have struggled to democratize them. It has provided financial support, legal counsel, and publicity to democratic elements in the labor movement.

The initiatives pursued by the AUD at the beginning of this century include litigation aimed at relaxing meeting attendance requirements for a member to run for office. These have historically been used to disqualify a very large percentage of union members from seeking union office. Also, the AUD has an education program that trains unionists in how to build democratic unions, and how to institute change from the grass roots. It has fought successfully to require unions to inform members of their legal rights vis-à-vis the union. It has been a strong presence in the movement for democracy and honesty in the Teamsters union.

The AUD, similar to other worker organizations that are not unions, is seldom mentioned in writings about the American labor movement. Needless to say, it has not been popular with the incumbent officials of unions, and neither has Herman Benson, its longtime leader. This, of course, is understandable. Leaders of labor unions are besieged by employers and government, and often by opposition within their unions. They are politicians who want to stay in office. The AUD is an almighty nuisance, stirring up the rank and file, or at least lending support to troublesome elements in the membership. Its revelations very often make unions look bad. It may give aid and comfort to the enemies of labor. Most recently, both Herman Benson and Clyde Summers, longtime AUD Board Member, testified in Congress in favor of legislation that is opposed by the AFL-CIO.

Yet it may be the glory of the American labor movement that an organization such as the AUD can prosper over the years. Although it may embarrass unions and their leaders at times, it is a tough and fearless watchdog for union democracy. It has been argued that unions, just like armies, cannot afford democracy (Goldberg 1959). However, without democracy the labor movement has no legitimacy. Unless it truly represents the interests of its members and is a credible spokesperson for them it has no reason to exist. It also seems reasonably clear that democratic unions are simply more effective than undemocratic ones (Strauss 1991). Gadflies are a nuisance, but they serve a crucial function. Their stings keep the labor movement truer to its cause than it would be without them.

The strategy of unions simply being better at their business is a mixture of Pure and Simple Unionism and Social Democratic Unionism. Making the union more efficient, honest, and democratic certainly fits within the goals of Pure and Simple unions. However, many of the arguments in favor of cleaning up unions see unions as part of a working-class movement. It is opposition to the betrayal of the labor movement as a social cause that gives much of the energy to the advocates of improved unions.

Associational Unionism. In his influential book, *The New Unionism* (1988), Charles Heckscher argues for a form of unionism that combines the logics of employee associations and unions. Similar to associations, such unions involve a number of employee groups acting in "shifting combinations," but still recognize the need for "organized pressure" (p. 10). The need for this comes from the rise of groups such as women's rights and civil rights organizations that have become more influential than unions, and the creation of a new body of rights by legislation. Heckscher sees associational unionism as "the structure needed to pull together these rights and interests – now confused and fractious – into a constructive system of representation" (p. 10).

Heckscher's associational unions have the following characteristics. They (1) are "based on universal rights guaranteed to all employees"; (2) "include varied employee groupings, based on job type, organizational level, geography, and other shared characteristics such as gender or race"; (3) "provide mechanisms of multilateral negotiation"; and (4) "encompass concerns about work structure and 'the quality of work life' on one hand, and about general policy on the other" (Heckscher 1988: 10–11). According to him, there are "traps" that need to be avoided by such organizations. These include failing to reduce the role of government in judging disputes (this should be done by local negotiations), assuming universal cooperation (ways must be provided to resolve disputes), and encouraging an explosion of litigation (it should be left to those involved to "work out interpretations of rights") (p. 11).

Arguing for the need for a different approach to employee representation, Heckscher says that the old distinction between those matters that affect workers and those that do not is obsolete. According to him, the old "two-stage" process, in which management makes a decision on economic grounds and the union then checks it for human effects, is too slow in the modern economy. The two-way balance of power model is also obsolete, as is a "rule-based" representational strategy. He claims that the worker attitudes and expectations that were the basis for the old Wagner Act system have changed. The white-collarization of the labor force has created a situation where many workers do not clearly fall on one side or the other of a line separating management and workers.

With white-collar workers the problem may not be that they lack solidarity, but that they have "a new form of solidarity that is not adequately addressed by existing structures" (p. 65). They want individualized rewards and promotions rather than group benefits. They tend toward forms of organization that differ from the mass organizations that came about in the 1930s. The solidarity and preferences of white-collar workers best find their expression in associations. Associations differ from unions in that they tend to be decentralized and participative, they minimize the role of bureaucracy, and they emphasize services to the members rather than demands on employers on their behalf. Where the members do have compelling collective interests, the association tends more toward using publicity than toward the strike.

White-collar unions, just like associations, tend to do some things that are not typical of unions. These include (1) bargaining only for minimum wage levels, leaving room for individual bargaining for wages above these levels; (2) encouraging other forms of participation along with bargaining; (3) down-playing emphasis on seniority and giving more importance to merit; (4) rarely seeking a fine specification of work rules; (5) minimizing the strike and emphasizing publicity and lobbying; and (6) being "relatively decentral-ized"(pp. 66–7).

Associational unions can gather together and rationalize the claims of multiple groups. This can provide the employer with a single representative with which to deal about a multiplicity of types of claims. This is the sort of thing that is done by true "general" unions. They provide "money, expertise and experience" (p. 211), which constitute the glue that holds together such diverse unions as the UAW and unions of hospital employees. Women's and minority caucuses within unions are examples of this phenomenon. One would expect associational unions to replace security in a particular job with security in having some job. They would free employee benefits from their ties to individual employers. In small firms, even with a small number of members, associational unions are capable of acting as pressure groups. In an industry of small employers, they can provide rationalization and coordina-tion to the industry.

Associational Unionism has much in common with craft and occupational unionism. It differs in that it models itself after the state employee associa-tions that were the precursors of the American Federation of State, County and Municipal Employees (AFSCME), and still exist in states that do not permit collective bargaining by state and local government employees. Given that they are by definition in the political realm, it is hardly surprising that public employee associations often employ publicity and political action rather than economic action. Whether this makes as much sense for private-sector workers is debatable. Also, this form takes a cue from the changing nature of the workforce – its white-collarization. Yet, as Heckscher recog-nizes, much white-collar work has become blue-collarized. Similar to the other forms previously outlined, it includes some interesting insights and opportunities, but seems not to be a solution that would be appropriate in all circumstances.

Associational Unionism is somewhat different from more traditional forms. It can be classed as Pure and Simple Unionism. However, similar to Social Democratic Unionism, it looks to politics for its power. It is, then, some-thing of a blend of these two types.

Reformist Unionism

Although Pure and Simple Unionism has been the dominant theme in American trade unionism, there has always been something of a Reformist subtheme. It flows rather naturally from the idea that the function of a labor movement is to improve the lives of workers. It also takes into account the need of labor to be seen as socially constructive – standing for something that is broader than the narrow self-interest of union members.

Social Unionism. What has historically been viewed as the polar opposite of craft unionism, social unionism, is perhaps the most talked about strategic choice these days. At the end of the nineteenth century the contest between these opposites took place in the form of competition between the Reformist Knights of Labor and the craft unions of the American Federation of Labor (AFL). The AFL won, and craft-style business unionism was the predominant form of union until the break out of industrial unionism in the 1930s. Now, at the beginning of the twenty-first century, these rival ideas are once again contending for dominance.

Social unionism has always had considerable intellectual appeal. On the surface at least, it seems more attractive than the more narrow, self-interested craft mode of organization. It particularly appeals to intellectuals and to those trade unionists who think in terms of a working class possessing broad common interests. A good part of the ideology of social unionism was picked up and used by the industrial unions as they organized the unskilled workers along with the skilled. Looking back to those days, Richard Belous of the Conference Board says,

Unions were at their best and most respected when they represented more than just the special interests of their members. In the golden days of unionism, the labor movement took on social causes, such as equity, justice, and the rights of those on the bottom rung of the economic ladder. Unionism prospers when it stands for more than a 3 percent raise and a cost-of-living increase (Belous 1987: 51).

Charles Heckscher, writing in favor of the general strategy of associational unionism (discussed previously), argues that where the union adopts resorting to the courts or using publicity as forms of pressure on an employer – unlike the situation in a strike – its success tends to depend upon considerations of reason and justice rather than on economic power. Moving into a broader forum than collective bargaining also allows unions to move to utilizing multiple party negotiations, involving such groups as environmental and human-rights organizations.

In an historical analysis of the union use of the community as a source of power, James Craft (1990) concludes that community action is only sometimes successful. There are examples of unions using the community as a whole as a basis for its power in disputes such as those over plant closings. Also, unions have linked with subgroups such as feminist, environmental, and civil-rights groups in organizing and in bargaining with employers. Local government has sometimes been brought in as an ally of labor in a dispute. At times unions have been able to make a case for community support, based on considerations of justice and equity.

There are, however, a number of barriers and limitations to unions drawing on the community as a power source. First, there is often little interest on the part of union members in establishing and maintaining long-term relationships with community groups. Second, there is often little coordination between community service and core union activities. Third, it is not clear that it is to the advantage of union leaders to spend their time on activities that the rank and file does not perceive to be related to their immediate interests. Fourth, the low esteem in which union leaders are held relative to business leaders may make it unrealistic to expect them to gain a great deal of community support (Craft 1990). There is the example of the International Association of Fire Fighters (IAFF) as a union that has long been effective in community affairs. It may be the case that for a union to be really effective in the community, and to gain advantage from it, it must make a commitment to making this an important part of the union's identity and activities, as has the IAFF. Yet this is difficult for many unions to do.

Despite the difficulties, community involvement in support of unions has been on the rise in the last year or so. This has often taken the form of a union or central labor body putting together a coalition of church and civic leaders, civil rights groups, and politicians. Especially encouraging is the revival of the old progressive alliance between organized labor and social action–oriented clergy.

In 1996, a group of California religious leaders organized Clergy and Laity United for Economic Justice (CLUE). This organization started out advocating that governments commit themselves to requiring a living wage to be paid to employees of their contractors. CLUE then joined in a fight for higher pay and better benefits for hotel workers, and in a dispute with the University of Southern California over its contracting out of jobs. CLUE is an instance of what has become a nationwide movement of "faith-based" activism. This arises out of an increasing awareness on the part of progressive religious leaders of a growing economic gap between rich and poor, and a belief that this is an "intolerable economic injustice" (Feingold 1998: p. E-8). Given their dependence upon the wealthy to support their religious institutions, taking the side of the poor is always a hazardous undertaking for religious leaders. Nevertheless, according to Rabbi Steven Jacobs, "There's an element in the religious community that's not going to be bowled over by princes and mayors" (Feingold 1998: p. E-8). These religious leaders see it as part of their mission to activate the consciences of decent persons, moving them to take action to eradicate injustices.

Early in the year 2000, a group of 1,500 Allegheny, Pennsylvania, registered nurses successfully organized a union with the support of a coalition of 13 community groups; labor leaders; state, local and national elected officials; and 3 clergy members. In California, a committee of religious and community leaders was put together by the Speaker of the State Assembly to monitor Catholic Healthcare West to make sure that its 5,000 workers had a free choice to join the SEIU. This committee, labeled The Fair Election Oversight Commission, includes the Dean of an Episcopal cathedral and the chair of the Chicano-Latino Caucus of the California Democratic Party (Voice@Work 2000). In an organizing campaign among workers at a Seattle hospital, the county labor council helped to form Northwest Neighbors for Fairness, which included neighborhood organizations and was supported by elected officials. This organization called for the employer to subscribe to a code of fair conduct that would constrain its conduct during the unionization campaign. The union prevailed in this campaign. Community support facilitated the organizing of graduate student employees at the University of Washington (Voice@Work 2001a).

There are numerous examples of community and religious leaders stepping forward in support of the rights of workers to decent conditions and pay, and the right to unionize. These range across the country from California to New York City to Boston and to Florida. These efforts have been publicized and encouraged by Voice@Work, a program of the AFL-CIO. The AFL-CIO has engaged in a highly publicized campaign in support of the right of workers to organize. The main theme of this campaign is that there is a secret war being waged by employers against workers, and that community leaders should respond to this by lending aid to the workers against whom this war is being perpetrated.

Also publicized by Voice@Work was the "Seven Days in June" campaign conducted by the AFL-CIO in June 2001. This involved a wide range of demonstrations and other forms of protest in support of organizing campaigns, good faith bargaining by employers where unions had won representation elections, living-wage ordinances, and the freedom of workers to organize a union and engage in union activity. These actions were organized at the local level, usually by a combination of a local central labor body of the AFL-CIO, groups of unions, religious leaders, politicians, and civic organizations. In Boston, a "justice trolley" containing activists visited the sites of two employers where workers were struggling to get initial collective-bargaining agreements after voting in a union (Voice@Work 2001b). In Columbia, South Carolina, several thousand workers and supporters rallied in support of the "Charleston Five," workers who were being prosecuted for felonies for alleged picket-line misconduct. In New Orleans, union and community activists protested at a shareholders' meeting of a company that fired several pro-union workers (Voice@Work 2001c). In Las Vegas a religious service was held during which "The Book of Shame," a list of employers who violated laws protecting workers' rights to organize, was released. The service was led by the Las Vegas Interfaith Council for Worker Justice (Voice@Work 2001d). In Houston the county central labor council gave "Justice Here" awards to the Oscar Romero Memorial Day Labor Center (named after the martyred El Salvador bishop) and the Central American Refugee Center, while naming an antiunion company as recipient of their "No Justice

Here" award (Voice@Work 2001e). Protests took place in several cities in California, Chicago, Washington, St. Paul, Portland, Miami, Cleveland, Little Rock, and a number of other cities across the country.

Justice for Janitors, an arm of the SEIU, held Justice for Janitors Day on June 15, 2001. For this thousands of supporters turned out across the country. The focus was immigrant rights. This featured a twenty-four-hour National Fast for Justice, for which a kickoff ceremony was held in front of the U.S. Capitol. The ceremony was attended by several members of Congress. Rallies were held in New York, Los Angeles, Baltimore, Chicago, Denver, Oakland, Portland, and Seattle (Voice@Work 2001f).

A characteristic aspect of social unionism is a focus on politics. This may even involve forming or supporting an independent labor party (Goldfield 1987; Pierce 1992; Rogers 1992). There have been calls for labor to "become a social and political movement," and to "stop behaving as an interest group and become an anti-establishment movement" (Navarro 1992: 57). It is argued that there should be a "labor-led strategy of industrial renewal focusing on worker training and work reorganization," providing services to members where there is no union certified to represent them, and creating and publicizing a "bill of rights for working Americans" (Rogers 1992). There is some evidence that workers will be attracted to unions that are instrumental to their political goals (Fiorito 1987). Even in decline, unions have sufficient funds to make a real difference in the political system. One of their greatest political successes in recent years was the 1998 defeat of a California ballot initiative that would have forced unions to obtain written permission from members before spending money for political purposes. This campaign showed that the traditional strength of labor – providing grassroots workers in large numbers – can still achieve some very powerful results. However, an enduring problem for labor in the political sphere is the ability of employers to outspend them by a very large margin. There is evidence that this margin is growing, not decreasing (Miller and Sifry 2000). Nevertheless, in the 2000 U.S. presidential election, labor proved its strength by swinging several key states to Democrat Al Gore, nearly carrying him to victory in the election.

A powerful progressive political movement has been launched by labor in California. At the heart of this movement is the Los Angeles County Federation of Labor, an AFL-CIO central labor council, led by Miguel Contreras. This is an alliance of labor and Latino activists, supported by religious and civic groups. It has helped to turn California into a progressive state in which the Democratic Party is predominant. In 2001, principally through local political action, it achieved such victories as the unionization of the workers of Gigante Supermarkets and the adoption of a living-wage ordinance in a traditionally conservative city. Working as a social union, it has become "the tribune not only for low-wage workers but for immigrant Californians generally" (Meyerson 2001).

In May 2001, the AFL-CIO launched the Alliance for Retired Americans. This is a political advocacy group on issues of interest to retirees. These issues include a secure income in retirement; good-quality housing; low-cost fuel and electricity; and good, affordable health care. This group initially consisted of retired union members who are enrolled by, and have their dues paid by, their unions. It started out with 2.5 million members. It does appear to have the potential for exerting substantial political influence on the U.S. Congress (Bureau of National Affairs 2001a).

Worker ownership, which will be discussed at length in Chapter 6, is another idea that has been historically associated with social unionism. This was an important concept of the Knights of Labor, who are considered further in Chapter 4. Although it was not practiced as actively as it was talked about, what the Knights called "cooperation," the establishment of worker cooperatives, was at the very core of the Knights' ideology. They wanted to turn back the clock to an earlier and better time before the advent of the wage system, which they wanted to abolish. The notion was that all "producers" should be owners.

As is noted in Chapter 6, a number of unions have opted for employee ownership as a practical response to threats to job security. This has often been "lemon socialism" – where a failing firm is taken over by its workers in an attempt to prevent a plant closing. Some unions, such as the United Steelworkers of America (Steelworkers), have become more proactive than this, however, sometimes actively seeking out successful firms that might be appropriate objects of a worker ownership attempt (Bernstein 1987).

The strategic direction of social unionism is essentially Reformist in nature. However, it does partake of some of the characteristics of Social Democratic Unionism.

Worker Rights Organizations. In addition to unions, there are a number of other organizations that concern themselves with worker rights and interests. They make up a lively and unconventional wing of a labor movement that has not always been known for these characteristics. These organizations mainly represent the low-wage, relatively unskilled workers at the bottom tier of the labor market. In the southeastern United States, where workers in general have low levels of rights and power, they include a wider band of the labor force.

These worker-rights groups are so diverse that it is difficult to generalize about them. They sometimes form on the basis of race or ethnicity. Some are purely geographical. Some focus only on employment relations issues, but most have somewhat broader goals. They are more akin to social unionism than to American bread-and-butter-style unionism. Some of them may even describe themselves in these terms, drawing a parallel to the Knights of Labor. Seldom do they engage in collective bargaining, although they may act to "soften up" organizing targets for unions that then bargain on behalf of the employees.

One grouping of these organizations is the Regional Economic Justice Network, located in the southeastern United States. It includes such organizations as South Carolina's Carolina Alliance for Fair Employment (CAFE), the Farm Labor Organizing Committee, and a group of University of North Carolina housekeepers. There is also a budding national network of ten to fifteen low-wage worker groups that includes an organization of Korean workers in Los Angeles and La Mujer Obera (The Woman Worker) in El Paso, Texas.

Perhaps listing these organizations is the best way to convey their variety: Chinese Staff and Workers' Association (restaurant workers in New York City); Latino Workers' Center (New York City); Black Workers for Justice (Rocky Mount, North Carolina); Movimiento Estudiantil Chicano de Aztlan (Chicano Student Movement of Aztlan – Aztlan is their name for the southwestern United States); Asian Immigrant Worker Advocates (Oakland, California); Atlanta Union of the Homeless; Community Voices Heard (New York City); Farm Labor Organizing Committee (Toledo, Ohio); Louisiana Injured Workers' Union (New Orleans); Northeast Citizen Action Resource Center (Cambridge, Massachusetts); Progreso Latino (Center Falls, Rhode Island); Tennessee Industrial Renewal Network (Nashville); UNC Housekeepers (Hillsborough, North Carolina); United Labor Agency of Bergen County (Hackensack, New Jersey); WEP Workers Organizing Center/ACORN (Brooklyn); Worker Organizing Committee (Portland, Oregon); Working Partnerships (San Jose, California); and Workplace Project (Hempstead, New York).

Worker rights organizations vary in their activities. Many of them are involved in one way or another in the problems of temporary workers. They lobby legislative bodies and engage in social protest actions such as picketing; educating and providing counseling to workers; and pressuring state labor and environmental agencies. They organize groups of workers in which unions may not be interested. On occasion they do preunion work, putting workers into motion in attempts to end their deprivations. This can sometimes carry them on a classic path to forming a union (see Wheeler 1985).

If one adopts Sidney and Beatrice Webb's (1911) traditional definition of a trade union – organizations of wage earners that seek to improve the conditions of their working lives – these groups might be considered unions. Certainly employer antiunion groups such as the South Carolina Chamber of Commerce consider them to be such. However, they do not do what we usually think of unions as doing – engage in collective bargaining. Neither do they ordinarily strike. Their weapons are much more likely to be political pressure, social protest, and publicity. What is clear is that these organizations are a part of any comprehensive definition of a labor movement in the United States. The fact that they have been little noted in the national news media or in scholarly literature does not mean that they are not important. One of them, CAFE, is the subject of Chapter 5. They are essentially Reformist in nature.

Cooperationist Unionism

Early in the last century, in 1915, a manager testifying before the Commission on Industrial Relations said, "We have come to the period of cooperation" (Smith 1986: 371). In 1920 a manager announced that the usefulness of "organizations of class antagonism" had come to an end (Smith 1986: 404). Were these statements, though untrue at the time, prescient with regard to the new realities of workplace relations that exist at the beginning of the twenty-first century? In addition to managers, many observers and trade unionists seem to think so.

Writing in 1988, John Stepp, who had been instrumental in working on labor-management cooperation programs in the Reagan administration's Labor Department, wrote that "many industries and unions . . . have been making the painful discovery that their traditional antagonistic relationships are self-defeating in today's global economy. At the same time however, they are discovering that cooperation is an important new direction" (Stepp 1988: 36). He argues that "the key to economic growth and sustained economic development thus lies in the process of establishing more productive labor-management relations" (p. 36). This involves a "new work environment . . . based on cooperation, mutuality, and a jointly crafted vision of the future" (p. 36). According to Stepp, employee-involvement programs and cooperative programs generally can lead to increased productivity and competitiveness. It is only by becoming "partners" with management that workers and unions can be a part of the solution to the problems of a modern economy. Debra Dinnocenzo, a management consultant, says,

Labor and management professionals are realizing that cooperative labor systems are more productive than adversarial ones, that worker involvement increases productivity and morale, and that job breadth and versatility can be good for both employer and employee (1989: 36).

According to Dinnocenzo, a necessary condition to success in a labor-management "partnership" is "a commitment to the philosophy of cooperation by both labor and management" (p. 36).

In a set of interviews by this writer with national union officials, conducted in Washington in 1997, one of the recurring themes was the need for "partnering" – meaning cooperation with management. Here is what these union leaders and union documents said.

Cooperation is happening because there is no alternative. *Bob Welsh, Executive Assistant to the President and Chief of Staff, AFL-CIO* (Welsh 1997).

This agreement specifically promotes the continued development of a labor management partnership fostered by openness, trust, and understanding resulting in a working environment which recognizes the full worth and dignity of all employees and facilitates their individual growth and accomplishments toward the continued needs for effective and efficient bakery operations. In striving toward the achievement of high performance workplaces, the Union and the Company are committed to maximizing company and employee profitability through the attainment of 5 core partnership elements: EMPOWERMENT, WORK REDESIGN, CHANGING ROLES & RESPONSIBILITIES, REWARDS. *Participative Work Agreement between Nabisco, Inc., and the Bakery, Confectionery, Tobacco Workers and Grain Millers International Union, 1995.*

I believe one particular path is very dangerous, and that is the path of neo-Taylorism, where the workers are further de-skilled, where their knowledge of their individual job is captured and bottled, leading to the demise of their job. The other path, however, could be advantageous. If workers can be truly valued for their skills and labor, and a program can be put in place where the workers receive advanced training (statistical processing, continuous improvement training, quality improvement training, etc.) resulting in an increased level of skills, and that the entire process can be governed by a negotiated framework, the results should be improved efficiencies, product consistency and quality, and employee satisfaction. The key to this path is for the workers to have an independent voice in the process, which is only guaranteed by a union. *Frank Hurt, International President, Bakery, Confectionery, Tobacco Workers and Grain Millers Union* (Hurt 1997).

We have to leverage internal [union] resources to influence decisions like high road v. low road, capital investment, jobs in 20 years, quality so that people will buy, the way work is organized, making sure jobs are not dead end, and more efficiency and productivity. . . . What should we engage in? Management decisions. . . . A study by the Foundation for the Study of Living and Working Conditions of the European Union, in Dublin, showed that after workplace participation was put in place, union participation doubled, and was by completely different people. Every story I hear is that opportunity and challenge are what workers say that they want. . . . We are so enterprise based that it's very hard for unions to have influence on enterprise decisions without becoming enterprise unions – without a broad industrial base and broad strength to build worker unity across enterprises. Otherwise, workers will identify more with their boss than with workers down the street. *Nancy Mills, Acting Director, Center for Workplace Democracy, AFL-CIO* (Mills 1997).

Our challenge is clear: Instead of relegating teachers to the role of production workers – with no say in organizing their schools for excellence – we need to enlist teachers as full partners, indeed, as co-managers of their schools. Instead of contracts that reduce flexibility and restrict change, we – and our schools – need contracts that empower and enable. . . . This new collaboration is not about sleeping with the enemy. It is about waking up to our shared stake in reinvigorating the public education enterprise. *Bob Chase, President, National Education Association. Remarks Before the National Press Club, Washington, DC, February 5, 1997* (Chase 1997).

We are working more toward partnering with employers. Unions that bring value to employers are those that will be around. . . . We will get there [partnering] because we have to. *M. E. Nichols, Vice President, Communication Workers of America* (Nichols 1997).

The Steelworkers have been actively engaged in setting up partnership-like relationships for about twenty years. Roy Murray, Director, Collective Bargaining Services Department, Steelworkers, described this experience at some length in a 1999 interview with this author. According to him, the beginning of intensive participation by steelworkers was in the 1980 Basic Steel Industry negotiations when the parties agreed to an experimental Labor Management Participation Teams (LMPT) process. The first formal Partnership Agreement was with National Steel in 1986.

What was labeled by the Steelworkers as "New Directions" bargaining in 1993 was built on two "core principles." They are (1) "no one has a greater stake in the ongoing success of an enterprise than its workers" and (2) "the best way to bring about . . . success is to involve workers and their union in the management and decision-making process, not perfunctorily or in appearance only, but in a fashion that everyone would recognize as meaningful and real" (Frankel 1993). New Directions bargaining included demands for long-term contracts with economic contract reopeners. It provided for partnership and workplace democracy to flow between the boardroom and the plant floor.

The idea of partnership is central to the Steelworkers' bargaining strategy. In the best cases union officers are actively involved in training workers. Union members control all of the elements of the job training. Employment security is guaranteed. According to Roy Murray, "It is the journey that changes the way that things are done" (Murray 1999: 4). This is because not everything can be put in explicit terms, and the important thing is to get along and not to fight over the specifics. The role of the union is seen by Murray as, after cooperating, working out how "the wealth should be shared with the bargaining unit" (Murray 1999: 5). Some of these partnerships have worked out quite well. Others have not. In Murray's view, employee ownership under an Employee Stock Ownership Plan (ESOP) does not affect the outcome. One positive outcome for the Steelworkers is to have union representatives on about twenty-six corporate boards of directors. He believes that this can be useful in passing on nonconfidential information to the union and the workers, and in speaking on their behalf to the board.

A qualitative scholarly study of union representation on corporate boards produced some interesting results on union influence. Larry W. Hunter (1998) found that there was very little advocacy of worker or union interests by union-appointed directors. Effectiveness of union directors in having influence on board decisions was found to depend on (1) the share of ownership held by the workers or union; (2) union support for the director(s); (3) the size of the firm (influence being greater in smaller firms); (4) the number of union directors (it was more effective to have more than one or two); and (5) management commitment to employee participation.

Why would managers, who have the whip hand under existing circumstances, want to act cooperatively with a union? This may be because real cooperation is possible only when workers have the ability to speak without fear of reprisal. As Charles Heckscher has argued, systems that are dependent entirely on management power are generally unable to protect managers against "deception and self-deception" (p. 254). This is because, even when management is attempting to operate in a nonoppressive manner, "it is quite common for management to miss hidden resistance, to believe that consensus is greater than it actually is, and to have too much faith in the power of charismatic leadership to sweep everyone along" (p. 254). Most companies, left to their own devices, adopt "half-measures" such as open-door policies and employee groups with only limited participation rights, rather than adopting the "real structural reforms" that are necessary to deliver the full benefits of participation.

Management resistance to cooperative systems is probably based, at least in part, on the unwillingness of management to share real power with unions or workers. There has also been resistance from some union leaders (Nichols 1988; Gould 1993). It has been argued that cooperation is an illusion, whereas the reality is unchecked management power (Verespej 1991). As Sar Levitan says, the management idea of cooperation may be "you coo and I'll operate" (quoted in Verespej 1991: 13). According to Reggie Newell of the International Association of Machinists, "we think they [management] are just trying to create an illusion of shop-floor empowerment and power sharing" (Verespej 1991: 14). Instead of cooperating, "Companies smell blood, and they are going for the kill" (Verespej 1991: 16). Indeed, it does appear that it is unrealistic to expect unions to act in partnership with managers who are at the same time trying to destroy them.

Participative mechanisms at the shop level have been growing in both union and nonunion firms. Union avoidance is often one of the motivations for participation in the nonunion setting. However, it is clear that for some companies it is part of a "high road" strategy for firm success. That strategy includes employee involvement, high wages, and a generally benevolent set of human-resource policies. For such firms, unions that accept mechanisms for individual worker participation can serve the function of making the firm's commitment to participation permanent. They do this by resisting its abandonment with the collective power of workers. The union can keep management honest. It can insure that the participation is genuine, and unfettered by fear of managers victimizing workers by punishing them for speaking out, or using their suggestions to eliminate their jobs.

On the other hand, participatory schemes are based on the assumption of common interests among workers, managers, and shareholders. The reality is more complex than this. Although there are common interests, there are also divergent interests. Pay is basically a cost to shareholders and a benefit to workers. The same can be said for staffing levels beyond those absolutely necessary to produce the goods or services. Therefore, at some point the adversarial nature of the union and management relationship will reveal itself (Gould 1993). What is required is a maturity of outlook on the part of both labor and management to be able to tolerate this complex situation. This is not all that difficult to obtain. It is very similar to what already goes on in mature collective-bargaining relationships, where there is an easy relationship between integrative matters, such as safety, where interests are the same, and distributive issues, such as wages, where they are not.

In a company such as Saturn, where cooperation and participation are at a very advanced stage, it may be that a very complex form of local union is required. One interesting study (Rubenstein 2001) concludes that the local union must not only add value to management by bringing substantive knowledge to bear upon problems and helping to produce quality results "through co-management and a dense communication network" (which the UAW local has done at Saturn) (Rubenstein 2001: 195). It must also manage to "bring worker interests to bear in the strategic choices made" and this must be visible and understood by the membership (p. 195). Otherwise workers will not believe that this form of representation has any value to them. In addition, the union needs to represent individual rights and concerns of workers as a worker advocate. The author of this study concludes that in this setting it makes sense for the union to tend toward being something of an American version of a Japanese enterprise union – tightly connected to the firm and dedicated to its success. Yet in the American environment, which is generally hostile to unionism, enterprise unions cannot by themselves effectively resist management pressure to drive down wages and standards in order to compete more effectively, or have the expertise and other resources necessary to survive. The crucial task of these unions – a difficult one – is to achieve a balance between collective and individual representation.

Essentially, labor-management cooperation is Cooperationist Unionism. This is an uncomfortable position for the basically Pure and Simple American unions. It contains traps such as loss of solidarity and militancy, but may be a necessary form where management is much more powerful than labor, as it is in the United States at present.

Collective Action by Managers: Intrafirm Network Groups. An interesting, but little noted, form of employee organization consists of networks of employees within a firm who are united by some common bond. African American network groups are described in a 1993 paper by Raymond A. Friedman and Donna Carter. These groups, which are generally for the benefit of managerial employees, have as their main goal assisting group members to "advance in their organizations in spite of lack of support from informal networks or acceptance by some members of the organization" (Friedman and

Carter 1993: ii). For African Americans these networks have been formed largely in response to the fact that the numbers of blacks in middle- and upper-management positions are disproportionately less than their representation in the population.

By the mid-1990s network groups of various types had been formed in one-third of Fortune and Service 500 companies (Friedman 1996). These groups have been put together by women, Blacks, Hispanics, Asians, American Indians, gays and lesbians, veterans, and the disabled. Their activities include social events, and discussions of new technology, firm strategy, and career progression systems. They tend to meet every month or two. Some of them organize annual conferences on such topics as selling techniques, personal finances, and Hispanic literature (Friedman and Craig 2000).

Corporate policy toward network groups has tended to be mildly approving. Some minor costs may be incurred by the firm, usually in the form of permitting the group to use the company photocopying machines and e-mail and permitting group leaders to meet during working hours (Friedman and Craig 2000). There is some evidence that nonmember managers fear that a network group may turn into a union or a pressure group. These fears, however, do not appear to be warranted (Friedman 1999).

Network groups tend to view themselves as performing the role of helping members build their careers through social networking, and providing knowledge and leadership opportunities. They have sometimes engaged in advocacy. For example, a Black caucus at Xerox uncovered and took action against some discriminatory practices. Gay and lesbian network groups have advocated domestic-partner fringe benefits. Yet, these groups are usually very leery of being seen as advocacy organizations of any kind, let alone as unions (Friedman and Craig 2000). They appear to be effective in improving the optimism with which Black managers view their careers, largely through positive effects on the mentoring that they receive (Friedman, Kane, and Cornfield 1998).

One of the things that makes network groups interesting is that they are a form of collective action by managers. Their rationale sometimes sounds very similar to that for rank-and-file employees. As one manager says, "When one person has a problem, no one listens. When there are lots of people complaining, they pay attention" (Friedman and Carter 1993: 9). However, at least according to one study (Friedman and Craig 2000), it appears that managers considering joining such a group may have somewhat different motivations from rank-and-file workers considering joining a union. Just like rank and filers, these managers are influenced by the perceived efficacy of the group and by feelings of solidarity with fellow members. However, unlike rank and filers, they do not appear to be motivated by dissatisfaction.

These groups evidence a demand for collective action that is not limited to "employees" as they are defined in the NLRA. The exclusion of supervisors in Section 2 (11) of the Act assumes that these employees do not have the same needs for representation as other employees. Even if this were true at one time (and this is doubtful) it would seem that this rule may now be obsolete. So, when we think of a labor movement it does not necessarily make sense to limit ourselves to thinking only of an order-taking working class, but also of the managers who are employees as well.

Intrafirm Network Groups are difficult to classify under our taxonomic framework. Just like Pure and Simple Unionism their chief aim is to improve the practical conditions of workers' working lives. They do not involve the use of politics, per se. However, they do depend upon government support in the form of antidiscrimination laws. Their consciousness is not that of a proletariat or even of an occupation, but rather of a racial, ethnic, or other group. They do not look to collective bargaining, but collective action is involved.

AMERICAN UNION TACTICS

The preceding discussion of broad strategic approaches sets up a consideration of the question of whether there are fundamental changes that need to be made in the general direction of the American labor movement. Whether or not this is the case, there would seem to be room for consideration of particular tactics that can make unions more successful. A number of tactical options have been discussed and experimented with since American unions began their decline in the mid-1950s. What this proves, if nothing else, is that unions and their friends have been active in seeking out new ways to survive and grow.

Most of the tactics discussed here – organizing, strikes, minority unions, corporate campaigns – are fundamentally consistent with Pure and Simple Unionism. Training is a bit different in that it partakes rather strongly of Social Democratic Unionism and, to a degree, of Reformist Unionism. Similarly, union action to regulate international trade, although aiming at bread-and-butter results, utilizes the forms of other types of unionism. Just like Social Democratic Unionism, it claims to benefit both American society as a whole and the international working class, and looks to government action rather than collective bargaining as its instrument of power.

APPROACHES TO ORGANIZING

On August 1, 2000, the AFL-CIO Executive Council approved a four-point program on organizing. The first point is a goal of adding one million new union members per year. The other points include national unions raising their organizing goals, periodic assessment of the organizing drive by a committee of the AFL-CIO Executive Council, and national unions keeping track of their organizing results (Bureau of National Affairs 2000b). This was followed in May 2001 by a new political/organizing mobilization program that involved the establishment of a fax/e-mail network with local unions and the assignment of AFL-CIO staff to organizing. This effort has also included efforts to change the political climate for organizing by building the commitment of politicians to changing the laws relative to organizing (Bureau of National Affairs 2001b).

In addition to simply spending more money and effort on organizing, there have been numerous ideas about new approaches to organizing. John Sweeney, the AFL-CIO under his leadership, and his home union (the SEIU), all advocate shifting the whole orientation of unions to a focus upon organizing. This is in contrast to the traditional role of unions as being primarily service organizations that negotiate contracts and handle grievances (Sweeney 2001). Sweeney speaks of the importance of building a "culture of organizing." This approach has led to calls for unions to devote an increased share of their resources to organizing. One union that has taken this challenge seriously is the Steelworkers. In their 1998 convention they voted to create a $40 million organizing fund, and to develop partnerships among local unions to facilitate organizing.

Even the historically closed building-trades unions have become active in organizing. Their tactic of using union members as "salts" in nonunion workplaces is an innovative one that has produced some positive results. "Salting" involves a union activist taking a job with a nonunion contractor for the express purpose of organizing (Tomsho 1993).

Organizing aimed at the special needs of particular groups of workers has become common. As previously noted, in early 1999, the SEIU won a representation election among 74,000 home health-care workers in Los Angeles. These workers work in patients' homes, a situation that makes them especially difficult to organize. The campaign was a mixture of politics and economics and was designed specifically for low-wage, immigrant workers.

As women make up an increasing proportion of the workforce, unions have devised strategies aimed at appealing to them. Interestingly, it is the AUD that may have come up with some of the best advice for unions on how to attract and hold onto women members. In the "Tips for Activists" in one of their newsletters, they advise women to set up a women's caucus, and tell them how to go about it (Association for Union Democracy 1994). It may be that it is precisely by facilitating women's influence within unions that the unions will come to attract them. If women's caucuses are successful in delivering union responsiveness to their needs, this should insure that the unions are in fact meeting the requirements of female members. This, more than any set of policies developed by the largely male union leadership, has the potential for improving organizing success among women.

Although also benefiting male workers, collectively bargained programs dealing with child care and other family concerns are particularly helpful to women employees. Ford Motor Company and the UAW have been leaders in setting up collectively negotiated child-care centers. The International Brotherhood of Electrical Workers (IBEW) and the Communication

Workers of America (CWA) negotiated a program called "Kids in the Workplace" that makes day care available at the workplace on days that children are not in school because of school holidays or other reasons (Lazarovici 2000a). Management officials have said that collective bargaining is a competitive advantage for their firm because of the positive effects of negotiated work-family programs. These programs have met employee needs, while at the same time helping employers solve problems of absenteeism (Lazarovici 2000b).

It has become increasingly apparent that in order for the American labor movement to survive it must find ways to attract more white-collar workers. Accomplishing this is partly a matter of image and partly a matter of what unions have to offer. In order for white-collar workers to find unions attractive, they must come to see unions in a positive light. This calls for more skillful use of public relations by unions. It has been argued that "labor has lost its voice" through not properly utilizing "the most bold weapons of the 90s: media" (Bynum 1992: 16). This also calls for unions to be democratic, honest, and competent.

Charles Craver, in his book *Can Unions Survive?* (1993), argues that a condition for union survival is for them "to develop programs designed to appeal to the burgeoning ranks of white-collar and service personnel," only 10 percent of whom were organized at the time of his writing (p. 82). According to him, this will require "an organizing revolution" (p. 82). The opportunity for organizing is there because of the "poor economic and environmental conditions associated with their positions" (p. 83). Also, in some of these jobs there need be no concern about organizing being squelched because of concern about the effects of foreign competition.

As argued by Craver, white-collar and professional workers have traditionally identified themselves with managers, believing that they have much in common with them. Given the differences in compensation and other indicators of social class, this is an illusion that has become increasingly difficult for management to maintain. In addition, the reality of the labor market is that, for most white-collar workers, there are only limited opportunities for advancement – something that these workers commonly want. In fact, the situations of white-collar and blue-collar workers have become very similar in the modern corporation, including in the important area of job security.

Craver suggests that Associational Unionism, as argued for by Heckscher, may be an answer to the difficulties of unions in organizing these workers. It would also seem that the experience of organizing and representing such workers in the public sector would be useful to unions in organizing them in the private sector. If nothing else, this should give them a cadre of organizers who have a great deal in common with the workers being organized.

It may be that changes in the NLRA are required in order to fit collective bargaining to the needs of professional employees. David Rabban, formerly legal counsel to the American Association of University Professors (AAUP), argues that the failure to require bargaining on what the NLRA considers only permissive (not mandatory) subjects of bargaining is out of sync with the concerns of professionals. It is just those subjects, involving basic policies of the work organization, with which professionals are most concerned. He also believes that exclusive representation and strictures against company-dominated unions are concepts that do not fit professionals well (Rabban 1989). Recent decisions of the NLRB do appear to clear away legal impediments to organizing both professors and graduate assistants in private colleges (*Academe* 2000). As John Sweeney (2001) notes, there have been some successes by unions in organizing college and university employees.

An intriguing idea that has arisen in recent years is the notion of professionals working in "guilds" that would send out teams to solve problems (Bureau of National Affairs 1993). These teams would report to work at client companies when called upon. They would be self-managed temporary work groups. This differs from workers being supplied by a temporary agency in that the professionals themselves would control the guild. This is similar in concept to the craft union hiring hall. The only example of something like this in the literature is of employees of Time-Life Inc. managing the publishing work of American Express Company. Such guilds could be unions, or could loosely affiliate themselves with unions or with the AFL-CIO.

An innovative approach called Voice@Work was initiated in 2000 by the AFL-CIO Organizing Department (Bureau of National Affairs 2000a). One major thrust of this tactic is to focus attention on the failings of American labor laws and the routine violation of these laws by employers. In its Labor Day 2000 newsletter, Voice@Work publicized a recent report by Human Rights Watch declaring that U.S. workers lacked the basic rights to organize, bargain collectively, and engage in strikes. It also announced an online Labor Day Festival.

Some efforts are being made to organize contingent employees, especially temporary employees, or "temps." In its 2000 convention the CWA dealt extensively with the potential for organizing contingent staff in high-tech industries. The CWA's president told the convention that the union was ready to organize "new economy" workers who often lack health care, pensions, seniority, and other workplace protections (Bureau of National Affairs 2000c).

The Washington Alliance of Technology Workers (WashTech), a small but energetic worker-rights organization in the Seattle area, has affiliated with the CWA. Its aim is worker advocacy rather than collective bargaining. This marrying of a worker-rights organization with a traditional union may offer an interesting new form of unionism. WashTech has exposed abusive practices in high-tech industry and lobbied for investigation and regulation of the temporary employment industry. The difficulties in organizing this highly independent, often highly paid, group of workers are considerable. As a

WashTech leader has said, it is necessary to "overcome the idea that labor unions were only for people who hated their jobs" (Moberg 2000a: 12). Yet, there are underlying issues of job security that may make unionization seem more attractive when the economy slows down a bit. John Sweeney (2001) believes that many of these workers are unhappy with their lack of grievance machinery, retirement plans, and training. According to him, "The challenge for the labor movement is how to reach these workers and convince them that true collective bargaining is able to address their issues" (p. 5).

There is a good model for organization of employees in very similar circumstances – skilled construction-trades workers. The union hiring hall and training systems that have worked well for carpenters and bricklayers might work equally well for software designers. The innovative California labor movement is trying this out in Silicon Valley. Under the leadership of Amy Dean, the South Bay AFL-CIO Labor Council in San Jose "has taken a leaf from the old guild model and offers training, benefits, and a hiring hall to the high-tech temps so beloved by new-economy employers" (Meyerson 2001).

WashTech is also working to establish a cooperative temp agency to be owned by the workers (Moberg 2000a). There is also an organization called Working Today, which is an amalgam of twenty-five associations of workers, that follows the craft union model to some degree. It attempts to control the supply of labor and works for "fair" prices for its members' products. Working Today is also experimenting with a portable benefit fund (Carre et al. 2000).

Unions have used collective bargaining as an instrument for organizing. This has mainly taken the form of neutrality or card-check agreements. In a neutrality agreement an employer that has both unionized and nonunionized operations, or a unionized employer who plans to open new operations, agrees to stand neutral in any organizing campaign involving the union and nonunionized work sites. It may even go so far as to agree to recognize the union on the basis of the union obtaining authorization cards from a majority of the employees – a card-check agreement. This bypasses the cumbersome and (for the union) risky election processes of the NLRB (Masters 1997).

The computer and the possibilities of e-mail and the Internet are beginning to be used very effectively by unions in organizing as well as in other facets of their operations (Shostak 1999). The new political/organizing mobilization network established by the AFL-CIO in 2001 was made possible by the computer. The initial experience with this has been very positive (Bureau of National Affairs 2001b).

Organizing, at least as practiced by American unions, is essentially a Pure and Simple union activity. Its aim is to strengthen the trade union as an organization. It does not necessarily call for a working-class consciousness or militant action. It does not look to political change, or even educating the producers in the society. Although it often takes on an appearance of Reformist or Social Democratic action, its announced and practically pursued goal is nearly always forming a unit of workers for the purpose of collective bargaining.

The Strike

Labor's oldest tactic has fallen into disuse in recent years, as the strike rate has fallen to historic lows. In 1999, in bargaining units of 1,000 or more workers, there were only 17 work stoppages involving 73,000 workers. These were the lowest numbers in the fifty-three years that the Bureau of Labor Statistics has been collecting these data. In 1998 there were only 34 stoppages involving 387,000 workers (Bureau of Labor Statistics 2000). This experience has led to talk of a labor movement without strikes. This idea was especially encouraged by the failure of many strikes in recent years, such as the one at Caterpillar. Employer use of permanent replacement of strikers, which places strikers' jobs at risk, seemed to be the ultimate employer weapon against unions. The failure of these strikes also did no good to organizing efforts.

What has changed in the last few years is that unions have won some highly visible strikes. The 1997 strike against United Parcel Service (UPS) by the Teamsters may have been the most dramatic labor victory in many years. Although it was explained away by many observers on the basis of special conditions at UPS, it nevertheless was seen by the public as a resounding victory for labor.

The results of strikes in both 1997 and 1998 were generally more favorable to unions than they had been in the recent past. The year 1998 saw major strikes at Northwest Airlines, General Motors, Bell Atlantic, and US West, all of which were union victories. In 1999 there was a successful strike against Verizon, a major wireless communication company. There has also been something of a revival of the general strike, a little-used weapon, in strikes in the New York City construction industry and in Puerto Rico.

The strike, at least as used by American unions, is clearly a tactic of Pure and Simple Unionism. American unions almost always strike in connection with demands made in collective bargaining. The demonstration or political strike that is common in other parts of the world is almost unknown in the American industrial relations system.

Union Membership Absent a Majority in a Bargaining Unit

American unions have traditionally represented workers only where they have been recognized by an employer, generally based upon a showing that the union is supported by a majority of the employees in the bargaining unit. In recent years this model has been challenged by two notions. One idea is associate membership. The other is nonmajority representation.

Associate membership is a mechanism for delivering some services to workers who are not in a bargaining unit represented by a union. It has been made available to prounion workers in a failed election, former union members who want to continue their affiliation with the union, and workers in antiunion settings who want some "personal affiliation with organized labor" (Shostak 1991: 63). This idea was given impetus by the 1985 AFL-CIO Executive Council Report, *The Changing Situation of Workers and Their Unions*. Pursuant to the conclusions of this report, the AFL-CIO set up the Union Privilege Benefit Program. This program made credit cards, vacation bargains, and other nonbargained benefits available to associate members, as well as to members.

One rationale for associate membership is to get workers "to begin to think of labor as a social support movement or a citizens' movement, and not just as a high-wages movement" (Shostak 1991: 64). This can be seen as expanding the concept of union membership as "moving in concentric circles from the core of dues-paying bargaining unit members to include all who might desire a union affiliation . . ." (Holter 1992: 40). Under this view membership is not an either/or matter, but instead a matter of degree. This would be a "step toward a much broader conception of what unions can do" (Edwards and Podgursky 1986: 53). Interestingly, this would also be a step back toward a preindustrial concept of unions as fraternal and benevolent organizations (Gould 1993).

Associate membership is not without its problems. If it substitutes for full membership, this is clearly not in the interests of unions. It may also constitute an unpredictable political bloc within the union – one that is made up of second-class citizens. Credit cards may create problems if associate members are found not to be credit worthy. Legal services may be the most promising of benefits (Gould 1993).

In an insightful law review article, Clyde Summers (1990) makes a powerful argument for union advocacy on behalf of employees in a nonmajority situation. As Summers notes, the giving of special status to a majority union by Section 9 (a) of the NLRA "in no way derogates from the section 7 rights of a union without a majority where there is no exclusive representative" (p. 531). Section 7 protects "other concerted activity" of workers as well as organizing and collective bargaining. A nonmajority union is protected in its right to present demands to an employer. Individual employees can claim the right not to discuss terms and conditions of employment with the employer, insisting upon the employer dealing with their union. Also, a nonmajority union can bargain out a collective-bargaining agreement covering its own members. A very useful role for a nonmajority union is providing assistance in learning about and enforcing individual rights provided by law. This, of course, parallels suggestions for legal services for associate members.

In addition to the notion of providing a broad set of services to associate members or nonmajority union members, there are proposals for having an expanded range of services available for regular members. Here again, the providing of legal services would seem to be the most crucial service for members, given the increasingly complex web of legal regulation that applies to the workplace (Higginson and Waxler 1990).

The idea of associate membership has been pursued very actively by a number of unions, with associate members now numbering in the hundreds of thousands. Similarly, the expansion of services is an idea that unions have taken up with some enthusiasm. As is noted in the following text, this idea has been taken up abroad, with labor movements in several European countries, particularly the Netherlands, expanding services. Legal services appear to be the most popular expanded benefit in the Netherlands and the United Kingdom.

What has not happened is the broad adoption of nonmajority representation. This is admittedly very difficult to do. The real problem is the practical ineffectiveness of the NLRA in providing protection to workers who assert their right to engage in this kind of protected activity. So long as the protections are illusory, this tactic may be too risky to be pursued. As noted in Chapter 5, this is a tactic tried, but eventually abandoned, by the worker-rights organization CAFE. As pragmatic organizations, American unions are unlikely to pursue this tactic very often unless it can be justified on practical grounds. It is not enough for the tactic to be appealing in theory. It *must* work.

It seems to this writer that American labor should, in spite of the difficulties, pursue nonmajority representation. The chief reason for this is the potential of this strategy for preparing workers for organizing for the purpose of collective bargaining. Workers organize when they become frustrated (Wheeler 1985). Frustration occurs only when workers take action to achieve their goals and are blocked by their employer. This means that they must somehow be put in motion toward their goals. If the employer refuses to grant a minority union's demands, or even to meet with it, this is a classic situation for worker frustration. It has a high potential for leading to unionization. If the employer grants what the minority union wants, this helps to create another crucial condition for organizing – perceptions on the part of workers that the union can be instrumental in achieving their goals. If the employer victimizes workers who engage in this action, this may well backfire against the employer – providing an occasion for unionization. So, the union wins, however the employer responds. This is clearly a tactic that, although risky, needs to be considered by American unions.

This tactic is one that should be classed as one of Pure and Simple Unionism.

The Corporate Campaign

In 1976, in the Amalgamated Clothing and Textile Workers Union (ACTWU) effort to organize the employees of J. P. Stevens, a new weapon was added to labor's arsenal. This weapon, the corporate campaign, has since been used on numerous occasions.

The term *corporate campaign* is used to describe a wide variety of tactics. In their comprehensive analysis of such campaigns up to 1990, Paul Jarley and Cheryl Maranto (1990) say that it is "no more than a label indicating the union's intent to utilize nontraditional tactics in an attempt to pressure the firm to change its behavior" (p. 507).

Jarley and Maranto construct a typology of campaigns based upon the situations in which they are utilized. The first type is to obtain representation rights, and is conducted in conjunction with an organizing campaign. The second is in aid of a strike. The third type is a substitute for a strike. They found that the first type – organizational – was the only one in which unions regularly experienced a reasonable degree of success, although there were some occasional successes with the other types. An earlier study by Charles Perry (1987) found that the prime determinants of success were the sensitivity of the employer to adverse publicity and the ability of the union to escalate the matter to something greater than an ordinary labor dispute.

In exploring the question of the nature of the corporate campaign, Jarley and Maranto (1990) rely upon Ray Rogers, the inventor of this tactic. Rogers described the Stevens campaign as having to do with the company's financial ties. According to him, a corporate campaign involves bringing secondary pressure to bear on directors, lenders, and other financial collaborators. Others have emphasized the public relations aspects of these campaigns, the strategy of influencing the firm's policy makers, the application of sophisticated public-relations techniques, or building coalitions with other interest groups. Arthur Shostak (1991) describes "comprehensive campaigns," as outlined by Robert F. Harbrant of the AFL-CIO Food and Allied Service Trades Department, as campaigns based upon extensive research on a company to identify fruitful pressure points. It seems to this writer that corporate campaigns may include any or all of the previously described characteristics.

Corporate campaigns, by their very nature, attract attention in the popular media, including the influential Wall Street Journal (see, e.g., Robert L. Rose 1993). Such activities as asking embarrassing questions at shareholders' meetings, sending pickets to an International Toy Fair dressed as children's television characters, or tracking down a renegade capitalist on the ski slopes of Switzerland, are bound to make good press. They are very costly, however, and often not successful.

The use of the corporate campaign declined in the late 1990s. However, it will likely remain one of a variety of weapons available for use by unions when warranted by the circumstances. Corporate campaigns seem especially appropriate for labor action that crosses national boundaries. This may make it the tactic of the future.

The corporate campaign is a Pure and Simple Unionism tactic. It aims either to organize for purposes of collective bargaining, or to achieve union collective bargaining goals.

Training

Although training is hardly a new idea for the American labor movement, a greater emphasis on it is one of the more promising current tactics. Training is an area of employment relations in which the United States trails a good bit of the developed world. Although major firms with enlightened policies recognize the need for training, when you look at small or nonunion companies, you find that surprisingly little of it is going on (Overman 1992). Because labor is seen primarily as a cost of doing business, and workers as resources can be replaced when they are worn out or become obsolete, many companies are reluctant to train. As previously noted, from an individual firm's perspective, this admittedly makes some sense with a mobile labor force. Workers trained by a firm become more marketable and may simply move elsewhere to use the skills in which they have been trained.

There are some unions and employers, particularly in industries facing great change, who have gotten together to make sure that the workers stay up to date. One example is the Alliance for Employee Growth and Development, Inc., which is a joint enterprise of AT&T, CWA, and the IBEW. The Alliance was founded in 1986 with the purpose of helping displaced workers. But by 1989, in at least some locations, it had turned to preparing workers to handle new technologies. The Alliance set up Technicians for Tomorrow in Chicago to help employees qualify for future jobs with the company. The IBEW and AT&T also have the Enhanced Training Opportunities Program (ETOP). This program very carefully determines the skills in which employees are to be trained, based on the jobs that are available in the particular community. This deals with a major weakness of many training programs – training workers for jobs that don't exist. ETOP offers courses in computers, accounting, electronics, clerical skills, and for the health-care professions. Other outstanding examples include UAW/General Motors Skills Centers and joint training programs of Ford Motor Co. and the UAW (Overman 1992).

It is perhaps not surprising that it is the building trades that have been leaders in developing new training programs and putting new emphasis on training. Bill Luddy, then Administrative Assistant to the President, United Brotherhood of Carpenters and Joiners (Carpenters), said in a 1997 interview that the construction industry is suffering from a critical shortage of skilled workers, particularly carpenters. He argues that this is because contractors, having weakened the unions, are finding that they have no good alternative source of labor. Particularly in an industry where workers regularly move from employer to employer, there is no incentive for any one employer to provide training. Although the industry as a whole needs trained workers, it runs contrary to the short-term interests of any one contractor to expend scarce funds on training that may end up benefiting its competitors. Nonunion contractor associations have attempted to make up for this by creating a training fund, but they have been unable to get a sufficient number of contractors to participate. According to Luddy, the only practical solution to this is union training (Luddy 1997).

Training has been described as "the ultimate union weapon" in a varied arsenal (Bradford 1990). The "centerpiece" of this in the early 1990s was the Construction Industry Labor-Management 1990s Committee. This is a cooperative effort between the building trades unions and unionized contractors. In 1990 unions and their contractors outspent the nonunion ABC on training $300 million to $6 million. This training is financed by special training-fund contributions. Some unions, such as the Plumbers, are developing highly specialized training programs. A particularly innovative program is one by the Laborers' International Union of North America (LIUNA) that trains its members in hazardous waste removal. LIUNA and other unions also provide basic skills and literacy education (Goodman 1992).

As will be argued in Chapter 7, union training efforts have the capacity to give labor a new face as well as a new strategy. By contributing to building up the stock of human capital in the society unions make an obvious contribution to the general national welfare. This is something that the labor movement must do in order to survive in the modern world. It must be viewed by the public as part of the solution, not part of the problem.

Training would seem to be essentially a Social Democratic Unionism tactic. It does aim to achieve practical workplace advantages to the members of the union, and hence partakes somewhat of Pure and Simple Unionism. However, it also speaks to the broader interests of the society, including employers, in having a good stock of human capital. It is this blend that makes it appealing as a tactic.

Labor Action on International Trade

The American labor movement has a long history of resisting the importing of foreign products into the American market, although the industrial unions were free trade advocates for a time immediately following World War II. Over most of its over two centuries of history it has been one of the most predictably protectionist institutions in American society. This may be because the unions, being essentially democratic institutions, have to reflect the views of the rank and file – and these views have usually been protectionist. A worker who believes his job is endangered by foreign-made goods is little inclined to accept assurances that he or she will find another job, or that in the long run everyone will be better off.

Organized labor unsuccessfully opposed the North American Free Trade Agreement (NAFTA), risking its relationship with an otherwise labor-friendly president, Bill Clinton. It has had more success in slowing down further expansion of trade by helping to put a stop to the "fast-track" authority of the president to open up trade with other countries. Also, it was able to combine with environmental groups to get some protection of labor and environmental standards in NAFTA. In 2001, it appears to have lost its fight to prevent China from being placed in a normal trading relationship with the United States. However, in the summer of 2001, the AFL-CIO led an effort to stall fast-track authority being given to President Bush. It did this through use of its new political/organizing network, which permitted it to fax and e-mail 6,000 local unions in 30 targeted congressional districts, having unionists contact their congressional representatives urging them to oppose fast track (Bureau of National Affairs 2001b).

American unions have supported the International Labour Organization's (ILO) position that "core labor standards" are fundamental human rights that must be respected by all nations. These standards seem to be a bare minimum. They include the right to freedom of association and collective bargaining, and freedom from exploitative forms of child labor, forced labor, and discrimination. Human Rights Watch has found that the legal system in the United States violates these standards, and therefore basic human rights of workers (Bureau of National Affairs 2000d). It seems clear that these rights should also include the rights to a living wage and a safe workplace.

Bringing pressure to bear on the World Trade Organization (WTO) and International Monetary Fund (IMF) is a tactic that is currently being used to forge links between international trading rights and labor standards. Unions joined in the "Battle in Seattle" in which massive protests were launched against the WTO, demanding that labor and environmental standards be part of the global trading system (Moberg 2000b; Mazur 2000). They followed this up by participating in demonstrations at a meeting of the IMF in Washington. Labor is a crucial part of a broad movement in the United States and other countries challenging the "Washington consensus" that completely free and unregulated trade has social consequences that are entirely acceptable (Mazur 2000). It may be that a crucial strategy of unions to build grass-roots support will be to "become more forceful as opponents of the dehumanizing advance of market forces" (Hyman 2001: 176).

Other International Tactics

The AFL-CIO under John Sweeney has consolidated the federation's international institutes into the new Solidarity Center. This new center is oriented toward assisting unions in developing countries. Unlike the old American Institute for Free Labor Development, it does not function as an arm of U.S. anticommunist governmental policy. At this writing its most recent program is working internationally to have the ILO Declaration on Fundamental Principles and Rights posted by employers in workplaces around the world. This is at least a step toward global unionism (Rodberg 2001).

American unions have become regular users of international pressures in support of collective bargaining and organizing. The 1997 UPS strike by the Teamsters was given significant support by trade unionists in other countries

(Mazur 2000). This was also true in the lockout of the Steelworkers by Ravenswood Aluminum Corporation in 1990 (Juravich and Bronfenbrenner 1999).

In numerous cases unions such as the Steelworkers and UAW have attempted to apply pressure on a foreign corporation in its home country in order to persuade it not to oppose unionization of American facilities. This has sometimes, as in the case of the manufacturer of BMW autos in South Carolina, included involving union representatives who are members of the corporate board of directors in the foreign country.

Crossing national borders in bringing pressure to bear on employers in collective bargaining and organizing disputes has become a standard operating procedure for many American unions. From being an extraordinary action just a few years ago, it has become an accepted tactic in dealing with employers.

CONCLUSIONS

Perhaps the most striking characteristic of this review of strategies and tactics of U.S. unions is their tremendous variety. What we see is a thoroughly pragmatic labor movement and its supporting cast of intellectuals searching intensely for answers to labor's problems. These range from broad changes in the very nature of the labor movement to relatively minor tinkering with its tactics.

It appears at first glance that the key question to be answered is what strategies and tactics have the greatest potential for success. Yet this is too simple a question to deal with the complex reality. One must ask what works for different purposes, and also under what circumstances. We find, for example, that craft unionism is excellent in building intensive solidarity, but does not do this extensively, and may be weak when it comes to building the public support necessary for keeping government friendly and supportive. Social Unionism is just the reverse as to strengths and weaknesses. Occupational unionism offers many of the strengths of craft unionism (indeed resembles it strongly), and may be more appropriate for low-wage, low-skill occupations. Associational Unionism may be highly congenial to modern conditions for white-collar and/or skilled workers. Intrafirm Network Groups fit managers. Worker-rights organizations are capable of providing support to the other forms of unionism and may be a form of labor organization that is well suited to operate effectively in extremely antiunion environments, such as my home state of South Carolina. Reform may be a necessary condition for a labor movement to draw support from the general public, itself a condition for having government support or tolerance.

All of the tactics noted in this chapter have some potential for contributing to the growth of the U.S. labor movement. Organizing is essential. Being an organizing-oriented organization may help a union to be the kind of lively organization that both attracts new members and serves the needs of existing members. Labor-management cooperation, whatever its limitations, appears to be necessary to keep employer opposition within the bounds necessary to allow the labor movement to survive at all. As previously noted, one leading staff member of the AFL-CIO has said, "Cooperation is happening because there is no alternative" (Welsh 1997). Corporate campaigns can be useful in some situations. An emphasis on training seems to offer some real advantages in providing benefits to workers that only unions can insure, meeting the needs of employers that they themselves cannot meet, and gaining public support as contributors to economic growth and prosperity.

Given that employers are overwhelmingly powerful under the situation that prevails at the beginning of this new century, getting around their opposition may be the most important condition against which to test any labor-movement strategy or tactic. I have become increasingly interested in worker ownership as a way of dealing with the problem of employer opposition. If it is true that the owners of capital have nearly all the power and – at least in the American corporate system – management serves only the needs of the holders of this capital (i.e., shareholders) it would seem to make sense to become the owners of capital. There is an American saying, "If you can't lick [defeat] them, join them." This should be changed to "If you can't lick them, become them." In the United States, workers already have a great deal of ownership, but this has not been translated into control. Converting this ownership into control, while admittedly requiring overcoming a number of obstacles, is something that American unions could do that would greatly increase worker influence while at the same time perhaps providing the "patient capital" that U.S. industry lacks.

As to coping with employer opposition, craft and occupational unions have the advantage of having the potential to provide skilled workers to an extent that employers are unable to do on their own. Training, labor-management cooperation, and corporate campaigns are also useful for dealing with employer opposition.

It should be recognized that in addition to the degree of employer opposition, other conditions are also important. Energetic and creative organizing is necessary to take advantage of whatever opportunities are created. Worker-rights organizations can not only help with this, but can also fill a need in strongly antiunion settings, and provide the labor movement with a lively group of rank-and-file activists who might not be willing to be part of a traditional union structure.

All of the strategic directions and tactics described in this book have advantages in certain situations. They should be viewed as an arsenal of weapons that are more or less effective depending on circumstances. This is a situation where the pragmatism of the American labor movement should be very useful. This is what gives it real hope for the future.

FOUR

The Old Reformist Unionism:
The Noble Order of the Knights of Labor

From the time of the first lockout, when Adam and Eve were locked out of Eden for indulging too freely in the alcohol contained in that apple, down to the present time there has been a labor question. There will always be a labor question, and today it is more intricate, more complex, and, apparently, less responsive to treatment than ever.

Terence Powderly, Grand Master Workman, Noble Order of the Knights of Labor, 1889

As the American labor movement searches for successful models at the beginning of the twenty-first century, it might consider turning back the clock to look at a Reformist organization that arose near the close of the nineteenth century. This is the Noble Order of the Knights of Labor, which grew to 700,000 members in 1886 before succumbing to assaults from employers and competition from the American Federation of Labor. It is generally believed that the failure of the Knights in the last century was caused by its being "contrary to the reality created by modern industrial forces" (Hoxie 1921: 93). If it is true that the Knights declined because they were unfit for the environment of old-style industrial capitalism, the demise of that system and the rise of postindustrial economies in the Western world may warrant a reconsideration of the Knights' ideas.

The Knights of Labor provide a fully articulated and well-documented example of a Reformist labor organization. A close look at the Knights and their experience furnishes a natural experiment that is revealing of the nature, strengths, and weaknesses of Reformist Unionism.

WHO WERE THE KNIGHTS?

Their ideas provide a good starting point for understanding what the Knights of Labor were all about. After looking at these ideas, we will consider their organizational structure, and their rise and fall.

The Ideology of the Knights

In the typology of trade unions previously cited, Robert Hoxie (1921) characterized the Knights as the prime example of "uplift unionism." Such unionism, according to Hoxie,

... aspires chiefly to elevate the moral, intellectual, and social life of the worker, to improve the conditions under which he works, to raise his material standards of living, give him a sense of personal worth and dignity, secure for him the leisure for culture, and insure him and his family against the loss of a decent livelihood ... (p. 47).

Although it will engage in collective bargaining, such a union is more interested in mutual insurance, political action, and "advocacy of cooperative enterprises, profit-sharing, and other idealistic plans for social regeneration" (p. 47). It does appear from the rather extensive literature about them that the principal ideas of the Knights were (1) that there needed to be fundamental reform in the order of things, rather than merely an amelioration of the effects of capitalism on workers; (2) broad solidarity among all producers; (3) the founding of producer cooperatives; and (4) education.

Reform. The reform of the economic system, principally by abolishing the wage system, was a core belief of the Knights. In his first annual address to the Knights, Terence Powderly, their leader during their heyday, said:

So long as the present order of things exist, just so long will the attempt to effect a lasting peace between the man who buys labor and the man who sells labor be fruitless. So long as it is in the interest of one kind of man to purchase labor at the lowest possible figure, and so long as it is to the interest of another kind of men to sell labor to the highest possible bidder, just so long will there exist an antagonism between the two which all the speakers and writers on labor cannot remove (Powderly 1940: 268).

Powderly believed that the contest was inevitably unequal:

... when the absolute ownership of machinery and the unlimited control of land are allowed to continue for the aggrandizement of the individual instead of for the welfare of the people, it will always be in the power of those who control to render the lot of the workman so burdensome that he will consent to violate the laws of the land and the laws of organizations in order to earn sufficient bread to sustain life (Powderly 1967: 264).

Consequently, he believed that merely shortening hours or raising pay without a change in the system would be fruitless. The trade unions were seen as limiting their goals to these outcomes and, therefore, not capable of permanently uplifting the producers.

Yet the Knights' leaders saw questions of hours and pay as important. Uriah S. Stephens, founder of the Knights, said:

Excess of labor and small pay stints, and blunts, and degrades, those god-like faculties, until the image of God, in which he is created and intended by his Great Creator
to exhibit, are scarcely discernable, and ignorance boldly asserts that it does not
exist (McNeil 1892: 403).

Unlike the trade unions, they believed that their goals could only be achieved
by abolishing the wage system and making "each man his own employer"
(Grob 1976: 38). The Knights saw the trade unions as having traded their lack
of support for revolutionary theories for "a respected though subordinate
position in the community" (Grob 1976: 9).

Solidarity. Norman Ware, one of the more insightful writers about the
Knights, says, "The one distinguishing characteristic of the Order was its
principle of solidarity, the belief that all trades should be brought under one
banner" (1959: 155). The well-known *History of Labor in the United States*
lists a "union of all trades" among the "First Principles" of the Knights that
were laid down by their founders (Commons et al. 1966).

This "one major idea or sentiment," solidarity, was expressed in the motto
of the Order, "An injury to one is the concern of all" (Ware 1959: xiv). This
notion was applied very broadly. Membership was not limited to the members
of a particular trade or craft. The Knights attempted to teach Americans that
they were wage-earners first and members of a particular craft, political party,
or religion second (Kealey and Palmer 1982). Powderly characterized this as
being concerned with the "rights of man," rather that the "rights of the trades-
man," to which the trade unions paid attention. This meant that "the rights
of the common, every-day laborer were to be considered by the new
Order . . ." (Powderly 1967: 84–5). Richard Ely, one of the founders of the
"Wisconsin School" of thought among labor economists, whose later
members tended to downplay the importance of the Knights, said admiringly
of the Knights:

They reason correctly that if they can elevate the lowest social stratum, they will
raise all other strata. It is in this that they put themselves in line with the precepts
of Christianity. The strong help to bear the infirmities of the weak, and no grander
conception of human brotherhood than that which they profess, characterizes any
movement of our times (Ely 1905: 77–8).

This was not entirely an altruistic stance on the part of the Knights,
however. Powderly believed that the invention of labor-saving machinery
had made it so that skilled workers would be in competition with "a boy,"
and that the boy would do the job better. He saw machinery "bringing the
machinist down to the level of the day laborer." His aim, accordingly, was to
"dignify the laborer" (Ely 1905: 78). Powderly believed that the Industrial
Revolution would largely destroy craft distinctions, creating a "dead level of
labor" (McLaurin 1978: xviii). This would form a basis for solidarity among
all workers. Similarly, the large aggregations of capital that were being assembled in the late nineteenth century, as well as the increase in government

activity, made it necessary to have a single unified labor movement to match these other centers of economic and political power (McLaurin 1978).

The Noble Order expressed its solidarity in symbols. No officer of the Knights ever occupied a seat on a platform higher than the members. It formed a brotherhood by means of rituals. An initiate described the ritual as "an impressive message of love for fellow man." Powderly described the Knights as a "pooling of heartbeats and throbbing intellects" (Powderly 1940: 54, 60). Uriah Stephens believed that the unity that was required could be produced among such a diverse workforce only through "religious senti-ment." So he attempted to create a universal brotherhood. This sentiment of brotherhood was the aim of the secrecy and ceremony of the Knights. Accord-ing to Stephens, the "Anti-Christ of civilization" was manifest in the "idola-try of wealth and the consequent degradation and social ostracism of [those not possessing wealth]" (Ware 1959: 74).

One of the more interesting aspects of the Knights' vision of solidarity is that it extended to all "producers." That is, it was not limited to persons in the role of employee. The Knights, as had the National Labor Union before them, saw the division in society as being between producers and the moneyed interests, not between employers and employees. Producers included all members of society who were not "parasites" – professional gamblers, lawyers, bankers, stockbrokers, and manufacturers and sellers of liquor. They were opposed to the moneyed interests, ". . . the bloodsuckers who don't work – who live by the sweat of other men's brows" (Kealey and Palmer 1982: 282). The Knights included white-collar workers and most professionals. Merchants and manufacturers who "showed respect for the dignity of labor (i.e., who sold union-made goods or employed union workers at union conditions) were welcomed into the Order" (Fink 1983: 9). This is considered a "pre-industrial concept of the work force that they wished to organize" (McLaurin 1978: 114). The nub of this concept is shown in the secret fraternal greeting ritual and passwords. One person was to say, "I am a worker," to which the other was to reply, "I too earn my bread with the sweat of my brow" (Kealey and Palmer 1982: 283–5). Historians have generally seen their inclusiveness as a source of problems for the Knights, making the national organization "heterogeneous beyond description and beyond control" (McLaurin 1978: 41).

Cooperation. The Knights' alternative to industrial capitalism was producer cooperatives. It was chiefly through these that they intended to abolish the wage system. Producers would unite in their persons both capital and labor, thereby returning them to the proprietary status that predated the Industrial Revolution. Laborers would save money from their wages and establish cooperatives owned by them (McLaurin 1978).

John R. Commons et al. (1966) say that "the deliberately planned policy of the Order as a whole, was directed chiefly at co-operation" (p. 430). This was reasonably well suited to periods of industrial depression when strikes were failing. Support for cooperatives came mainly from the older, skilled, members of the Knights who furnished the leadership of the Order. As did Powderly, they saw themselves as middle class. The Knights had set up 135 cooperatives by the end of 1887, the largest numbers being in mining, cooperage, and shoe manufacturing – all industries where little capital was needed. The national Knights provided some funding as well as advice for cooperative governance and management. There was opposition to the cooperatives by railroads and other major capitalist enterprises. By 1888 the cooperatives had generally failed. Commons et al. (1966) say that:

The failure was definite and final. Not since this time has the American labor movement ventured upon co-operation. The year 1888 marks the closing of the age of middle-class panaceas, and consequently the beginning of the wage-conscious period (p. 438).

Philip Foner (1955), viewing the experience from a different (Marxist) perspective, generally agrees with the Commons et al. analysis. He emphasizes the damage done to the Knights' cooperatives by the capitalists. His conclusion is that the Knights learned that "cooperation on a modest scale was doomed to failure" (Foner 1955: 77). Norman Ware (1959) says that the Knights never really invested much money or energy in cooperatives. He believes that the growth of large-scale production caused the cooperatives to become "increasingly anachronistic" (p. 320).

Education. Included in the preamble to the Knights' constitution is the statement that its purpose is organizing, educating, and directing the powers of the industrial masses (Hoxie 1921). Terence Powderly strongly supported an emphasis on education. He quotes with approval a statement of William Sylvis of the National Labor Union saying:

. . . I have always held it to be unwise and eminently foolish to enforce the [eight-hour day] system by strikes. What we want is agitation, education, and legislation. Convince the people that it is right, and then demand the necessary legislation (Powderly 1967: 241).

Commons et al. (1966) list education among the "First Principles" of the Knights.

Philip Foner quotes a leaflet of the Knights as saying, "The fundamental principle of the Knights of Labor is *Education*" (Foner 1955: 75). According to him, the Knights believed that workers needed to be properly educated before they could lead the society. Many workers had not had much schooling. In the eyes of the Knights, those who did have education had been taught procapitalist and antilabor misinformation. So the Knights set up their own educational program, mainly teaching practical economics so that "the fallacies which have so long prevented the people from knowing what hurt them" would be countered (Foner 1955: 76). They believed that "To propagate sound economic doctrine is our holiest mission" (Foner 1955: 76). Only after the members had learned their lessons in "economic science" would action be appropriate. They established libraries and reading rooms and had lectures and discussions at local assembly meetings. However, according to Foner (1955), "Unfortunately, to the leaders of the Order education became a substitute for action" (p. 76). While workers wanted action to solve their immediate problems, the leaders of the Knights were focused upon long-term educational goals and the utopian dream of cooperatives.

Organizational Structure of the Knights

On paper, the Knights of Labor were a highly centralized national organization. In reality, however, many local organizations did pretty much as they pleased (Ware 1959). At the local level they consisted of either trade assemblies that contained only members of a particular trade, or mixed assemblies that contained all kinds of workers and even employers (Grob 1976). At the Knights' peak in 1886, 1,088 of the local organizations were trade assemblies and 1,279 were mixed assemblies. The mixed assemblies were mainly study and debating groups. They could engage in agitation or politics, but were not suited to collective bargaining.

Rise of the Knights

The Knights rose to power in the highly disturbed environment of the 1880s. The early part of this decade saw general prosperity and rising prices. Unions of craftsmen struggled with their employers to get better terms, but there was no general workers' social movement. However, the Depression of 1884–5 saw a radical change in the labor movement. Unskilled and semiskilled workers came into labor organizations. These organizations became "real class movements." This development was the product of some "far-reaching economic changes" that had occurred over the years following the Civil War (Commons et al. 1966: 357). Following the war, in the 1860s, a national market was created. Then there was the "marvelous industrial expansion" of the 1880s, in which machinery was introduced into production in "unprecedented scale." This led to an increase in unskilled and semiskilled labor, who had little bargaining power. With rapidly expanding markets, manufacturers engaged in "a cutthroat competition, low prices, low profits, and consequently a steady and insistent [downward] pressure on wages." Manufacturers formed combinations, but these tended to be unstable. Immigration increased, supplying a flood of new, unskilled, workers. All this led to large reductions in wages. It was during the worst of these times, which ended gradually in 1886 and 1887, that the Knights of Labor rose to national prominence (Commons et al. 1966: 358–61).

The Knights' actions during the mid-1880s "marked the awakening of all democratic elements in society and their uniting in a common effort to combat plutocracy" (Commons et al. 1966: 362). Some scholars see the key to the power of the Knights being that:

workers cherished values different from the acquisitive individualism espoused by their employers. As an 1880 parade banner of the Detroit coopers' union put the point:

> Each for himself is the bosses' plea
> Union for all will make you free (Montgomery 1980: 502).

Although they started with skilled tradesmen, and always included skilled workers as a crucial element, the Knights formed for the first time a unified voice for the entire American working class. In consequence, "all previous labor movements in the United States seem insignificant in contrast to the K. of L" (Foner 1955: 47).

The Knights of Labor grew steadily from 1881 to 1884, by which time they claimed a membership of 71,326 (Foner 1955). The tremendous growth of the Knights to the level of 700,000 members in 1886 was credited by Terence Powderly to two things for which the Knights were not responsible. The first was the eight-hour-day movement and the second was "the spread of an extravagant idea of the strength of the Order" (Hoxie 1921: 93). A successful 1885 strike against leading capitalist Jay Gould's Wabash Railroad, and a few other strikes, led workers to flock to the Knights. As Philip Foner (1955) says, "The spectacular triumph over one of the greatest capitalists of the day brought thousands of new workers into the ranks of the K. of L" (p. 53). At its peak, it had assemblies in Canada, Australia, New Zealand, Belgium, France, England, Ireland, and Italy (Foner 1955).

Decline of the Knights

After peaking at 700,000 members in 1886, the Knights immediately began a steep decline. By July 1, 1887, they were down to 510,351 members. They continued to steadily lose members for several years. By the end of the century, there was only a remnant of the once powerful Noble Order (Commons et al. 1966). The reasons for the demise are worth considering. These appear to include the effects of a particular event with which they had nothing to do (The Haymarket Riot), attacks by employers, competition from the newly born American Federation of Labor (AFL) and its constituent unions, and internal weaknesses of both organization and leadership.

The Haymarket Riot of 1886 was an event that shocked the national consciousness. The riot occurred when a group of International Harvester strikers, led by some anarchists, held a demonstration that the Chicago police broke up. It resulted in the death of several police officers. It was highly

publicized. It turned public opinion against labor, the most visible representative of which was the Knights of Labor. The fact that the Haymarket
meeting and the resultant riot were led by anarchists who were not Knights
appears not to have saved the Knights from the wrath of the press, the clergy,
and the public (Powderly 1967; Ware 1959).

Employer suppression played no small part in the demise of the Knights.
During the period of their decline, employers engaged in systematic discrimination against members of labor organizations. Employers organized
both nationally and by industry sector to eradicate worker organizations.
They used lockouts, "iron-clad" agreements of workers not to join unions, the
blacklist, and labor spies (mainly Pinkertons). All of this antiunion activity
focused primarily on the Knights of Labor (Commons et al. 1966).

The Knights' fall coincided with the birth and growth of the AFL. Competition with this confederation of craft unions probably had as much to
do with the Knights' disappearance as anything else. In the first place, the
Knights, which contained many trade unions and trade unionists, became
embroiled in a great deal of conflict with these unions. Their Richmond
Assembly of 1887 took antiunion positions, leading the trade unions to reciprocate (Commons et al. 1966). Second, and most importantly, it became clear
that trade unions were better able to operate successfully, not only to survive but also to achieve some real benefits for workers. As a result, there
was a "veritable rush," "a stampede," for workers to organize by trade in 1887
(Commons et al. 1966: 427–8).

According to Gerald Grob (1976), the trade unions were popular because:

"The workers' loss of identity and status prepared the ground for the rise of trade
unionism. While accepting industrial society, the unions set to work to replace the
community that had disintegrated. Thus the workers again became members of a
social group having common interests" (p. 190).

As Grob (1976) argues, the trade unions were much more homogeneous.
As they were made up of workers who, because of their skills, had both
economic and social ties, they were "more stable . . . and were therefore able
to enforce a much greater degree of discipline" (p. 120). In a "rapidly expanding and acquisitive society" such organizations were better suited to their
environment than the Knights (p. 120).

As also suggested by Grob (1976), the unions' objectives were consistent
with the "middle-class psychology of American laborers" that saw American
society as harmonious rather than as a venue for class struggle. Although
Samuel Gompers and other labor leaders privately expressed class-based
views, the rationale for unions was framed in terms of material gain that did
not conflict with "the workers' dreams of rising to a middle-class status" (p.
189). One way of looking at the survival of the trade unions and the AFL at
a time when the Knights were dying is to see craft unionism not as an advance
for American labor, but as "a strategic retreat of a few craft unionists dis-

turbed for their own safety by the remarkable but 'unhealthy' growth of the One Big Union" (Ware 1959: xii).

Clearly, internal weaknesses contributed to the fall of the Knights of Labor. Some historians blame the incompetence of the Knights' leaders, particularly Terence Powderly, for the Knights' failure (Falzone 1978). Powderly is described as "a windbag whose place was on a street corner rousing the rabble to concert pitch and providing emotional compensation to dull lives" (Ware 1959: xvi). According to Norman Ware, Powderly was retained as head of the Knights "in spite of obvious disqualification for the job" (p. xvi). Under his leadership, "the labor movement of the eighties was not a business but a religion . . . a vague, primitive, embryonic sentiment, a religion in the making" (Ware 1959: xvi). In contrast, the trade unions generally had very good leadership (Grob 1976).

For an organization that reached its greatest strength based on its success in striking, it is ironic that its policy and practice with regard to strikes were major causes of their undoing. The Knights' leaders were opposed to strikes. When they got involved in them they were poor bargainers and were unwilling to spend money or energy on actions that they saw as a waste of resources that could be better spent on education and cooperatives. The Chicago stockyards strike of 1886 and some railroad strikes, including on Jay Gould's Southwestern Railway, revealed very clearly the weakness of the Knights in leading strikes. In addition, the mixed assemblies of the Knights, while useful as debating societies and for political action, were next to useless for engaging in collective bargaining and conducting strikes (Commons et al. 1966; Ware 1959).

THE KNIGHTS AND THE ENABLING CONDITIONS

Although it is always interesting, at least to some of us, to read about historical phenomena, it is not particularly useful unless we can answer the question, "Who cares?" This section of this chapter will attempt to provide an answer to this crucial question by analyzing the extent to which the Knights' model is capable of contributing to the conditions that would enable the American labor movement to succeed under modern circumstances. These enabling conditions are set out and discussed in Chapter 1.

Importance of the Work Role

A major item of faith for the Knights was that workers were workers first and other things, such as members of a particular craft, political party, or religion, second. They saw the role of worker as being the central one. Also, their concept of the work role was more comprehensive than that of the trade unions of their day. The Knights were unwilling to accept the capitalist notion of workers as mere "hands." Instead, they were "producers," those who created goods for society by the sweat of their brows. So, for society as well as for the individual worker, the human being in the work role was at the heart of a productive system.

Solidarity

One would think that, given the centrality of the motto, "An injury to one is the concern of all," the Knights' great strength would lie in its contribution to the condition of solidarity. Certainly this idea, combined with the broad reach of the Knights to a wide variety of persons, is an important one as to having extensive solidarity. The "one" and "all" of the Knights' motto referred to the class of producers, a broader class than employees. This makes for extreme heterogeneity among the "us" of the Knights. The strength of this is that it includes nearly everyone in the society. Unfortunately, this is a weakness as well, for it creates problems for intensive solidarity. It was precisely the failing of intensive solidarity that contributed mightily to its failure to compete effectively with the AFL trade unions. The question is whether a group defined so broadly can have sufficient feelings of common interests and affection to enable its members to act together when mutual support and real sacrifice are required. So, as to solidarity, the Knights' philosophy has both advantages and disadvantages.

Perceptions of Distinct Worker Interests

Whether one believes that the Knights' ideas can contribute to perceptions of distinct, discrete, worker interests depends upon how the term *worker* is defined. The Knights' view was that the distinct interest was that of producers, and that this differed from nonproducers. As previously noted, this does not make the modern-day distinction between employers and employees.

The term *producer* carries with it some normative connotations that the term *employee* does not. Implicit in the term *producer* is the basic premise that underlies the classical economists' labor theory of value, a view that was used by Karl Marx (Marx and Engels 1848). It holds that all value in goods and services derives from the labor that produced them. Marx used this idea to draw the conclusion that those who create value should not be exploited, but should enjoy the fruits of their labor (this was the view of the Knights as well). Productive members of society being entitled to the benefits of their economic achievements is an idea that still has considerable appeal.

A previously noted problem with regard to solidarity is where to draw the line between the producers ("us") and the nonproducers ("them"). The Knights' password refers to earning bread by the sweat of one's own brow. Does this mean that persons who earn their living by the sweat of the brows of others are not "producers"? Managers would seem to fit into this category if one sees management as solely directing the work of others. One could make a distinction between those who actually perform hands-on productive work to a significant degree and those who are completely, or nearly completely, involved only in directing others.

Owners of capital would also go into the category of nonproducer because their "constant capital" (Marx's term) produces profits only by means of the labor of others. In a world where many rank-and-file workers own shares of their employer and benefit from pension funds that invest in many companies, this is a bit complicated. However, it would be possible to classify persons based upon the proportion of their income or wealth that comes from wages or salaries versus income from investments in capitalist enterprises. It may make more sense, however, to classify them on the basis of their perceptions as to whether they identify themselves primarily with labor or capital.

It appears that the cutting point for determining whether one is or is not a "producer" in either an industrial or office environment may not be greatly different from the existing distinction between "employee" and "supervisor" under Section 2 (11), National Labor Relations Act (NLRA). The chief practical difference would be the inclusion of independent contracting workers within the definition of producer. There is, however, a difference in what is claimed for the worker role as opposed to the roles of manager and owner. *Producer* is a positive term that connotes contribution to society. *Employee* is not. The latter term buys into, or at least fails to challenge, capitalist claims of being the moving force in society by "creating jobs." The distinction between *producer* and *nonproducer* may be a useful one for drawing the line between *us* and *them*. This might help to solve the solidarity problem of modern labor movements. The producer/nonproducer distinction drawn from a pre–Industrial Revolution model may make sense post–Industrial Revolution.

Benefits of Collective Action

The broad, community-based, organizational structure of the Knights of Labor would seem to be highly useful for collective political action. The notion of drawing community groups ranging from local trade unions to single-issue groups such as women's and minority rights action groups together under a single umbrella is a good one. There are many ways that such a group can be put together by unions and their natural allies. Perhaps a "Local Assembly" consisting of unions, minority rights groups, environmental groups, and others in a particular community could provide a useful instrument for collective political and social action.

For purposes of collective bargaining the Knights' community-based, mixed-assembly style of organization would appear to be less useful. However, it is not necessary for every part of the labor movement to serve every purpose. *Instead of a modern equivalent of mixed assemblies competing with unions, they could perform mutually complementary roles.*

Mixed assemblies of the type suggested here would go beyond the bounds of including only persons who are acting in the role of worker. Members of women's rights groups, for example, may be primarily concerned with their role as citizens, mothers, or feminists. However, the common ground for members of the new local mixed assemblies should be their concerns about work and workplace issues. So, in this sense, these assemblies would have as their *raison d'etre* serving the producer's, or worker's, interest.

Education, another of the fundamental principles of the Knights, should serve to improve both political and collective-bargaining outcomes. Workers' votes can be a powerful political force, but only if the votes are informed. They need to understand the whys of political action and economics. The misinformation that the Knights denounced in the last century is still being spread. It is debilitating to workers who are responsible citizens to not understand the usefulness to society of their unions. This is a high purpose of a labor movement – to educate the organized as well as the unorganized.

Containing Employer Opposition

Under current circumstances both large multinational corporations and smaller businesses hold enormous power in American society. Therefore, it would seem to be especially important for a labor movement to either be perceived as nonthreatening by business or so powerful as to discourage challenges to it, or somehow render management opposition irrelevant. Terence Powderly correctly saw the need for a unified labor movement to match the power of employers and government. Unfortunately, by doing so the Knights brought down upon themselves the full weight of employer opposition.

Historically, trade unions have endured in the United States in part because they have challenged neither the fundamental right of management to manage nor the right of owners of capital to be the primary beneficiaries of corporate success. As Powderly alleged, they received what they believed was a secure, if subordinate, place in the society in consideration of their giving up notions of radical reform. This worked reasonably well for several decades. Yet, it has not earned them the tolerance of management in the modern world. Even the most responsible and limited of unions have been subjected to attacks by managements once believed to be friendly to labor.

Workers turned to more revolutionary philosophies in the nineteenth century when, due to economic circumstances, collective bargaining through traditional business unions wasn't working. They may do so once again for similar reasons. If collective bargaining does not produce adequate results, it is reasonable to consider other alternatives. If employers are violently opposed even to moderate business trade unions, nothing can be lost by pursuing revolutionary, or reformist, ideas. If employers will strongly oppose *any* form of labor movement, workers may as well attempt to change society in a fundamental way. It is not that a more Reformist labor movement will not face vigorous employer opposition. It is simply that it is hard to imagine employer opposition being much stronger than it already is.

Another way to deal with employer opposition is to become the employer. That is, a cooperative owned by the workers, or even a corporation in which the workers own a substantial proportion of the stock, is less likely to oppose an organization desired by these same workers. This may be the ultimate answer to employer opposition.

Obtaining Government Support

Whether government support is present is dependent mainly upon the political strength of labor. A broad, socially conscious, labor movement with a vision of a better society is probably more likely to attract political support than a narrow, self-interested, one. To the extent that labor is perceived by policy makers and the public as just one more interest group fighting for its share of the pie to the detriment of other interest groups, not much public support is going to be forthcoming. On the other hand, a movement that dreams of what might be a better society (Kealey and Palmer 1982) has some chance of capturing the public imagination.

The cooperative strategy of the Knights is not so different from what a number of American unions, including the United Steelworkers of America, have been doing with respect to employee ownership. In general, employee ownership is an idea that has considerable appeal. If it were pursued systematically and publicly as an alternative work structure, it might provide a major theme for a resurgent labor movement.

THE KNIGHTS AND THE CURRENT ENVIRONMENT

Given that the conditions under which the modern, New Deal model, labor movement came into being have changed in the ways previously indicated in this book, what is it about the Knights that might lead us to believe that they might succeed where current unions have failed? As previously noted, these conditions include high competition in product markets, focus on quality, and the development of new forms of work organization that include broader, more flexible job descriptions; increased use of temporary and part-time employees and independent contractors; and increased diversity in the workforce. This means that the old verities of oligopolistic product markets, narrowly defined jobs, full-time permanent jobs as the norm, and a relatively homogeneous workforce, no longer hold. Unlike the set of enabling conditions for the existence of a strong labor movement previously analyzed, these are clearly unreceptive to change by the labor movement. What follows, therefore, is a consideration of the potential for several of the main ideas of the Knights for delivering improved results for labor given these circumstances.

Worker Ownership

The Knights' idea of fundamental reform of the productive system is one that is worthy of attention. Workers owning the means of production may be the only way to maintain the movement to worker participation in the long term. The American corporation is both legally and practically required to serve the interests of shareholders to the exclusion of other stakeholders. Worker interests can be given weight only insofar as they contribute to the bottom line – and the bottom line is profits for shareholders. How, then, can it be possible to maintain the impression of a real concern for worker interests?

Although it may be possible for debt-financed corporations (e.g., such as the Japanese) to be run in a fashion that is more consistent with worker needs, equity-financed corporations that have to constantly improve profitability are severely limited in their ability to do this. While an employer will provide high wages and good conditions when the labor market requires it and its competitive situation allows it, when labor markets are loose or competition is sharp, the real purpose of the corporation (to serve the interests of shareholders) is bound to be revealed.

It may be the case that Powderly and the Knights were right in judging that in the long run trade unions would not be able to successfully achieve their goals because of the necessity of their being in opposition to the persons with the greatest power in the society – the owners of capital and their agents. As Powderly argued, the power of the owner of the means of production will always be such that workers will be forced to "violate the laws of the land and the laws of organizations in order to earn sufficient bread to sustain life" (Powderly 1967: 264). It can be argued that the unique conditions of the 1930s that led to the one great surge of private-sector unionization were peculiar to that time, and that the more normal situation is the one that pertains at present, with capitalists riding high. If this is true, the labor movement must adopt radically new forms to survive and prosper. The simple answer would seem to be that, having failed to lick the capitalists, workers should join them and become owners of the means of production.

There is one aspect of the modern global economy that favors worker ownership in the form of cooperatives. This is the increasing advantage of small-scale operations over unwieldy large enterprises in surviving in the new global economic environment. If it is true, as suggested by Norman Ware (1959), that what doomed cooperatives was the growth of large-scale production, then the revival of the competitiveness of small-scale production should create new opportunities for such an organization.

Solidarity among "Producers"

The Knights' vision of solidarity is one that offers many advantages. It was utilized by the industrial unions in their rise to power in the 1930s, and has always formed a crucial part of the philosophy of American unions of the Left. "An injury to one is the concern of all" is an attractive slogan. The call to community in collective action, although running contrary to some strains of American cultural thought, is inherently appealing to human beings. Also, a broad concept of solidarity is more compatible with the modern reality of much work being done by temporary and part-time employees, and especially by independent contractors. A computer programmer working on contract with a Silicon Valley firm, or a physician, is better described as a "producer" than as an "employee" or as a "worker."

As indicated, the difficulty with solidarity lies in defining the community. The Knights adopted the widest possible definition, excluding only "parasites" from membership. The trade unions drew the boundaries of "us" much more narrowly, including only members of a particular craft or trade, and really only including skilled workers. The industrial unions, although including both the skilled and the unskilled, were historically limited to a particular industry. In fact most modern American unions are now general unions, drawing no craft or industrial lines.

Drawing on the thoughts of the Knights of Labor, it makes sense to define the persons for whom the labor movement exists as the "producers." This includes all workers, blue-collar, professional, and white-collar clerical, who are directly involved in the process of producing goods or services. Those who earn their bread by the sweat of the brows of others, namely persons with authority over others, would be excluded. Where the line is drawn could depend upon the propinquity of the job to the productive process, and the physical and social distance of the job occupant from the rank-and-file worker. A first-level supervisor in an industrial establishment, for example, may be so intimately involved in production as to be included among the producers. This is of necessity a matter of degree. An individual independent contractor would be included. Those who direct the work of others would generally be excluded. They are normally more highly paid and have other privileges of rank. At certain levels of management differences in social class become quite evident. However, including employers is probably not warranted. This would lead to such a degree of heterogeneity as to make policies for such a group impossible to develop, and would make likely the dominance of the producer organization by employers.

One important benefit of having "producers" as the "us" is that the label makes a moral statement. If "we" are the persons who are producing the wealth of society, it follows quite naturally that "we" have a solid claim on a hefty share of that wealth. From this it is rather easy to move to arguments that society benefits from a wide dispersion of wealth, and that the society benefits from the high consumer demand that results from ordinary workers receiving high pay. This also fits quite nicely with current ideas about rank-and-file workers participating in making what were formerly managerial decisions. If the producers are organizing the work as well as doing it, their claim to the fruits of it is so much the stronger.

The Knights' vision of "us" is one that is powerful for building solidarity on an extensive basis. Its weakness is in providing solidarity of sufficient intensity, a strength of craft unionism. Intensive solidarity is especially important where worker organizations are under attack by employers. However, there is no reason why the labor movement as a whole cannot have it both ways. Although the idea of a labor movement is broader than just labor unions, it nevertheless must have unions as its core. There is no good reason why there cannot be an overall umbrella body that has as its goal advancing the interests of all producers, while also having individual trade unions that pursue the interests of particular groups of workers. Indeed, this is the way that the Knights were actually organized, including trade unions as well as individual members.

The failure of the Knights as an umbrella body, including its failure to work out an accommodation with the trade unions, may have been as much a matter of conflicting egos and personalities as of necessary structural conflict. The Knights and the trade unions had come to view themselves as competitors rather than as allies, partly because the Knights could not bring themselves to give support to collective bargaining and strikes. This inclination to view differing approaches to the labor problem as competing rather than complementary was repeated later in the conflicts between Communist and non-Communist unionists.

The old wars between competing ideologies no longer exist, and the personalities are long gone. Given the rather desperate condition of the American labor movement, and the inclination of the traditional unions to try new strategies (including worker ownership and labor-management cooperation), the time may be ripe for a major rethinking of what the American labor movement should be. There is no reason that it cannot at one level be a union of all producers, while at the same time include trade unions that look out for the interests of workers in a particular craft or industry. Indeed, it could become both more general and more particular at the same time, with units of general unions being formed to serve the very particular needs of distinctive groups of workers (e.g., construction workers within the Steelworkers).

Worker Education

Education is a crucial function for a labor movement. As university labor educators know, not only the rank-and-file union members, but also the lower-level and mid-level union leaders, are woefully lacking in knowledge of the "whys" of a labor movement. Neo-classical economics has penetrated to all levels of society. Practical institutional economics and neo-institutional economics is seldom heard from in our classrooms or in public discourse. Workers need to know why a labor union makes sense for society. Rosalynn Noonan, a teacher unionist in the highly disturbed industrial relations environment of New Zealand, described to this writer the power of her union educating its members as to the union's importance. As she and other leaders of her union learned, in order for these professionals to act effectively as trade unionists, they need to be confident that what they are doing is good for society (Noonan 1994). Some research on union organizing has shown that, at least in regions where unions are weak, the attitude of workers toward unions in general is a powerful determinant of their willingness to support a union at their workplace (McClendon, Wheeler, and Weikle 1998). Unlike the Knights, the current American labor movement should not use the need for education as an excuse for inaction, but should engage in education and other action simultaneously.

The success, at least from an American perspective, of the free-market global economy has given the ideology of laissez faire capitalism tremendous credibility. Yet there are weaknesses in both its logic and its real effects. The situation is not unlike the one described by the Knights where workers as well as the public in general hear nothing but unalloyed and uncritical praise for free markets. There is another point of view. It is conceding important ground to capital to allow the only message being heard to be the one that serves the interests of capital. This is, of course, a long-range strategy, and change will not come overnight. However, at least the members of labor organizations should be provided with knowledge that confirms the social usefulness of their institutions.

Inclusion of Allied Groups

A lesson that can be learned from the structure of the Knights is that local organizations such as their mixed assemblies can have their uses. This is not to say that this should be a substitute for either collective bargaining or political action by unions. It is, rather, the idea of a deliberate effort to establish across the nation "Local Assemblies" of groups and individuals with progressive leanings. This would be neither a city central labor organization nor a political party, but a broad-based coalition of progressives. As local politics has increased in importance in the United States, the necessity for local political and social action has increased. Union action for progressive causes on the local level should help to re-polish American labor's badly tarnished image.

If participative processes are necessary for the survival of firms under modern competitive conditions, a good case can be made for worker-owned organizations providing a more friendly environment for these processes, particularly in the long run. This solves the dilemma of needing commitment from workers but not being able to reciprocate with commitment to those workers. In capitalist firms the interests of shareholders must ultimately prevail and, as a practical and legal matter, trump any commitments made to employees. The broad umbrella of an organization such as the Knights would seem ideal for a highly diverse workforce. This suits current conditions quite well.

The conditions at the end of the twentieth century bear considerable resemblance to those at the end of the nineteenth century in that in both cases the ground upon which old verities were based was shifting dramatically. Just as forms of worker organization evolved to meet the conditions of the early twentieth century, different forms will evolve to meet the conditions of the early twenty-first century. This is a time when both old and new ideas can reasonably be given a look. The Knights of Labor provide a distinctive model of unionism that has considerable appeal.

In the next two chapters we will examine two modern versions of Reformist Unionism strategy. In Chapter 5 is a description and analysis of a worker-rights organization, the Carolina Alliance for Fair Employment (CAFE), which is essentially Reformist in nature. Chapter 6 takes up the subject of worker ownership in its contemporary form. As previously noted, ownership by the producers was one of the prime tenets of the Reformism of the Knights of Labor.

FIVE

The New Reformist Unionism: CAFE

We, at CAFE, believe that everyone has a moral right to fair employment –
to work that is free from bias, dishonesty, and injustice. It is reasonable and
right to expect fair employment. The key to fair employment is having strong
worker organizations.

Carolina Alliance for Fair Employment, undated

As one surveys the American labor movement it is easy to miss a part of it
that is given little attention in the news media and the scholarly literature.
These are the worker-rights organizations discussed in Chapter 3. They are
important not so much for their numbers, which are small relative to those
of traditional unions, but because it is in these organizations that the
American labor movement looks most like the social working-class movement
long dreamed of by left-leaning intellectuals and reformers. They are more
akin to the Knights of Labor of the nineteenth century than to modern labor
unions. Indeed, they appear to be a new version of Reformist Unionism.

In its modern incarnation, Reformism in the form of worker-rights organizations has many, but not all, of the characteristics of the Knights of Labor.
Just like the Knights, these organizations have a very broad vision of the
group among whom solidarity is envisioned, and they tend to have education
as a major priority. Just like the Knights, they do not see collective bargaining as an organizational goal, although assistance to the formation of collective bargaining units is actively engaged in. Although they do not tend to
speak of changing society in a broad way, their focus on changing laws does
involve changing societal institutions. Only a few of them are interested in
setting up worker cooperatives. What is most interesting about them is that
they play a theme that is distinctive from the dominant one of American
unionism, but yet has its source deep in American labor history.

As was noted in Chapter 3, worker-rights organizations are extremely
diverse. Yet without knowing some of the details it is impossible to fully

appreciate the complex reality that these organizations represent. Accordingly, in this book one of these organizations is singled out for intensive description. This organization, the Carolina Alliance for Fair Employment (CAFE), is chosen chiefly because the author is most familiar with it and has access to data regarding it. In addition, it is especially interesting because it has flourished in South Carolina, where the societal setting is as averse to worker organizations as anyplace in the United States. The United States is arguably the leader of antiunionism among developed nations. From a union standpoint South Carolina is the veritable "belly of the beast" – the center of the employer antiunion movement in this country.

CAFE originated in the work of Southerners for Economic Justice (SEJ) in South Carolina in the 1970s. SEJ had the declared aim of extending civil rights that had been newly achieved in the political system to the workplace. It started by acting in support of an organizing campaign by what was then the Amalgamated Clothing and Textile Workers' Union (ACTWU) of employees of J. P. Stevens & Co. J. P. Stevens is a large multistate textile manufacturer that employed several thousand workers in and around Greenville, South Carolina. The ACTWU campaign ended with no J. P. Stevens workers in South Carolina unionized. The general workforce in South Carolina also remained virtually union free.

SEJ decided to continue its work beyond the J. P. Stevens campaign by launching the Workers' Rights Project (WRP) in 1980. This was done with the help of a grant from an agency of the Roman Catholic Church. WRP sought to find ways to empower workers in the absence of labor unions. It soon became independent of SEJ and, after nearly a decade of work, transformed into an organization known as CAFE. CAFE's founding purpose was building a constituency through local organizing (Sanders 1986; Taylor 1990). CAFE proceeded to build a statewide organization of over 1,000 families, scattered among fourteen local chapters in different South Carolina cities. CAFE considers 1980, when WRP was founded, as the year of its birth.

CAFE'S MENU OF PROGRAMS

CAFE and its predecessor organization (WRP) have created an extraordinary variety of programs for achieving fair employment conditions for South Carolina workers. In no case have they engaged in collective bargaining or attempted to do so. This, however, is one of the few limits to their broad pursuit of employee rights. Among other things, they have assisted unions in organizing campaigns, engaged in protected concerted activity, taken political action at both state and national levels, educated workers as to their legal rights; litigated; led various community action campaigns with respect to the environment and schools; and put forward a nationally recognized program on temporary workers. They have acted against racism and sexism, and have both a membership and a set of officers that are biracial and balanced as to sex.

CAFE and the Unions

Given its origins in the J. P. Stevens union-organizing campaign, it is hardly surprising that CAFE has included assistance to unions among its core activities. In its literature one finds numerous references to the desirability of collective bargaining and CAFE's support of unions. However, until 1996 it had a policy of not accepting financial support from unions. This policy was adopted in order to avoid the appearance of being a front for unions. In fact, in 1990 it sued the Western Carolina Sewer Authority for defamation for labeling it a "union" (Faris 1990). However, in 1996 CAFE's Board of Directors declared that CAFE had matured to the point where no one could doubt its independence. Therefore, given CAFE's strong support for the right of workers to form unions, the board decided to accept union financial help to defray the costs of particular joint projects with unions. The attitudes of South Carolina trade unionists toward CAFE have been mixed. The State AFL-CIO leadership has been favorably disposed toward CAFE, but this has not always been true of local officials of the various national unions.

Protest on the Plantation – Hilton Head. In 1994, employees from Melrose Resort on Daufuskie Island, at Hilton Head, South Carolina, contacted CAFE about problems that they were having with their employer. CAFE put them in touch with the International Union of Operating Engineers (IUOE). This led to a three-month organizing campaign in which the IUOE and CAFE worked together. CAFE published a newsletter on problems at Melrose and other hotels in the area and distributed a letter from Jesse Jackson. In a National Labor Relations Board (NLRB) election held on October 27, 1994, Melrose employees voted ninety-eight to forty-five for representation by the union.

When negotiations began they were supported by protests by the Ministerial Alliance, the National Association for the Advancement of Colored People (NAACP), and the local Democratic Club. Unfair labor practice charges filed with the NLRB by IUOE resulted in Melrose being found to have failed to bargain in good faith with the union. This ruling was followed in May, 1996, by a "week of action" during the nationally publicized MCI golf tournament. The AFL-CIO and grassroots groups from several states joined CAFE and the IUOE in these protests. The idea was "to let tourists know that their plantation vacation comes at somebody's else's expense" (*Point* 1996). Protesters passed out thousands of leaflets, slowed down traffic, and picketed using a giant inflatable rat named "Mickey Melrose." Protesters conducted "union schools" on buses transporting workers. Guests arriving at Melrose by boat were greeted by chants of "Hey, hey, hey, how many slaves did you buy today?" At the eighteenth hole of the tournament's golf course, a loudspeaker on a boat blasted out songs and testimony from Melrose workers until it was chased away by the U.S. Coast Guard. On the final day of the tournament, a boat wired for sound serenaded people with songs, and an airplane flew over with a banner saying, "Melrose employees deserve a fair contract now" (*Point* 1996).

In mid-August, 1996, a collective-bargaining agreement was reached between Melrose and the IUOE that gave workers a raise of $.40 per hour in wages, a travel allowance of $1.50 per day, and an insurance program. However, new owners took over the resort soon after the agreement was signed, renamed it the Daufuskie Island Resort, and got rid of the workers. Daufuskie Island Resort then hired only 37 of the 140 former Melrose employees. The IUOE filed unfair labor practice charges with the NLRB. CAFE stayed on during the pendency of the NLRB charges. One of its organizers, David Kennedy, continued to work with the Melrose workers. The NLRB eventually ruled in favor of the union. In May 2000 the U.S. Court of Appeals for the District of Columbia Circuit granted enforcement of an NLRB order for the employer to reinstate all of the former Melrose workers with backpay and recognize the union. Barring a successful appeal to the U.S. Supreme Court, the IUOE will, after four years of struggle, have the right to represent these workers and bargain with the successor employer, Daufuskie Island Resort.

The Melrose campaign led to a broader set of worker actions in Hilton Head. CAFE publicized and protested the practice of the Hyatt Regency and other hotels of charging banquet customers a 17 percent gratuity and not passing it on to the employees who performed the services.

CAFE worked with employees of the Hilton Head city government, successfully advocating a grievance procedure. They assisted the IUOE in successfully organizing waste haulers at ECO Services. They helped employees of the Hilton Head Wal-Mart in a concerted action protesting discrimination in hiring. Another concerted action was by employees of a small clothing retailer. These employees got rid of an unpopular manager and replaced him with the leader of the employees' concerted action. CAFE gave support to a protest by bus drivers who had held a "sick-out" over low wages and other problems.

Betwixt and Between – Citadel Workers. In 1991, food service employees of Aramack, a private company providing food service at The Citadel, a state military academy, attempted to form a union. They petitioned the NLRB for an election that would allow them to choose the Hotel Employees and Restaurant Employees Union (HERE) as their representative. However, the employer successfully defended against this petition by obtaining a ruling from the NLRB that, because their wages and benefits were controlled by the state of South Carolina, they were state employees and therefore exempt from coverage under the National Labor Relations Act (NLRA). Ironically, these employees had lost the advantages of being state employees (pension, grievance procedure, etc.) twenty-five years earlier when The Citadel's food service was privatized. So, they were in a no man's land between public- and private-sector employment where they received the advantages of neither.

CAFE's role in this matter was to hold the collective organization together until the NLRB changed its mind. Isiah Bennett, a CAFE organizer, continued to meet with the workers monthly and kept track of workplace developments. With his help they raised money, sent flowers to sick workers, and held social gatherings. CAFE represented these workers before the South Carolina State Procurement Review Panel in an unsuccessful attempt to claim that the employees were entitled to state employee benefits (Taylor 1997). Finally, in 1997, in response to a petition by the IUOE, the NLRB ruled that the Aramack employees were not state employees, and permitted an election to take place (Blakeney 1997). This election was won by the IUOE. A collective-bargaining agreement was reached between the union and Aramack effective March 1, 2000. What appears to be a reasonably constructive bargaining relationship has been established.

Other Collaboration with Unions. In addition to the campaigns at Melrose and The Citadel, CAFE has worked in cooperation with unions in other ways. The early instances of concerted action, which are discussed in the following text, had the aim of eventually leading to unionization. Also, CAFE and the South Carolina AFL-CIO are longtime allies in state politics. In 1996, an AFL-CIO Union Summer program in South Carolina was directed by Simon Greer, a CAFE staffer. Early in its history, in 1981 and again in 1983, CAFE (as WRP) picketed the Greater Greenville Chamber of Commerce when it conducted union avoidance seminars (Steinle 1981; Matthews 1983).

CAFE has the same enemies as the unions. The South Carolina Chamber of Commerce, for example, considers CAFE to be a union. The Chamber monitors CAFE's activities and denounces it as it does unions. Charles Taylor, then CAFE's State Coordinator, has described CAFE as an organization that "rose from the ashes of failed union drives" (Ocasio 1990: 1). Steve Henry, a Greenville attorney and one of the founders of CAFE, argues that CAFE can be an effective preunion group to stir things up and even file NLRB charges. He believes that the unions have made a mistake in not working more often with CAFE to facilitate organizing (Henry 2000).

Protected Concerted Action

The NLRA protects not only activity directed toward forming and joining a union, but also "concerted activity for . . . mutual aid and protection" (Section 7, NLRA). An early strategy of CAFE's predecessor organization, the WRP, was to form employee advocacy groups comprised of a minority of employees in each of a number of firms. The idea was to bring these groups into existence, make improvements at the workplace, and then knit the groups together into a citywide organization. This would take place under the shelter of the concerted activity protections of Section 7. The strength of this approach is that, unlike collective bargaining, protected concerted activity does not require a majority of the employees of a particular employer at a particular location. Its weakness is that it does not impose upon the employer the duty to bargain.

The first concerted action campaign by CAFE (as WRP) took place between 1983 and 1984 at a food distributor in Greenville. A group of delivery truck workers approached WRP because of a number of workplace problems. The workers had written an anonymous letter to corporate head-quarters saying that there were problems in the region, and that a union would be formed if the problems were not solved. The company responded by having some top corporate officials come to Greenville to meet with a committee of the workers. After two of the workers who attended the meeting were fired and a third given two disciplinary warnings, the workers turned to WRP. About thirty of the fifty drivers became WRP members. WRP then instructed the employees on the techniques of concerted action. The workers proceeded to file group grievance letters and petitions to raise all of their concerns in a protected manner. The company first responded by trying to divide the workers by having meetings in several locations simultaneously. When this failed to produce any result, it fired an unpopular supervisor and transferred the local manager. According to Charles Taylor, the new manager was a "back slapper" who was friendly to the employees. He asked them to give the company a chance to resolve things. The company then corrected many of the problems.

WRP contacted the International Brotherhood of Teamsters (IBT) to see if they would be interested in organizing these workers. The union sent representatives to talk with the workers. After considering union representation, the workers decided against it. At this point WRP concluded that there was nothing further that could be done through concerted activity and withdrew. About a year later the employees called WRP, saying that there were problems once again. WRP declined to get involved this time.

A second concerted action campaign was at a textile plant. After some initial organizing by workers who had been early members of WRP, a group of about twenty-five employees began meeting on a regular basis. They produced an in-plant newsletter that included articles on job problems and safety hazards. WRP staff printed and distributed the newsletter. This produced some changes in working conditions by the company. However, when two-thirds of the workers showed up at work on a "Button Day" wearing WRP buttons, the employer changed tactics and, according to Charles Taylor, began to harass certain key WRP leaders by issuing warnings to them. WRP responded by filing unfair labor practice charges with the NLRB that caused the warnings to be removed from the workers' files. However, unfair labor practice charges filed on behalf of a worker who was only "marginally involved" with WRP failed and, according to Charles Taylor, the employer began harassing employees who had testified on her behalf. WRP lost a case that challenged the firing of one of these employees. At this point the workers lost interest in WRP and the organization withdrew from the plant.

From its experience with concerted action, CAFE concluded that this strategy involved a high degree of risk for workers. It was also extremely labor intensive for the CAFE staff. It had failed to produce enduring results. Consequently, WRP decided to abandon this strategy.

Political Action

CAFE's first foray into politics came in 1984 when it took up the cause of workers who had been laid off by a Greenville manufacturer. The company had terminated sixty-seven workers while at the same time hiring some twenty temporary workers. It had also applied to the Greenville City Council for $8.3 million in revenue bonds to support its operations in the area. In its application the company had represented that it would employ 150 workers. WRP organized large turnouts of terminated workers and testimony by them at City Council meetings, generating publicity on this issue. Although it was too late in the bond approval process to block it, WRP was successful in instituting reforms in the bond process. New rules were adopted requiring firms applying for bond approval to give notice of layoffs and report at six-month intervals on employment levels. According to Charles Taylor, this experience persuaded WRP that it was easier to operate in the political arena than to take on the "hardest, meanest, management by intimidation, hard ball guys in these textile mills" (Taylor 1999: 6).

Although WRP had engaged in public discussions criticizing state law permitting the use of polygraphs (lie detectors) in 1982 (Taylor 1982), it had not attempted to be politically active at the state level in a significant way until it began a statewide issue campaign on workers' compensation laws in 1985. At issue was the retaliatory firing of workers' compensation claimants, which was permitted under state law. According to Charles Taylor, there were horror stories of workers being told by their employer that they had a choice between filing a workers' compensation claim and keeping their job, and of workers being fired while in their hospital beds.

Ben Bowen, a Greenville attorney who was an early supporter of WRP, set up a meeting between WRP representatives and State Senator Isadore Lourie of Columbia, who was the head of a South Carolina House/Senate Study Committee on workers' compensation. Senator Lourie was receptive to the idea of holding hearings. WRP wrote the proposed legislation and Senator Lourie set up field hearings in Greenville, Columbia, Charleston, and Florence, the four largest cities in the state. WRP worked on turnout for the hearings, receiving help from local chapters of the American Civil Liberties Union (ACLU) and NAACP, the AFL-CIO, and the trial lawyers. A total of 400 to 600 persons attended the four hearings. Testimony at the hearings was dramatic and media coverage was extensive. This was followed up by lobbying at the legislature in cooperation with the AFL-CIO and other organizations. The result was a statute that now provides some protection to the approximately 1.5 million workers covered by workers' compensation in South Carolina.

Subsequent to the 1985 workers' compensation legislation campaign, WRP and then CAFE have remained active in state politics. In 1987 WRP publicly criticized the South Carolina Department of Labor for favoring employer interests over those of employees, and opposed legislation weakening workers' compensation laws. In 1989 it fought for legislation giving workers' compensation claimants a choice of physicians. In 1990 CAFE undertook a major lobbying effort in support of the Wrongful Discharge Act, which would make it unlawful to fire a worker without good cause. One interesting twist on CAFE's approach to this issue was to sponsor legislation that would prohibit an employer from firing an employee who missed work because of being a victim of a crime. This was aimed at conservative legislators who often express concern over victims' rights (as opposed to the rights of persons accused of crime).

An extensive legislative platform was adopted by CAFE in 1996. This set of ideas still represents its legislative program. Under the heading of *countering the decline in wages* it includes support for education and training, improved severance pay and transition assistance for displaced workers, repeal of the Right to Work law, curbing abuses of temporary employees, opposition to privatization that lowers pay and benefits, government subsidies going to a company only if it creates higher-wage jobs, and increases in both state and federal minimum wages. Under *increasing job security* it supports replacing at will employment with a "fair cause" system, employee access to personnel records, increasing job security for sheriffs' deputies, strengthening protections for workers who file health and safety complaints, and broad whistleblower protections. Under *defending and expanding the rights of injured workers* it includes workers having a more meaningful say in their medical treatment, strong antiretaliation provisions in the workers' compensation laws, and opposition to diminishing existing rights of injured workers. Finally, it aims *"to enable working families to participate more fully in public life"* by increasing worker participation in the making of public policy, campaign finance reform, and the creation of job-protected leaves for employees who run for public office (Carolina Alliance for Fair Employment 1986).

CAFE's activities in state politics over the last decade have included challenging the appointment of a corporate executive as a workers' compensation judge, continuing to advocate an employee's choice of physician in workers' compensation cases, and opposing attempts on the part of employers to weaken the workers' compensation statute. It was also involved in closing a loophole in the South Carolina workers' compensation statute that allowed employers to opt out of its coverage. In 1999 it actively pursued the cause of giving employees the right to examine their own personnel records.

Worker Rights Education

Educating workers about their legal rights has been an ongoing activity of WRP and CAFE since 1985. It was in 1985 that WRP announced a job-rights campaign of holding five seminars in different South Carolina cities (Kelly 1985). These were in fact held in ten cities between 1985 and 1987. Steve Henry, the attorney previously mentioned, conducted these workshops. They were free, one-and-one-half to two-hour programs. Workshops averaged fifty people in attendance. Nearly all were successful. According to Henry (2000) those attending the workshops were interested in their own problems – not particularly in helping others or in making broad changes in the law.

Although CAFE no longer holds these workshops, it is still very much in the business of advising workers about their legal rights. This is often a topic in their meetings. CAFE's office regularly answers inquiries on job rights. Perhaps most importantly, it continues to publish the *Basic Guide to Workers' Rights in South Carolina* (Carolina Alliance for Fair Employment 1994), a highly useful description of federal and state employment law written in laymen's terms.

Community Issues

Consistent with its Reformist social-movement orientation, CAFE has been active in issues affecting the community as a whole rather than limiting itself to workplace concerns. These have chiefly had to do with the ever-sensitive topics of race and the environment.

At this writing, CAFE's most recent involvement in a racially related issue was taking a stand against the flying of the Confederate flag on the state capitol. This has created strains within the organization, and is one of the factors that may account for a recent decrease in the proportion of white members. For an organization that prides itself on racial balance, and on being one of those rare progressive organizations that appeals to white working-class men, this is a serious problem.

Other actions in the area of race include a 1997 protest at a Darlington nursing home against racist treatment of employees. This was led by CAFE organizer David Kennedy. In 1996, Kennedy helped lead a protest against the Redneck Shop in Laurens, South Carolina, which was selling racist materials. Jesse Jackson, a South Carolina native, joined in this action. CAFE organizer Carol Bishop led a fight in Darlington County schools to reduce racial discrimination in their gifted and talented program, and discrimination in the handling of students with emotional problems and physical disabilities (Carolina Alliance for Fair Employment 1997). The CAFE chapter in Abbeyville/Greenwood has been involved in efforts to end racial discrimination in employment in the Abbeyville County School system (Carolina Alliance for Fair Employment 1998a).

The most visible action on the environment was a fight to clean up Langley Pond. Beginning in 1987, CAFE has led efforts to solve severe environmental problems in this pond, which is located in a working-class neighborhood. In the rural community of Mullins, CAFE joined in an effort to solve sewage treatment problems. In Charleston, CAFE representatives serve on the board dealing with environmental problems arising from the closing of the Charleston Naval Yard.

Temporary Workers

CAFE has gained national recognition for its innovative work on behalf of temporary workers. It started in 1994 with a "Temp School." CAFE hired twenty temporary workers. It then taught them about job rights and obtained information from them about temporary employment policies in the Greenville area. It also published a newsletter for temporary workers, but this was soon discontinued because of distribution problems. CAFE put together Principles of Fair Conduct for temporary help agencies and shared this with other worker-rights organizations across the country.

In 1995 and 1996, CAFE ran its Temp Testing Project. It hired temporary employees to register with selected temporary help agencies and go out on job assignments for at least one day. The employees were then to report back to CAFE. Thirty-two of the sixty Greenville temporary help agencies were tested. Later, in 1997, CAFE tested seven temporary help agencies in four South Carolina cities. The two "questionable practices" that they found were (1) failure to provide written notice of wages when sending them out on assignments (state law requires such a notice); and (2) asking medical questions prior to making a job offer (the Federal Americans with Disabilities Act prohibits this). These problems, particularly the failure to give notice of wages, were found to be quite widespread (Taylor 1999).

Based on the findings of the Temp Testing Project, CAFE filed complaints with the South Carolina Department of Labor alleging violations of the wage notice law by seven temporary help agencies. The Department of Labor found three of the seven guilty of violating this law. However, it took the position that adequate notice was given if the agency advised employees that they would be paid at least the minimum wage, and that pay would vary according to the assignment (*Poverty & Race* 1997). CAFE sued the Department of Labor, claiming that the Department of Labor was wrong in its interpretation of the law. In 1999 the South Carolina Court of Appeals affirmed a trial court ruling in favor of the Department of Labor (*The State* 1999). Claims of violations of the Americans with Disabilities Act are still being pursued at this writing.

Having gained a great deal of knowledge in its Temp School and Temp Testing Project, CAFE embarked on a national campaign for temporary employee rights, working with other worker-rights organizations. Its strategy is to persuade temporary help agencies to subscribe to principles of fair conduct. Employee rights groups in Milwaukee and New Jersey have modified the "Principles of Fair Conduct for Temp Agencies" produced by CAFE in 1994. As modified, these are the basis for the national campaign on temporary employee rights (Carolina Alliance for Fair Employment 1998b). CAFE staffers have made presentations at national meetings to tell the story of their work with temporary workers.

Other CAFE Actions

A film, *The Uprising of '34*, sparked a controversy in which CAFE became involved. This film, the story of the 1934 textile strike, had been shown nationally on National Public Television, but South Carolina Educational Television refused to carry it. In 1998, CAFE had reserved a room at the Easley, South Carolina, Chamber of Commerce building to show *The Uprising of '34*, only to have the room reservation cancelled (Nye 1998). This was followed a week later by the cancellation of facilities reservations in a training center in Easley where CAFE intended to show this film. Protests of these cancellations led to the arrest of CAFE's then State Coordinator, Charles Taylor (Stokes 1998).

In 1995, a five-week public interest course at Spartanburg Technical College was scheduled to include a showing of *The Uprising of '34*. The instructor of this course was to have been Simon Greer, a CAFE staffer. However, before the course could begin, Greer was first interrogated by college officials about his political views and then told that the course was cancelled because it was "politically unwise" because certain textile and auto industry executives believed that Greer would teach employees "how to uprise." Greer was told that the school received a great deal of money from industry, and that industry leaders did not want it to teach workers their rights (Beacham 1995). The course at Spartanburg Technical College was cancelled, but CAFE managed to teach it at another location. A lawsuit by CAFE that challenged the legality of the course cancellation failed.

Litigation

In 1984 and 1985 the WRP operated a litigation project, funded by the Public Interest Law Foundation at Columbia University. This project included two types of cases: "(1) those with the potential for creating favorable state employment law precedents, and (2) those in which a person had a winable (sic) employment case under an existing law but was financially unable to pursue the case" (Taylor 1990: 115). Of the eight cases initiated during this period, the six that attempted to create new precedent were lost, while the two to enforce existing law were won.

According to Charles Taylor (1990) the litigation project was important because it led WRP to think in terms of state law and was their first organized effort to make new employment law in South Carolina's court system. Taylor believes, however, that this strategy has significant weaknesses. These include the difficulty of including rank-and-file workers in the process, given that trials are held during the day when they are at work; the extremely lengthy processes of the law; and the limited role that workers can play in the litigation. In his view such a strategy can attract public attention and change public policy, but lacks the potential for empowering workers that is present in organization building.

Steve Henry, an attorney who is one of the founders of CAFE, disagrees with Charles Taylor as to the effectiveness of the litigation strategy. He cites key people, such as David Kennedy, who came to CAFE as a result of litigation. His view is that CAFE's best strategy is to litigate and organize around the litigation. In litigation a concrete issue and a real person are involved. People can understand and care about the issues. He cites the CAFE temporary workers project as a good idea in general terms, but one that has "no heart" because it is not as concrete as a lawsuit. According to him, an employer or government agency will "take the bait every time" when CAFE leaders expose themselves to retribution and, like Br'er Rabbit, ask "not to be thrown in the briar patch." In his view, this creates a controversy that has the power to move people (Henry 2000).

SNAPSHOTS OF TWO FOUNDERS

Among the founders of CAFE are two men with very different sets of abilities – Charles Taylor and Steve Henry. They combined their talents to plant the seed that grew into CAFE, and tended it in its early years. One of them, Charles Taylor, until recently held the title of State Coordinator, which is CAFE's chief administrative office. Steve Henry, while not now as active as he was in the past, still lends his legal expertise to CAFE and remains a key supporter. A number of other men and women also made very significant contributions to the birth and growth of CAFE. Focusing on Taylor and Henry is not intended as a slight to such important figures as Greenville attorney Ben Bowen, Isiah Bennett, Carol Nichols, David Kennedy, and others. It is simply a way to give the reader some impression of the people who made CAFE.

Taylor, the son of a Methodist minister, grew up in one of South Carolina's medium-sized cities in the upstate region. While a college student at Davidson College in North Carolina he worked for a summer as the

Director of Compassion House, which he describes as a "flop house for winos." After graduating from college, in 1979 he became a supervisor for Milliken & Company in their textile mills in Williamston, and then Greenville, South Carolina. In 1981, after working two years as a supervisor, he resigned in protest of what he believed was bad treatment of hourly employees by the company. He then went to work as a volunteer for WRP. In 1982 WRP received a grant from a small Catholic religious order and hired Taylor as an organizer. He became Director of WRP in June 1982, and continued to head WRP and then CAFE until 2000. His energy, imagination, and organizational skills have been indispensable to CAFE.

Steve Henry, a Michigan native, came to Columbia, South Carolina, in 1972. He skipped his college graduation ceremony to start a job with Richland House, a facility for juvenile offenders. He had previously worked in a psychiatric hospital. While in Columbia, he entered law school at the University of South Carolina, graduating in 1977. He worked at the South Carolina Legislature for several months while awaiting bar examination results. Upon passing the South Carolina State Bar he took a job as Deputy Public Defender in Greenville County, South Carolina. He left this job in 1981 and went into private practice. It was at this time that he began working with SEJ in a "funky little place," and then with WRP (Henry 2000). According to Charles Taylor, Henry joining in this work was a "real key" to its success (Taylor 1999). For several years Steve Henry was legal counsel for CAFE, bringing and defending a series of cases on its behalf. He now continues to do work for CAFE, but on a volunteer basis. He worked with Charles Taylor on the concerted activities campaigns and conducted the job-rights work-shops. At this writing he is defending Charles Taylor on charges, previously mentioned, arising from the protests regarding the refusal of officials in the city of Easley to permit a showing of the film *The Uprising of '34.*

Steve Henry and Charles Taylor have complementary skills. Whereas Charles has kept the organization running and fostered a number of initia-tives, Steve has supplied crucial skills and knowledge relating to the law, along with his own views on strategy. Although differing in their approaches, they have been an effective team. Steve Henry favors litigation as the prime approach for building CAFE, whereas Charles Taylor is less optimistic about the potential of litigation for organization building. In fact CAFE has used both litigation and a variety of other approaches, often with the leadership of such CAFE activists as Isiah Bennett, Carol Nichols, and David Kennedy. It is the energy and courage of all these individuals, as well as a number of others, that account for CAFE's success. In South Carolina, the "belly of the beast" of American antiunionism, it takes individuals of superlative quality to lead a worker-rights organization. These very special human beings have been crucial to its success.

In 2000, Charles Taylor retired from his position of State Coordinator of CAFE. He was succeeded by long-time activist Carol Nichols. This means that for the first time CAFE, which has a large Black membership, will have a Black woman as its principal officer.

CAFE fits into our taxonomy as a Reformist labor organization. It has broader goals than Pure and Simple unions, reaching considerably beyond wages and conditions of work to social class and community concerns. It is organized on a geographic basis. It actively forms coalitions with other progressive groups. It does not aim to engage in collective bargaining, although it acts to facilitate the forming of collective-bargaining relationships by unions. Its emphasis on education is reminiscent of the Reformist Knights of Labor. Its focus on the law as the instrument of worker power gives it something of a Social Democratic flavor.

It is interesting to note that CAFE arrived at its strategic orientation largely by trial and error. In the hands of leaders that had a strong social-work flavor to their backgrounds, and arising from the failures of trade unions in the very harsh environment of South Carolina, it evolved a set of strategies and activities that seemed to work out in practice. The move into politics from concerted action campaigns occurred because the experience with politics (first in dealing with the City of Greenville) was more successful than dealing with South Carolina employers. What we observe, then, is the development of a strategic thrust not by a predetermined philosophy of worker organization, but by trial and error and experience. This is what makes CAFE such an interesting model for worker organizations operating in extremely adverse social settings.

Testing CAFE against our enabling conditions for the existence of a strong labor movement produces mixed results. First, it does not particularly lead to greater perceptions of centrality of work, given that its appeal and programs are not limited to the workplace. Second, it is powerful for building extensive solidarity, given the broad reach of its membership. By the same token, however, similar to the Reformist Knights before them, they would not be expected to be strong in building intensive solidarity. Third, as to building perceptions of a distinct worker interest, one does not see this being articulated by CAFE. It is more a social-class organization than one limited to workers. Still, it does regularly deal with workplace issues, taking the side of the worker in opposition to the forces of capital. Fourth, it has produced benefits for its members and society at relatively low cost. This has been the result of nearly heroic efforts on the part of its officers and activists. Fifth, employer opposition has been strong, at least in terms of the position relative to CAFE taken by the South Carolina Chamber of Commerce. However, it must be said that employers have had a difficult time finding a way to fight CAFE. Because it does not aim at collective bargaining, the traditionally powerful weapons of employers and their organizations are not as effective as they are against traditional unions. Sixth, government support for its political positions has been sporadic. As an organization it at least has not yet attracted the unfriendly eye of state policy makers. As a political and social action organization it is probably reasonably well protected from adverse government action by constitutional guarantees and social norms of free speech and free association.

In sum, it is clear that CAFE, and similar worker-rights organizations, have some strengths that other forms of worker organizations lack. They may be especially well fitted for an extremely hostile environment. CAFE has served very effectively as an educator of workers; a spokesperson for their rights and interests before legislative bodies; a source of expertise on and pressure for temporary workers; and a general-purpose worker organization. Above all, CAFE is experimental and opportunistic in following whatever paths are open in forwarding worker interests. A great deal can be learned from their successes and failures. For example, the use of concerted protected activities appears less attractive once one sees CAFE's experience with this tactic. On the other hand, the comparative success in politics suggests that this is an attractive avenue for worker power in a setting such as South Carolina. The parallel with the Social Democratic Social Dialogue in the European Community (EC), as described in Chapter 7, is an interesting one. In the EC, as in South Carolina, where collective bargaining (in the EC case at European level) is resisted very strongly by employers, a strategic approach that aims at government action may be the one most likely to achieve results.

In the Knights of Labor we see an example of an historic Reformist union organization. In CAFE, we see a contemporary one. Next we will look at a current expression of a basic principle of Reformist Unionism – ownership of enterprises by the employees (or producers, to use the terminology of the Knights).

SIX

A New Version of an Old Reformist Strategy:
Employee Ownership

> ... one of the exciting opportunities employee ownership presents is to reach a new and higher level of economic democracy, a long-time labor objective. ...
>
> *Lynn Williams, Former President, United Steelworkers of America, 2000*

Worker ownership is an idea whose time may have finally come. Paradoxically, employee ownership of the enterprise in which they work is at once the oldest and the newest labor strategy. In its historic form of producer co-operatives, which was advocated by the Knights of Labor, is a core strategy of Reformist Unionism. In recent years it has been put into practice frequently, but in a manner that has been largely haphazard and opportunistic. Yet, it appears to be one of the few general strategic directions that offers to unions the ability to organize and represent the winners as well as the losers in the modern global economy. This chapter will briefly review the idea of employee ownership, take a look at its current state, and evaluate its potential as a major strategic union thrust.

THE IDEA OF EMPLOYEE OWNERSHIP

The concept of employee ownership has many fathers. Perhaps the most obvious American source of thinking and practice in the area of employee ownership is the Knights of Labor. As noted in Chapter 4, employee ownership in the form of producer cooperatives was at the very heart of their ideology. The Knights' notion was to replace the wage system with one where the "producer" was also the owner. This would unite, and therefore do away with the conflict between capital and labor. It would ensure that the producer received the just fruits of his labor (McLaurin 1978).

Marxist theory holds that the relations of production are crucial in determining economic and social systems (Engels 1894). The key to these relations

118

is ownership of the means of production. Collective ownership of the instruments and mechanisms of production is a necessary condition for a socialist society (Balinky 1970). Although this was interpreted in the major Communist countries to mean state ownership, it has sometimes been operationalized as employee control (e.g., in the former Yugoslavia).

The ideas of Louis Kelso have been influential in forming the current legal framework for employee ownership in the United States. Kelso theorized that access to owning capital "is as fundamental a human right as the right to the fruits of one's labor" (Kurland and Brohawn 1999/2000: 6). He believed that an ideal market system would guarantee to all the ability to acquire capital. This would lead to a distribution of rewards according to the contributions that each person's labor and capital made to society. His "Value-Based Management" would spread capital ownership, and therefore risks and rewards, broadly among a firm's workers. In the 1950s he observed that in the United States only the few owned the chief source of wealth – stock in corporations. This led to vast disparities in wealth among American citizens. His principal solution was the Employee Stock Ownership Plan (ESOP), which would give ordinary workers the opportunity to acquire capital in the form of corporate stock. Kelso's signal importance arises primarily from the fact that he had the good fortune to sell this idea to one of the most powerful persons in the United States Senate, Russell Long. In 1974 Long translated Kelso's ideas into federal legislation in the Employee Retirement Income Security Act (ERISA) (Rosen 1991).

THE STATE OF EMPLOYEE OWNERSHIP IN THE UNITED STATES

At the present time employee ownership is much more widespread than is commonly recognized. Except for the publicity given a few prominent cases, such as United Airlines, there is relatively little media attention to this important phenomenon. Perhaps this is because it is relatively uncontroversial, drawing support from across the political spectrum.

According to the latest Department of Labor statistics collected in 1998, there are about 11,000 ESOP plans or their equivalent, covering over 10 million employees. These numbers have grown rather steadily since 1975, although the number of employees leveled off from 1997 to 1998. In 1998 these plans had assets of about $500 billion. Most (85 percent) were in privately held companies (whose stock is not publicly traded). The median percentage of employee ownership in private companies that have employee ownership is 30 to 40 percent. In publicly held firms it is 10 to 15 percent. Taking into account both ESOPs and other forms of employee ownership, about $800 billion worth of stock is held by employees in the United States, amounting to approximately 8 percent of the total (Rosen 1998). In 1990, types of employee ownership other than ESOPs made up nearly half of the 1,000 largest employee ownership plans (Blasi and Kruse 1991). In 1998, one of these types, 401 (k) plans, owned about $300 billion worth of stock, primarily in publicly traded companies (Rosen 1998).

The ten largest majority employee–owned companies in the United States are United Parcel Services (UPS) (344,000 employees), Publix Supermarkets (109,000 employees), United Airlines (95,000 employees), Hy-Vee (supermarkets – 46,000 employees), Science Applications International (research and development, computer systems – 41,000 employees), TTC Inc. (employee leasing – 26,000 employees), Tharaldson Motels (18,000 employees), Dyncorp (technical services – 17,000 employees), Parsons Corporate (engineering, construction – 12,000 employees), and CH2M Hill, Inc. (engineering and architecture – 10,250 employees). The remaining top 100 employee-owned companies are widely dispersed, both geographically and across industries (National Center for Employee Ownership 2001).

TYPES OF EMPLOYEE OWNERSHIP PLANS

Louis Kelso's ESOP is the most common form of employee ownership. An ESOP is a defined-contribution retirement plan, and is covered by the ERISA of 1974 (29 U.S.C. Secs. 1001–1461). It is established to invest primarily, often exclusively, in the stock of the employing corporation. Usually an ESOP trust borrows money to buy an employer's stock. The repayment of the loan is guaranteed by the employer. Over a period of five to ten years, payments are made by the employer to the trust so that it can repay the loan. As parts of the loan are repaid, a proportional number of shares of stock is allocated to particular employees' individual investment accounts.

There are a number of federal tax advantages to the corporation in this arrangement. First, the principal as well as the interest on the loan is deductible from taxes as an employee benefit. The upper limit on this is 25 percent of employee compensation, significantly higher than it is for other benefits. Second, dividends paid on the stock, which can be used to repay the loan, are also tax deductible. This provision is probably the crucial tax benefit (Blasi and Kruse 1991). In addition, until 1996, 50 percent of the interest paid was nontaxable to the lender, allowing lenders to loan money to ESOPs at low rates (Carberry 1998).

401 (k) plans are growing rapidly. This has been given a recent boost by changes in federal law permitting automatic enrollment of employees. The 401 (k) plans use pretax employee contributions to purchase company stock, and match these contributions either with cash or additional company stock (Blasi and Kruse 1991; Rosen 1998). The 401 (k) plans invest the majority of their funds in company stock but, unlike ESOPs, do diversify their investments. Most of the investments in the stock of the employing company occur in large companies. In 1993, $250 billion of the $447 billion of 401 (k) plan assets were invested in the stock of the employees' own company, a larger figure than the total amount invested in own-company stock by ESOPs at the time. However, few of the companies with large holdings of their own stock in 401 (k) plans think of themselves as employee ownership companies. If present trends continue this may change, as in a few years employees in such plans will come to own in the neighborhood of 20 percent of some large public companies (Rosen 1998).

Deferred profit-sharing plans give rise to employee ownership by investing profit-sharing plan money in a retirement trust fund. This trust then purchases the company's stock. A large percentage of profit-sharing plans are of this type (Blasi and Kruse 1991).

Employee stock-purchase plans sell stock to employees, often at a discount, sometimes matching the employee stock purchases or paying brokerage fees. There are no tax advantages to such a plan (Blasi and Kruse 1991).

Broad stock options, virtually unknown prior to the 1980s, have become increasingly popular. For firms that do not want the restrictions inherent in the "qualified" plans (ESOP and 401 [k]) that are required for their tax advantages, this may be an attractive way to put ownership into the hands of employees (Rosen 1998). Recently there has been a great deal of attention given to providing tax breaks for these plans. In 2000, Congress speedily passed the Worker Economic Opportunity Act, which exempts stock option awards from the overtime pay requirements of the Fair Labor Standards Act. This removes a source of complexity in figuring overtime pay rates for rank-and-file employees who are granted such options (National Center for Employee Ownership 2000a). In addition, on June 21, 2000, the House Committee on Education and the Workforce approved, by voice vote, the Wealth through the Workplace Act. If passed by Congress, it would permit nonexecutive employees to delay taxation on options until the underlying stock is sold (rather than when the option is exercised) and allow a limited tax deduction to employers granting stock options to employees (Bureau of National Affairs 2000).

Cooperatives of producers, the preferred mode of organization of the Knights of Labor, have a long history in the United States. They have seen something of a renaissance in recent years (United Steelworkers of America undated a). The organizational structure developed by the Industrial Co-operative Association of America gives one share to each member, who must be a worker at the cooperative. The share value is a membership fee, and does not reflect the market value of the enterprise. Each year a share of the net earnings is allocated to the account of each member. These accounts earn a modest rate of interest. When the member leaves the cooperative the accumulated amount in the account is paid to the member. Also, each year the cooperative pays some portion of the net earnings to the members. The cooperative is governed on a one-share, one-vote basis. The laws of several states deal specifically with cooperatives. Where such special laws do not exist, organization is done under the corporate form and the cooperative operates as a corporation (United Steelworkers of America undated a).

WORKER OWNERSHIP IN OTHER COUNTRIES

The worker cooperative is the main form of worker ownership outside the United States. Many countries have strong traditions of worker, as well as other types of, cooperatives. The best known of these is the Mondragon group in Spain's Basque region. It has about 20,000 worker-members. It has its own bank. Among other activities, the bank assists in developing new cooperative enterprises. It funds schools, as well as research and development activities.

Both Italy and France have strong cooperative movements involving tens of thousands of workers (Durso and Rothblatt 1991). There is a very extensive cooperative system in India (Durso and Rothblatt 1991; Sinha 2000). Israel's famous kibbutz movement has recently been going through some major changes, but remains an important example of a producers' cooperative (Galor 2000). A related institution in Israel consists of the very large number of enterprises owned by the Histadrut, the Israeli national labor federation.

Plans for corporate stock ownership are not so common abroad, but have been the subject of increasing interest in a number of countries. The flexibility of the corporate form of ownership is the chief attraction (Durso and Rothblatt 1991). This is also consistent with the virtually worldwide triumph of the capitalist system. ESOPs or ESOP-like plans have come into existence in the United Kingdom, Ireland, Australia, and, to a limited extent, in Canada. Germany has seen some growth in employee ownership, although this was, at least initially, mainly through nonvoting forms of financial participation (Durso and Rothblatt 1991). There has been some movement toward employee stock ownership in Egypt and South Africa. In Asia, the one country that has moved actively into employee ownership is the Philippines (Durso and Rothblatt 1991).

At its September 2000 convention the Swedish national peak labor federation, the LO, decided to reconsider its long-standing policy opposing worker ownership. It based this change in attitude on the changes in capital requirements of firms to involve less physical capital and more intellectual capital, and the increasingly common practice for employees to receive stock or stock options as part of their compensation (Aahlstrom 2000). In 2001 France broadened its already rather comprehensive law that regulated and encouraged employee share ownership (*European Industrial Relations Review* 2001).

Advocates of worker ownership have taken note of the increasing interest of international agencies – International Labor Organization (ILO), World Bank, and International Monetary Fund (IMF) – in poverty reduction. This fits nicely with the employee ownership goal of moderating the wide disparity of income and wealth between the economically privileged and the poor. It may provide an opportunity for employee ownership to make its way onto the agendas of these agencies (Clem 2000).

Japan provides an interesting case of something similar to worker ownership – what has been termed "quasi-employee-managed firms" (Kuwahara 2000: 77). Japanese firms in the post–World War II period came to be controlled by a combination of employees and bankers, with shareholder power being minimized. This resulted in something similar to employee governance, albeit in the absence of ownership. In addition, in recent years, many Japanese firms have instituted stock ownership plans at the initiative of management. Furthermore, to a limited degree, unions have moved to acquire ownership stakes in companies (Kuwahara 2000).

SHOULD AMERICAN UNIONS ADVOCATE WORKER OWNERSHIP?

For the purposes of this book the crucial question about worker ownership is whether it makes sense as a strategy for American unions. The answer to this chiefly depends, in turn, upon whether it is a viable strategy for employee power and influence on corporate policy. Furthermore, it is probably not feasible if it has negative effects upon productivity and profits.

Employee Ownership and Employee Power

In the U.S. legal system the corporation is owned by its shareholders. The shareholders elect the board of directors, who appoint the top executives, who in turn control the hiring of other employees and are responsible for conducting the business of the firm. There is a legal obligation on the part of the directors and executives to manage the organization for the shareholders' benefit. Although the extent to which managers actually serve shareholder interests has been often debated, there is a clear line of responsibility drawn by the law from the shareholders to the directors to the executives. In addition, there is a general social expectation that managers serve shareholder interests. This is their social role, and managers who do not fulfill this role place their jobs in jeopardy. Therefore, to be a shareholder places power over management into the hands of the person holding the corporate stock.

The degree to which employee ownership places shareholder power in the hands of workers varies with the type of employee ownership. Employee Stock-Purchase Plans and Stock Option Plans (after the option is exercised) put employee owners in the same position as other shareholders. They participate in the election of directors and vote on some matters of corporate policy. This is not the case with 401 (k) plans or ESOPs. The stock in a 401 (k) plan is voted by the plan's trustee, although he or she is under a fiduciary obligation to act in the interests of the members of the plan.

In the case of ESOPs the law is more complex. Here, there are two types of shares – those that have been allocated to the employees' individual investment accounts and those that have not. Different rules apply to each type. Voting rights also vary according to whether the corporation is privately held or publicly traded. It is to worker influence through ESOP stock that we will now turn our attention.

ESOPs and Employee Power. The ability of employee-owners to exercise influence on corporate policy depends upon a number of factors. The most important of these are the right of employees to direct the ESOP trustee as to how stock is to be voted, and the total proportion of stock held by the ESOP or by employees.

Because legal ownership of the stock in an ESOP is vested in a trustee, it is the trustee who actually votes the stock. The crucial questions are who (if anyone) directs the trustee how to vote, and what considerations must, or may, the trustee legally take into account in voting. In order to be eligible for favorable federal tax treatment, the plan is required by U.S. Internal Revenue Code, Section 409 (e), to pass through to employees certain voting rights. Section 409 (e) (2) requires that, for publicly traded securities, "each participant . . . is entitled to direct the plan as to the manner in which the securities of the employer which are entitled to vote and are allocated to the account of such participant . . . are to be voted." For privately held securities, Section 409 (e) (3) requires that

. . . each participant . . . is entitled to direct the plan as to the manner in which voting rights under securities of the employer which are allocated to the account of such participants are to be exercised *with respect to any corporate matter which involves the voting of such shares with respect to the approval or disapproval of any corporate merger or consolidation, recapitalization, reclassification, liquidation, dissolution, sale of substantially all assets of a trade or business, or [similar transactions]* (emphasis added).

So, for securities that have been allocated to the employee's account, the employee has the right to direct the trustee how to vote – on all issues in a publicly held company and on a more limited set of issues in a privately held one. However, ERISA, Section 403 (a), provides that the "trustee . . . shall have exclusive authority and discretion to manage and control the assets of the plan." The only exceptions stated are where the "plan expressly provides that the . . . trustees are subject to the direction of a named fiduciary who is not a trustee . . ." or the authority to manage the plan has been delegated to an investment manager. This power is to be exercised under fiduciary duties imposed by Section 404, requiring that the "exclusive purpose" be "providing benefits to participants and their beneficiaries" and paying the costs of administration. This is to be done with the care of a "prudent man."

Although the case law is not entirely clear on this, the Department of Labor has issued an advice letter that states that, if a plan specifically provides that the trustee must accept the direction of employees as to allocated shares, the employee becomes a "named fiduciary" whose direction the trustee *must* take (Sec. 403, Internal Revenue Code). However, the trustee must assure that the plan's procedures are followed, that there has been no "coercion or undue pressure" on the employees, that "necessary information" is provided to them, and that clearly false information has either not been distributed to them or, if distributed, is corrected (RIA 1996: 97, 502). As such pass-through rights are required by the Internal Revenue Code, this would indicate that, in general, trustees may be required to take directions from the employees as to voting allocated shares.

As to unallocated shares, the plan need not provide for a pass-through of voting rights. For these, the trustee must follow the strictures of ERISA and vote for the exclusive benefit of the employees, and in a prudent fashion. If the plan does in fact provide for a pass-through of voting power for unallo-cated shares, it is the opinion of the Department of Labor that the trustee must follow the employees' directions unless the trustee "can articulate well-founded reasons why doing so would give rise to a violation [of ERISA]" (RIA 1996: 97, 503). These reasons include imprudence.

Where there is no pass-through, and the trustee is voting the stock in his/her discretion, it is clear that he/she must, as previously indicated, act for the exclusive purpose of providing benefits to the employees, and act pru-dently (ERISA, Sec. 404). This means that he or she must make an indepen-dent investigation and gather as much information as is necessary before acting (Carberry 1998). An important question for our purposes is what the trustee may take into account in making a decision. Does "providing bene-fits" to employees mean only retirement income? Can their interests as workers be considered along with their interests as investors? How about their interest in job security?

The law is not clear as to the boundaries of the factors that the trustee must, or may, consider in voting employees' stock. There have been ERISA Opinion Letters from the Department of Labor indicating that there may be some flexibility. Decisions to make investments in construction projects that would stimulate the industry in which the employer is situated were found not to violate ERISA so long as the investments were not more risky than other investments. A decision to make investments in home mortgages in areas in which a local union's members were located did not violate ERISA so long as investments were made on the basis of factors relating to the par-ticipants' retirement income (RIA 1998). However, it is probably the case that under the present state of the law a trustee could reasonably refuse to take into account a broader set of factors that were unrelated to retirement income. Therefore, a desirable change in the law from the standpoint of employee influence over corporate policy would be to allow, or even require, trustees to take into account the interests of the employees *as employees* in voting unallocated shares of stock.

It appears, then, that as to allocated shares of stock in an ESOP, there is the potential for employee influence as shareholders. As to unallocated shares it would take a change in the law to make this true unless the plan provides for employee direction to the trustee. Even if the plan so provides, however, a trustee could refuse to follow employee directions if he/she believed the directions to be imprudent *with respect to maximizing retirement benefits.* ERISA appears to focus the duties of trustees rather narrowly on maximizing the value of employee stock, and requires them to stick to financial issues, rather than taking into account the interests of the employees in corporate governance (Carberry 1998).

Employee Shareholders and Corporate Governance. What difference does it make for employees to be shareholders? How, if at all, is corporate governance affected? Corporate governance has been defined as follows:

In general, corporate governance refers to the legal mechanisms and cultural beliefs that determine who controls the way wealth is generated in a company and how this wealth is distributed to the various parties involved in the company's operation. It most often refers to how power is exercised and decisions made by boards of directors, shareholders, and management (Carberry 1996: 2).

It is influence upon corporate policy at this high level that is, from the standpoints of workers and unions, a potentially fruitful goal of employee ownership.

One impediment to meaningful participation in corporate governance by employees is that management has traditionally been reluctant to cede power over corporate policy to them. This is partly because of fears that this will result in decisions that are "too political or that favor short-term employee interests" (Carberry 1996: 1). Very importantly, the financial establishment has generally been unfriendly to employee involvement in governance at the corporate level (Carberry 1996).

There is some evidence that a pass-through of voting rights that gives employees the full powers of shareholders produces few changes in corporate policy. However, voting rights may create "a symbolic acknowledgment of ownership," have a positive impact on communications, and cause management to be "more attuned to the employees because they could get voted out" (Ivancic undated: 30). Some research has reached similar conclusions where there is employee representation on corporate boards. Employees electing corporate directors does appear to create "an atmosphere of mutual cooperation between management and non-management employees," but not "sharp divisions or voting blocks within the board" (Carberry 1996: 19).

Blasi and Kruse (1991) have an interesting analytical structure for understanding corporate governance in the presence of employee ownership. According to them, public corporations approach employee ownership in five different ways – that is, there are five different corporate cultures with regard to employee ownership. They are feudal culture, investor culture, participatory culture, shareholder culture, and entrepreneurial culture.

The first of these, a *feudal culture*, exists where employee ownership is completely under the domination of senior executives. These firms, which constitute about 20 to 30 percent of the top 1,000 employee ownership companies, see employee ownership simply as a way to fund employee benefits. Corporate governance prerogatives are jealously guarded, and employees receive only the financial benefits of stock ownership.

Another 65 to 70 percent of the top 1,000 companies have an *investor culture*. Here, the firm proudly acclaims itself as an employee ownership company, but employee-owners are viewed as mere passive holders of stock. Employee investors are seen as employees who should accept managerial guidance in corporate governance just as they do in the workplace. They function mainly as a source of patient, long-term capital that frees management to some degree from demands that profits increase each and every quarter.

An estimated 5 percent of the top 1,000 firms has a *participatory culture*. In these organizations the link between ownership and employee participation in lower-level decisions is recognized. Accordingly, they emphasize worker participation programs such as teams and quality circles.

Even more rare (about .5 percent of the top 1,000) is a *shareholder culture*. This culture treats employees as full-blown shareholders. It accords them the same degree of power and respect that any other shareholder who owned say, 20 percent, of the company's shares would receive. Board representation is common. Management perceives employee-owners as being among the principals for whom managers are agents. The workability of this culture has been demonstrated by the employee shareholders of Weirton Steel taking a shareholder perspective by agreeing to take cuts in profit sharing in order to increase capital investment. In this type of firm, worker ownership rights are a part of a current general movement for shareholder rights.

The last of these cultures is an *entrepreneurial culture*, of which there are no current examples. These would be companies in which employee ownership is a central part of the strategy to make the firm both the "top competitor in its business and the best possible organization for which to work" (Blasi and Kruse 1991: 215). A few privately held companies are thought by Blasi and Kruse to be headed in this direction.

The culture of the firm with respect to the consequences and appurtenances of employee ownership is, in theory, a matter to be determined at the highest level of the firm – the board of directors. However, as with many other aspects of corporate governance, those who in fact select, and cause the appointment of, directors – senior management – are likely to be the true power behind such a decision. Also, this is clearly at least a permissive subject of collective bargaining under the National Labor Relations Act (NLRA). In 1988, the Steelworkers adopted a policy resolution supporting, among other changes in the NLRA, making both the existence and structure of ESOPs (including voting rights) to be mandatory subjects of collective bargaining (United Steelworkers of America undated b).

The issue of governance at the highest corporate level is inextricably linked to the broader question of what is the proper role for employees in the decision-making structure of the firm. Christopher Mackin and Fred Freundlich (1995) have posited a framework for thinking about this more general question in the context of employee ownership. For majority-employee owned firms, they advocate a rather complex structure of employee representation that varies according to the type of decision being made. They make a distinction between the external structure of employee ownership and its internal structure. The external structure is seen as having the value of "economic justice – allocating the risks and rewards of production to those who produce it," and the internal structure as having to do with "social or organizational justice – the effective and fair management of power" (Mackin and Freundlich 1995: 5). They argue that power is a fundamental problem in this, given that in most organizations employees are seen solely as the objects of power exercised by managers.

Mackin and Freundlich have created a framework that differentiates among the possible employee participation structures that would be appropriate for various kinds of work organization decisions. That is, they argue that the appropriate kind of participation depends upon the issue involved. They have two guiding principles in deciding what type of participation fits what issue. The first principle is expertise ("Decisions should be made primarily by people with the requisite expertise to make them"). The second is inclusion, regardless of responsibility and expertise (even for the most technical of decisions there is room for "Consultative Influence") (Mackin and Freundlich 1995: 11). Borrowing a set of issues, and the categorization of them, from an earlier study, they set these out as shown in Figure 1. In Figure 2 they assign to each class of issues a type of participation.

What we see from these figures is that decisions that have to do *with performing the work itself* are appropriate for work teams that are subject to *direct influence* from the employee-owners. Decisions having to do *with local policy, planning, and coordination* are fit subjects for employee participation as *shared influence*. A number of decisions on *overall company policy and future strategic decisions* are for advisory boards, councils, committees, etc., as avenues for *consultative influence*. The very highest levels of *overall company policy and future strategic decisions* (fate of the company, election of board of directors) are appropriate for voting for the board of directors and stockholder voting as a means of *representative influence and voting*. The strength of this framework is that it speaks in a practical manner to the entire range of instruments of organizational democracy that make sense in an employee-owned firm.

As Mackin and Freundlich recognize, it is when one gets to the point of talking about *group* representation that the subject of worker representation becomes controversial. Where a collective worker body comes into being it could be an "Ownership Committee" or perhaps a union. A complicating factor here is these authors' argument that managers should be included. If

Corporate	*Overall Company Policy and Future Strategic Decisions*	21. Fate of the company: merger, acquisition, sale, closing, major location changes 20. Election of board of directors, advisory boards, employees' committees, etc. 19. Distribution of net profits to investment, employee-owners, outside stockholders 18. Long-term product, technology, and investment strategy 17. Long-term marketing and advertising strategy 16. Raising capital, relationships with banks and investment groups 15. Relationships among divisions and plants 14. Annual corporate business plan 13. Executive compensation and promotion 12. Job security, layoff policy 11. Policy for compensation, benefits, promotion, hiring, firing
Division, Plant, Department	*Local Policy, Planning, and Coordination*	10. Develop local annual business plan (capital budgets, quality processes, cost, volume, staffing) 9. Coordinate departments, teams, and individuals 8. Manage progress toward goals for quality, cost, volume, staffing – plan and take remedial action 7. Maintain external customer and supplier relations 6. Coordinate equipment layout 5. Determine training needs and perform training
Work Teams	*Performing the Work Itself*	4. Determine how work is done; scheduling; job assignments; quality standards and measurement; speed; maintenance; group/individual work; autonomy 3. Hiring, supervision, basic discipline, evaluation 2. Safety rules and practices 1. Physical working conditions

Figure 1. Types of Issues for Decision Making. *Source*: Adapted from Paul Bernstein, *Workplace Democratization*. Reprinted with permission from Christopher Mackin and Fred Freundlich, 1995. "Representative Structures in Employee-Owned Firms." *Journal of Employee Ownership Law and Finance* 7, 2 (Spring): 1–25 (12).

supervisors are included, the union becomes an inappropriate spokesperson for the employee-owners as a group. However, it is possible that the NLRA might be amended to permit this. This is an example of the obsolescence of the supervisor versus nonsupervisor distinction in the law (see Wheeler and Kochan 1977).

It appears that employee ownership has the potential for opening channels for employee influence over managerial and corporate decisions.

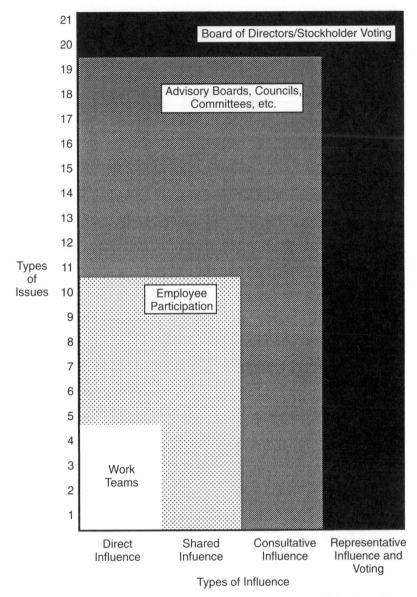

Figure 2. Types of Issues, Types of Influence, and Types of Participation. *Source*: Reprinted with permission from Christopher Mackin and Fred Freundlich, 1995. "Representative Structures in Employee-Owned Firms." *Journal of Employee Ownership Law and Finance* 7, 2 (Spring): 1–25 (13).

However, it remains to be seen how attractive this alternative is to managers, workers, and unions.

Pros and Cons of Employee Ownership

For Managers. Why would managers be attracted to employee ownership? From the standpoint of their own power to do as they please within the organization, it would not seem that there would be anything in it for them. It not only places power in the hands of workers, but it also locates that power in the highest source of authority in the corporate structure – the shareholders. In effect, it turns the managerial hierarchy upside down, with the manager being responsible to the same persons that he/she supervises. The obvious thing for managers to do with employee ownership, if anything, is to adopt a feudal position that creates the illusion of worker control without the reality of it.

Yet, employee ownership accompanied by some employee control may have some appeal to managers. This is because it can contribute to the bottom line. The conclusion that one can draw from a large number of studies by various researchers is that employee ownership does have positive effects on productivity and profitability, if only when combined with worker participation (National Center for Employee Ownership 1998). If this is true it would seem to indicate that ownership motivates, but that participation is necessary to give the increased motivation an opportunity to express itself.

Given that it is the role of managers to serve the bottom-line interests of shareholders, they might be attracted to a combination of ownership and participation. There is another reason that ownership may fit modern management very well. This stems from the popularity of worker participation in work teams, quality circles, and the like. It can be argued that such exercises in participation are ultimately doomed to failure in the United States because of a fundamental flaw. This flaw is that they are founded upon the assumption of a commonality of interests between employees and owners. Yet, this is not true, and cannot be true, in a capitalist corporation that comes into existence, and remains in existence, for the sole purpose of serving the interests of the shareholders who are not also employees.

It is possible to paper over the inherent conflict of interest between capital and labor in good times. Sooner or later, however, a day of reckoning comes when managers are forced to choose between the efficiency needs of shareholders and the pay and security interests of workers. As many downsized workers can attest, this choice can have only one outcome – management serving the interests of capital. What then happens to all the fine talk of partnership and cooperation? It is exposed as the fraud that it is. Deep alienation and conflict are likely to follow. Workers who do not expect to be treated as citizens of the industrial enterprise, or "associates" rather than employees, may not be shocked when they are discarded as expendable resources.

However, how would an "associate" be expected to react when told that he/she is being *disassociated* because the interests of the shareholders are more important than his/her interests?

In order to maintain worker participation it may be necessary to resort to meaningful employee ownership. Uniting labor and capital in the same persons may be the only way to solve the contradictions inherent in employee participation under capitalism. It also appears to be useful for the bottom line.

For Workers. Perhaps the most important question to ask in deciding whether to make employee ownership a major union strategy is what employees think of employee ownership. Do they want it? What are the advantages and disadvantages of it for them?

Public-opinion poll results generally support the view that employees would like to have an ownership stake in the firm that employs them. A 1975 Peter Hart poll found that 66 percent of its sample said that a program for employee stock ownership would do more good than harm. Sixty-six percent said they would prefer working for an employee-owned company. In 1985, a Bureau of National Affairs/National Center for Employee Ownership/Bruskin poll found that 57 percent of their respondents said that they would trade their next pay increase for an ownership stake in the company. A later Roper poll showed 40 percent saying that they would put some of their next raise in company stock if they had a choice.

In 1989 a Gallup/Employee Benefit Research Institute poll showed that 44 percent said that they would be willing to take their next pay increase in an ownership share that "could be cashed out at retirement." The same percentage said that they would not. Thirty-nine percent said that they preferred an ownership stake to having input into decisions (29 percent preferred input). However, the same poll in 1994 showed 64 percent preferring input. Twenty-nine percent said that they preferred an ownership stake that could be cashed out at retirement, compared to 23 percent who preferred a higher pay check and 46 percent who preferred employer-paid pension benefits.

A review of these polling results concludes that, as to employee ownership, "people seem favorable to the idea, so much that a majority say they would give up a pay increase for stock. Given other uses for that money, however, stock becomes the choice of a minority, albeit a substantial one" (National Center for Employee Ownership 1999).

Why would some employees prefer stock to wages or other forms of compensation? One very good reason is that it is likely to produce greater wealth over time. It has been argued that over the last twenty-five years the stock market has increased to eleven times its value, while the real median wage has "inched up only a few percent" (National Center for Employee Ownership 2000a). By this view, over the last 100 years wages have increased only a fraction of the increases in returns on stock investments. Also, "If capital and technology matter so much more [than labor] to creating economic value, it stands to reason that those who own it will do better than they ever have before" (National Center for Employee Ownership 1999: 15).

Along similar lines, it also stands to reason that if the managers who run the corporation serve capital, and capital is becoming increasingly powerful in the modern global economy, it is a good idea to own capital. In the terminology of Mackin and Freundlich (1995), this goes not only to external concerns of division of wealth, but also to internal concerns of "the effective and fair management of power" (p. 5). It seems clear that one of the main effects of globalization has been to strengthen capital and weaken labor. To regain some power within the organization and escape being simply the objects of the exercise of managerial power, labor may have to become capital. If workers want power and autonomy within the work organization, they may need to have some capital power to go along with their labor power.

It would seem that workers would benefit by having better informed and sounder decisions by management regarding the welfare of the firm. The employee inputs made possible by employee ownership and its accompanying structures should provide managers with improved information upon which to act. To the extent that employee ownership translates into employee influence over corporate policy, employees would gain the advantage of having crucial employee interests such as job security at least taken into account in decisions such as whether to close a plant. If there are employee- or union-selected members of the board of directors, this is an avenue for employee ideas and opinions to be expressed to the board. An employee-owned firm would be expected to be less likely to take extreme actions to avoid or bust unions. Employee ownership might also be able to influence corporate policy away from support of antiworker politicians and extreme antiunion groups in the employer community.

For Unions. Although this is changing, mainstream American unions have historically opposed employee ownership. The logic of American Pure and Simple Unionism emphasizes the separation of the interests of labor and capital. It sees the function of unions as consisting of the representation of the inherently adversarial interests of workers in a struggle against the interests of capital. It calls for workers to identify with fellow workers (and their union), not with management or the owners of the organization. Any blurring of this distinction is to be avoided because of the danger of workers losing their militancy and their willingness to take economic action against their employer. What sense does a strike make if it is a strike against one's self (Barbash 1984)?

In the early years of the American Federation of Labor (AFL), a policy decision was made to pursue collective bargaining as labor's strategy, and not to take the path of establishing worker-owned cooperatives (Stern et al.

1983). In part this was a rejection of one of the primary ideas of the AFL's chief competitor, the Knights of Labor. Also, there was some discomfort with being involved in the finances of corporations, on grounds of principle. The founding father of the AFL, Samuel Gompers, declared:

It is labor and industry which create values, money included. In finance, as in all things, the created thing should never be greater than its creator. The Frankenstein, the power of finance which the people in the past created, has been given its proper limitations and power, and with intelligence it will no longer threaten death or destruction to those who gave it the breath of life (1919: 94).

Also on principle, unions traditionally have been opposed to workers assuming the risks of the enterprise, believing that this is more properly the burden of capital. There is evidence that union leaders have continued to be concerned about the loss of the adversarial relationship (Stern et al. 1983). In the 1970s there came a wave of situations where there was a choice between worker ownership to save failing firms and unemployment for the workers. For a time, "the apparent contradiction between collective bargaining and employee ownership immobilized them" (Stern et al. 1983: 82). They were also hindered by a fear of the unknown and conflicts between local union leaders who were willing to agree to almost anything to save jobs and national union leaders who were concerned about preserving national patterns. There were also fears that ESOPs offered only the illusion of ownership at the cost of weakening the commitment of workers to the union. However, subsequent to the mid-1970s the attitudes of unionists appeared to change in the direction of favoring worker ownership, particularly among those who had some experience with it (Stern et al. 1983).

Unions are skeptical about ESOPs for several other reasons. First, most unions are proud of their pension plans, and are not inclined to substitute less secure stock ownership plans for well-funded, government-guaranteed pensions. Second, some union leaders believe that companies turn to employee ownership only when a company is failing and the stock is not worth very much. Third, they are familiar with situations where employees have been led to have exaggerated expectations of ESOPs, and have become disillusioned when the ESOP fails to deliver the benefits promised. Fourth, union leaders are wary of "playing on management's home turf" where they do not have a solid understanding of the rules. Fifth, there is the previously noted concern about a loss of worker militancy, and workers perhaps concluding that as owners they no longer need a union (Hester 1988: 268).

However, this distinction between labor and capital interests has never been entirely clear-cut, and is becoming less so in the modern economic system. Unions have always recognized broad areas of common interests with employers. Profitability is necessary for the survival of the private corporation. Survival of the corporation is necessary for the preservation of job security. The current emphasis upon worker participation at lower levels of the organization certainly runs counter to the idea of workers and managers being in opposition to one another. Union/management "partnership" agreements emphasize the commonality of interests between workers (and unions) and owners. The reality of modern industrial life may be that unions do not have sufficient power to operate as adversaries to businesses and must of necessity move into a more cooperative mode of behavior.

Unlike some other forms of participation, ownership offers opportunities for real power to be placed in the hands of the employees. Ownership is the ultimate "empowerment," of which American managers claim to be so fond these days. Unions can aggregate the capital power of workers as well as their labor power. The idea of collective action, upon which unions are based, can accommodate to a new basis for action – the ownership of capital.

At least one major labor leader, Lynn Williams, now former president of the Steelworkers, has stated his approval of employee ownership. He views it as not being a threat to unions. According to him:

In essence then we must recognize that the worker-owner has two sets of interests arising out of his separate roles of worker and investor. Business managers, even if the worker helps select them through stock voting processes, cannot effectively re-present workers interests *as workers*. The need for unions will therefore continue, and unions will continue because workers will continue to perceive the need for them. I certainly would not fear for the future of the USWA if every employer in the United States became an ESOP company (quoted in Hester 1988: 279).

UNION EXPERIENCE WITH EMPLOYEE OWNERSHIP

American unions have accumulated considerable experience with employee ownership over the last several decades. An analysis of the Bureau of National Affairs (BNA) sample of collective-bargaining agreements in 1998 showed that 68 percent contained 401 (k) plans, and 11 percent had ESOPs (Bureau of National Affairs 1998). Some unions, such as the Steelworkers, have refused to substitute ESOPs for pension benefits, preferring rather to trade off other types of compensation. Where a major company in a troubled industry, such as Eastern Air Lines, TWA, Chrysler, or one of a number of steel companies, has claimed a need for wage concessions as a basis for substituting stock for wages, unions have generally required the company to open its books to union-paid experts to verify the claims of financial distress (Hester 1988).

Voting rights is an area where unions have clearly made a difference. A "principal difference" between collectively bargained ESOPs and others is that union plans tend to give broad voting rights to employees (Hester 1988: 272). There is room for negotiations to enlarge voting rights because the law (Internal Revenue Code Sec. 409 [e]) does not require pass-through of voting rights for unallocated employee shares in an ESOP for a publicly held company, and requires voting rights only on certain issues even on allocated shares in a closely held company. "Voting programs negotiated by unions have generally extended to all of the stock held in the ESOP program whether or not allocated or vested" (Hester 1988: 272). In the Eastern Airlines ESOP voting rights were aggregated in a union-appointed trustee (being covered by the Railway Labor Act, airline unions are not covered by Taft-Hartley Act restrictions on payments to union agents). In a Kaiser Aluminum ESOP the Steelworkers negotiated an agreement that the trustee was required to vote shares for which he/she received no direction in the same proportion as the shares for which he/she did receive direction. This is important because of the relatively low participation rate of employees in such voting (Hester 1988).

How have unions behaved as agents of shareholders, or as shareholders in their own right? An interesting paper by Stewart J. Schwab and Randall Thomas (1997) looks at this question in some depth. These authors believe that unions are "making waves" as "the most aggressive shareholder proponents of corporate governance reforms in major American corporations" (p. 1). They see as "enormous" the potential for changes in corporate governance if unions are "seeking a long-term alignment with shareholders against management" (p. 3).

The chief danger noted by critics of this union strategy is that the unions will assert the interests of workers to the disadvantage of other groups of shareholders. Schwab and Thomas argue that several "forces" effectively limit a union's ability to do this. First, as to union pension funds, there are Taft-Hartley Act requirements of a fiduciary obligation to serve the interests of the shareholders who are the beneficiaries of the pension fund. Second, the market for the stock will severely punish any corporate action that "deviates too far from maximizing shareholder profits" (p. 3). Third, union efforts will generally come to naught unless they can attract the support of other shareholders. These authors suggest that unions can accomplish this if they focus their efforts on such areas as protesting executive compensation "where they have special advantages in monitoring management" (p. 3). Unions have the ability to gather information on the routine workplace-level operations of the firm, and have reason to be motivated to expend the time and energy to do this. They, and corporate directors appointed by them, are also more likely to be willing to challenge management on such questions as executive compensation than are directors who owe their appointment to management and may themselves be high executives in other firms.

Unions have sometimes acted by sponsoring shareholder proposals at company annual meetings. Research has shown that labor-sponsored proposals do about as well as proposals sponsored by public institutions, and better than those advocated by individual shareholders (Schwab and Thomas 1997). It appears that unions will be successful in these actions to the extent that they are able to convince other shareholders that their interests as well as the workers interests would be served.

Schwab and Thomas (1997) conclude:

If labor can demonstrate to other shareholders that it is using its monitoring advantages to take actions to increase firm value by policing management shirking and reducing the agency costs of equity, other shareholders will be more willing to follow its lead in future voting initiatives. This opens up the possibility that labor union shareholders could reinvigorate some currently ineffectual corporate governance systems" (p. 57).

"Union" pension funds appear on their face to be a highly useful source of union power over corporate governance. What is usually referred to by this label are joint union-employer trustee plans that are permitted as an exception to Taft-Hartley Act prohibitions against employers making payments to union-controlled funds. These funds are required to have equal numbers of employer and union trustees. However, in fact the union trustees generally control these funds. Such funds, holding shares in publicly held companies with values totaling in the billions of dollars, would seem to be a promising source of union power. However, both the Taft-Hartley Act and ERISA impose fiduciary duties on trustees that impede the use of this power to serve the full range of interests of employees. The ERISA requirements have "greater bite" in that they impose a prudent man requirement upon trustee conduct and require diversified investments (ESOPs are effectively exempted from this last requirement). It appears that union pension funds may choose to invest in projects that benefit workers in a general way so long as the risk and return are approximately the same as alternative investments (Schwab and Thomas 1997).

For our immediate purposes, a more interesting question is whether trustees of union pension funds can become activist shareholders who pursue worker interests that extend beyond return on investment. In 1991, the AFL-CIO adopted policies that urged member unions to increase their activism as investors. In 1994, the Industrial Union Department (IUD) of the AFL-CIO passed resolutions calling for, among other things, "responsible proxy voting by pension plans" (quoted in Schwab and Thomas 1997: 51).

The U.S. Department of Labor (DOL) appears to have encouraged labor investor activism in its proxy voting guidelines issued in 1994. The DOL suggests that board of director candidates' qualifications and independence; compensation of executives; long-term business plans; and merger and acquisition policies, were all issues that could be raised in shareholder proposals (Schwab and Thomas 1997). Schwab and Thomas (1997) conclude on this issue:

In short, ERISA does impose some limits on how far union pension funds can push shareholder resolutions. Cost-justified expenditures on resolutions dealing with corporate governance issues are allowable. But union pension funds risk ERISA litigation when they sponsor resolutions that clearly can be shown to provide little returns (p. 51).

The AFL-CIO continues to pursue this avenue of union and worker influence. Ron Blackwell, AFL-CIO Director of Corporate Affairs, says that pension funds "are managed by people who act as though they need a high rate of short term return." According to him, "This is nonsense for pension investments." Labor wants the influence of pension fund stock on the side of a "high road" corporate strategy and favors "drawing a bright line between managers who manage that way and those that don't" (Blackwell 1997).

The influence of pension fund shareholding on corporate governance is potentially powerful. However, it is not at all the same thing as employee ownership. In some ways it may be more advantageous for unions, because it does not tie the welfare of the worker to the success of his or her employer. It thereby avoids the chief objections of advocates of traditional Pure and Simple Unionism. On the other hand, it does not do anything to give employees power over the policies of their own employer, which would be more immediately beneficial to them than influence on the policies of other employers. One of the problems with unions pursuing influence on corporate governance is that workers may not see the benefit of it. This problem is attenuated in the case of pension funds that by law (unlike ESOPs) must have diversified holdings.

The Steelworkers Worker-Ownership Institute

By 1994, the Steelworkers found themselves involved with a number of companies that had become worker-owned during the period from 1982 to 1993. These were all cases of firms that responded to economic distress by instituting ESOPs or other forms of employee ownership (Householder and Dolmajer 1999; Davis 1999). The Steelworkers' leadership believed that there were "unique problems of collective bargaining in an ESOP environment" that arose in these firms (Householder and Dolmajer 1999: 1).

The Steelworkers' answer to this challenge was to establish the Worker-Ownership Institute (WOI). WOI solutions to the problems of worker-owned firms include building trust; instituting and supporting participatory systems; dealing with competitive pressure on the firms; assisting workers and shop-floor managers to change roles to respond to worker ownership; providing an understanding of business fundamentals; and instituting new work systems. Accomplishing all of this chiefly involved training. WOI "was formed as a self-help institute to supply help, guidance, and shared experience" (Davis 1999).

WOI was created under the joint sponsorship of the Steelworkers and the managements of companies that were wholly or partly employee-owned and employed union members. The Federal Mediation and Conciliation Service (FMCS) assisted WOI's start-up with a $100,000 grant.

Training programs conducted by WOI have included a collective-bargaining workshop; board of directors training; programs on new work systems; financial training; a program on repurchase liability and stock evaluation; training of trainers in "Open Book Management"; and programs on participation. Through the FMCS, programs were offered on Relationships by Objectives (a FMCS program for improving labor-management relation-ships), labor-management committees, and Interest-Based Bargaining (a bargaining technique encouraged by FMCS). With the help of the Ohio Employee Ownership Center, WOI produced a book on participatory employee ownership. It also had its own Web site.

At its peak in 1998 WOI included thirteen companies employing approximately 22,000 employee-owners. However, in 1999 a number of companies (including the largest) dropped out as a result of changes in ownership (ESOPs ended), bankruptcy, or other reasons. This left just four companies employing approximately 1,200 employee-owners. With these lower numbers the WOI board decided to scale down operations, closing its separate office and assigning the management of WOI to a Steelworker representative – Richard Davis, Vice President for Administration (Householder and Dolmajer 1999; Davis 1999).

It is difficult to evaluate the Steelworker experience with the WOI. Richard Davis believes that the overall experience with ESOPs and WOI has been good. Yet some of these companies went bankrupt and others were sold in such a way as to end the ESOPs. Given that most of these companies were in financial difficulty when the ESOPs were instituted, perhaps it is enough to expect that they were kept afloat for a time or sold in a way that was more advantageous to employees than an earlier layoff would have been. What is impossible to know is what would have been the result if this had not been "lemon socialism," involving failing companies, but rather part of a broad strategy to acquire employee ownership in sound companies.

SOME CASE EXPERIENCES

By far the most highly publicized recent union experience with employee ownership is the case of United Airlines. In 1994, several unions led by the Airline Pilots Association (ALPA) gained majority ownership of the airline for employees. Employees represented by ALPA and the International Association of Machinists (IAM), along with salaried employees, received 55 percent of the company's stock in exchange for wage concessions. Flight attendants chose not to take part. A new board of directors was set up to include representatives of the participating unions and salaried employees. The board also contained independent directors, and representatives of the public stockholders. "Task teams" were set up to deal with operating issues (Carberry 1996).

How did this work out? For one thing, there is some evidence that United took employee-owner input sufficiently seriously to listen to their opposition to a purchase of USAir that United considered in 1995 (Carberry 1996). However, the National Center for Employee Ownership (NCEO) writes in its newsletter that the results in this very large ESOP have been "mixed." According to NCEO:

The company was never able to establish an 'ownership culture,' but employees were able to influence key corporate decisions and the company experienced more labor peace than did other carriers during the same period (National Center for Employee Ownership 2000b: 13).

Nevertheless, at this writing it appears that the United ESOP will come to an end. Management took the position in collective bargaining that it would only extend the ESOP if the unions were willing to make further concessions, and the unions would not agree to this. However, employees will retain seats on the board of directors until the proportion of employee ownership goes below 20 percent, which is likely to happen within a few years.

Northwest Airlines and TWA also instituted substantial employee ownership systems. Both exchanged approximately 30 percent of their shares for concessions by their employees. Unlike United, where the Airline Flight Attendants (AFA) refused to join in the deal, all of the unions were involved, and each received a seat on the boards of directors. At least up to 1996, both companies prospered under this degree of employee ownership (Carberry 1996).

Another oft-cited example of employee ownership is Weirton Steel of Weirton, West Virginia. In 1984 Weirton's 8,000 employees bought all of the stock in the company, setting up an ESOP. Their union, the Independent Steel Workers Union (ISU), was involved in negotiating this deal. Workers agreed to cuts in wages, wage freezes in the future, and loans. A new board of directors was formed consisting of the Chief Executive Officer (CEO), up to two managers chosen by him/her, three members of the union, and seven outside directors. After an early turnaround under employee ownership, the company ran into some of the same difficulties experienced by other firms in the industry. New shares were issued, and by 1996 employees owned only 29 percent of the stock and had less than a majority (49 percent) of the voting power. Weirton still survives as a viable company, a significant achievement in its industry (Carberry 1996).

Republic Steel, through negotiations with the Steelworkers, became employee-owned through an ESOP in 1989. Just like Weirton Steel, it has performed well, and went public again in 1994 (Carberry 1996).

Beginning in the 1970s, a number of other employee buyouts occurred, many of which were attempts to save failing companies. Rath Packing, Hyatt-Clark, and Atlas Chain were all unionized firms that became employee-owned but then, for various reasons, went out of business. However, other companies with either complete or otherwise significant employee ownership had some success. These include such examples as O & O Supermarkets, an employee-owned company set up by the United Food and Commercial Workers (UFCW), and several steel companies working with the Steelworkers (United Steelworkers of America undated c). Southwest Airlines is a more recent example of a successful unionized company that has a substantial amount of employee ownership (10 percent), albeit through a profit-sharing plan that invests in company stock rather than through an ESOP (National Center for Employee Ownership 2000c). In 1999 the Paper, Allied-Industrial, Chemical and Energy Workers (PACE) worked out the buyout of seven plants owned by Champion International Paper Mills by an ESOP that shared ownership with an investment fund (KPS Special Situations Fund). Workers agreed to a cut of 15 percent in labor costs in exchange for an ownership share and the continued operation of these plants (Bureau of National Affairs 1999).

CONCLUSIONS

In their *Union Guide* (United Steelworkers of America undated d), the NCEO makes a detailed and persuasive argument for a "Broad Employee Ownership Strategy" for unions. They argue that worker-owned firms have a competitive advantage for two main reasons. First, worker-owners tend to put extra effort into their work. Second, the firms' need for outside capital is reduced to the extent that employee compensation is in the form of stock. This form of compensation has the unique characteristic of staying within the company until the employee quits or retires. This author would add as a third advantage that worker ownership facilitates other forms of participation by legitimizing them. Also, there is rather clear evidence that a combination of worker ownership and other forms of participation has the potential for improving profitability. If, as some critics of employee ownership claim, this will undermine wages and solidarity in other unionized firms in an industry, the solution is to convert the entire industry to employee ownership.

Unions are in a good position to spread worker ownership across an industry or indeed a whole economy. Unions "have the financial and organizational resources, and they have the ideological commitment to workers' interests" to make this happen (United Steelworkers of America undated d: 45). A union operating on an industry-wide basis could negotiate for better ESOPs. It could bargain for stock in addition to, not in place of, pensions. It could negotiate to have a greater proportion of an ESOP's holdings to be in cash, giving some protection against the company's stock sinking too low.

There are a number of technical plan features that could be bargained for that would be to the employees' advantage. These include: (1) providing written options allowing the employees to sell stock at a given price (put options); (2) actuarial planning standards for funding the liability of the ESOP for repurchasing stock upon an employee leaving the plan; (3) providing for early withdrawal in emergencies; (4) guarantees that their ownership share will not be diluted by the issuance of new stock; and (5) pension guarantee plans. Quite importantly for our concerns in this chapter, a union could also bargain for employee or union representation of the board of directors, and the broadest possible voting rights for employees while their stock is in an ESOP. The right of first refusal in case of a sale of the company could also be negotiated.

The NCEO believes that employee ownership can be a basis for union organizing. According to them:

> If employee owned companies are more profitable and productive than others, and create more jobs than others, as studies indicate they do, the labor movement could gain a great deal from leading a crusade to convert the union sector of the economy en masse to worker ownership (United Steelworkers of America undated d: 46).

The NCEO notes that the International Union of Operating Engineers (IUOE) and the Bricklayers are using the idea of worker ownership as part of their organizing strategies.

An organizing campaign in which it is argued that the company is a good company, in fact so good that employees should own a share of it, could be very powerful. It allows unions to have a chance to organize the winners in the economy as well as the losers. In such a campaign the union does not have to rely upon fanning the flames of discontent in all cases. How to organize the contented worker is a central problem of American labor at the present time. Advocating employee ownership of a kind that provides maximum benefit to the employees may be an answer to this question.

Also importantly, this type of organizing effort may not engender as much employer opposition as the traditional campaign that, by its very nature, is an attack upon management. This is helped by the fact that firms that combine employee ownership with employee participation appear to be more profitable. A more subtle aspect of this strategy is that, unlike traditional organizing efforts, the union is proposing a structure that will tie employees more closely to the company, something modern management wants that is important in a time of tight labor markets.

As NCEO says, for an employee to identify more with his or her employer does not necessarily mean less identification with fellow union members. Ownership could become "a major new birthright demand of union members" as pensions were in an earlier day (United Steelworkers of America undated d: 46).

NCEO envisions ESOPs making it possible for unions "to increase their clout by using other people's money" (United Steelworkers of America undated d: 46). This could be done by the union using an ESOP to perform, or threaten to perform, a hostile takeover of a company whose management needs to be replaced. NCEO suggests that unions could "evolve a new set of labor strategies which seek to subordinate capital to labor's control" (p. 47). This could be done by "linking" employee ownership to cooperative banks, credit unions and loan funds.

NCEO admits that the experience in industries that have moved to employee ownership "on a wholesale basis" – airlines, trucking, and steel – "has not been, on the whole, spectacular" (United Steelworkers of America undated d: 47). However, it has not been a disaster either. Also, as they say, we do not have an experience that shows what this would look like in a healthy industry.

In summary, NCEO asserts:

> We believe that employee ownership can revitalize the labor movement by providing a means of influencing the movement of capital and a framework for increasing worker participation and control. Employee ownership can also serve as a foundation for new organizing drives through its ability to provide new jobs and financially significant ownership in start-up companies (United Steelworkers of America undated d: 47).

Employee ownership is a strategy that has enormous potential for the American labor movement. It is a means of gaining real power for workers. There has been a great deal of discussion of employees having a "voice" in corporate decisions (Freeman and Medoff 1984). Much better than a mere voice is the ability to influence management to act in ways that are in the interests of employees, whether or not they are in the interests of managers. The difference between voice (even collective voice) and real power is similar to the distinction made by public-sector unions between "collective begging" and collective bargaining. As a union can aggregate the labor power of employees as workers, it can also aggregate the capital power of employees as owners.

Testing employee ownership under our enabling conditions set out in Chapter 1, we find that it has some real strengths with respect to some of them, but not as to others. With respect to contributing to the first condition, centrality of the work role, it is at best neutral. It may even lead in the opposite direction, creating the role of owner of capital for workers, thereby lessening the importance of the role of worker. It would not likely contribute to greater solidarity among workers, but would instead blur the distinction between them and owners of capital. The same could be said of the condition of worker perceptions of a distinct worker interest.

It is with respect to the other enabling conditions that worker ownership would be expected to make a positive contribution. Its benefits would appear to more than equal its costs in most cases. If pursued properly it has the potential for lessening employer opposition to the labor movement, especially in the long run. This can be a powerful force for truly uniting capital and labor, thereby causing managers to be more responsive to the needs of workers who possess capital.

The enabling condition of obtaining government support should flow naturally to a labor movement that expresses itself as a positive, collaborative force in society. By definition, this strategy downplays the aggressive, combative image of labor and emphasizes its more attractive positive side. Insofar as it advances industrial democracy, it fits the general democratic values of American society.

Employee ownership is a strategy that is especially timely in light of current conditions. It fits the present situation where, with globalization, capital has almost unlimited power. It does this by placing the most powerful instrument for influence over corporate policy in the hands of workers. This is real empowerment.

It is difficult to estimate the effects that an extensive system of union-sponsored employee ownership would have on the relations between unions and their partners in the political arena. It should be possible for union influence to make corporations more receptive to the needs of civil rights and environmental rights groups. Having some influence on corporate policy could provide labor with the power to reciprocate for the support of other progressives in its legislative program. It is much better for environmental groups to have an ally that has some power in the economic system. Such an ally would be very useful to have.

Employee ownership is a policy that should add to the positive public image of labor unions. Where labor is powerful within the councils of organizations, and therefore able to truly cooperate with management, it should find itself seen in a more favorable light by members of the public. To the extent that this is seen as a move away from extreme adversarialism it makes for a more congenial image. Support from public opinion might translate into political support, thereby making government more responsive to the needs of unions.

At this point, we have considered Reformist strategies of the American labor movement, both as they have historically been pursued and in their modern forms. What we now move to is a survey and analysis of the strategies of the traditionally Social Democratic labor movements of Western Europe. This will be followed by an in-depth look at one particular Social Democratic union strategy – assistance to economic development – as it has been followed in both Western Europe and the United States.

SEVEN

Social Democratic Unionism in Action: Strategies of European Trade Unions

We must make a politics of quality. We cannot look only at the losers in change, but also at the winners.

*Wilhelm Adamy, International Affairs, DGB
(German Labor Federation), 1994*

In attempting to identify a range of possible strategies that might be useful to the American labor movement, it is helpful to view strategic approaches utilized by trade unions in countries where the national cultures bear at least a general resemblance to that of the United States. Also, Western European labor movements have recently been quite innovative. Europe provides an interesting set of national laboratories for the testing of strategies by a different type of unionism – Social Democratic Unionism – in a somewhat different setting. In addition, there is an important experiment in cross-national industrial relations currently going on in the European Community (EC).

Social Democratic Unionism, similar to Reformist Unionism, is a path not often taken by American trade unions. In the next two chapters, we will look at Social Democratic Unionism. First, in this chapter, we will examine a wide range of strategies and tactics employed in recent years by the traditionally Social Democratic labor movements of Western Europe. Second, in the next chapter, we will look at a particular Social Democratic strategy – contributing to regional economic development – that has been adopted in both Europe and North America.

As was done in Chapter 3 with strategies of American unions, national-level strategies of Western European trade unions are categorized according to the typology laid out in Chapter 1. That is, strategies are labeled as examples of Social Democratic Unionism, Pure and Simple Unionism, Militant Radical Unionism, Cooperationist Unionism, or Reformist Unionism. It should be emphasized that what is being classified are strategies, not unions. That is, it is clear that even when pursuing a variety of strategies, Western European unions remain fundamentally Social Democratic.

In addition to national-level strategies, European trade unions have developed an interesting set of strategies at the regional level. The EC offers unique opportunities for trade union action at the level of Europe as a whole. Indeed, the increasing ties among European countries, most recently given a healthy push by the creation of a common currency, the Euro, probably make it inevitable that European unions will continue to develop strategy at this level.

In this chapter, the national strategies will be discussed first. Our attention will then move to a Europe-wide or cross-national perspective. The material in this chapter is drawn from the English-language literature and from a series of interviews conducted by the author in Europe in 1994. In the following chapter (Chapter 8) special attention will be given to a particular Social Democratic strategy – unions assisting in regional economic development. This is a strategy whose chief example is European – the Trade Union Regional Network (TURN), but of which there are important examples in North America as well.

It is beyond the scope of these chapters to comprehensively describe the full range of strategies and tactics of Western European labor movements. Instead, what is intended is to identify and briefly analyze some of the strategies pursued over about the last decade that are believed to be of interest to American trade unionists and scholars.

NATIONAL STRATEGIES

Social Democratic Unionism

As one would expect in Europe, many examples are found of Social Democratic strategies. These are spread across virtually all of the countries from which data were gathered. In a number of countries, including most clearly Austria and Belgium, trade unions have adopted a policy of Social Democratic corporatist concertation by setting national policy through consultation with government and employers (Blaschke, Kirschner, and Traxler 2000; Van Guys, DeWitte, and van der Hallen 2000). In the early 1990s, Italian trade unions returned to social concertation as a general strategy after moving away from it, and have continued to prosper relative to unions in other European countries (Regini and Regalia 2000). Indeed, driven by the single market and common currency, in a number of European countries there has been a revival of "corporatist-style concertation" since the mid-1980s (R. Hoffmann 2000).

Perhaps the greatest achievement of Western European Social Democratic Unionism is the writing into law of instruments of worker participation in, and power over, corporate decision making. Works councils exist in most

European countries. These worker representation bodies, required by law, give workers a variety of powers and opportunities for voice. Also significant are statutory requirements for worker representation on company boards of directors. This exists in Denmark, France, Germany, Luxembourg, and the Netherlands. The German case is the best known. At least in some industries, it provides for equal representation of workers (Bridgford and Stirling 1994).

Although unions initially feared that works councils would replace them, their experience has largely been that they are able to work through works councils in ways that are to their advantage (Adams 1995). For example, in Austria they have been said to "form the backbone of trade union organization" (Blaschke, Kirschner, and Traxler 2000: 96). In Germany, unions have been able to "incorporate [the works council] into their activities" and the works council "plays a complementary role" to that of the union (J. Hoffmann 2000: 251). However, in France, works councils may have had deleterious effects on the influence and legitimacy of unions (Boulin 2000).

A Variety of Social Democratic Programs. In *the Netherlands*, the Christian labor federation (CNV) has taken the position that unions should be involved in discussions of the environment, working conditions, and sustainable development (van den Toren 1994). Dutch unions see themselves as representing everyone, not just their members or employed workers. This is believed to give them a legitimacy that cannot be ignored. But, as Tom Etty of the Socialist labor federation (FNV) says,

This is a paradox. Our broad social-minded attitude is based in self-interest. The benefit is not more union members, but more support in society for what you are doing, so government can't go over your head. Influence on political parties and government is the payoff (1994).

Also, according to Tom Etty, "Unions must make a visible contribution to economic growth. Narrow interest representation is not a good method for that" (1994). From the perspective of the CNV, van den Toren believes that, in the Netherlands,

Unions have become a partner in the economy, helping with difficult problems such as cutting social insurance for retirees. Unlike five or six years ago, employers and government see unions as having a place, especially in wage moderation (van den Toren 1994).

Luxembourg has a unique legal structure for employment relations. This includes a national "Chamber of Labor" that oversees issues relating to workers. It has a Solidarity Employment Fund that avoids unemployment by funding public-works employment for employees while they remain on their employer's payroll. Through these and other mechanisms, Luxembourg has elaborate processes for dealing with social conflict arising from work (Mielke,

Rutters, and Tudyka 1994). In this setting all workers might be expected to believe that the unions work on their behalf.

Luxembourg unions are very much a part of the daily lives of their members. It is seen as a "natural thing" for "workers to be in the union" (Pizzaferri 1994). Unions work with children, and with whole families on such matters as vacations. They assist their members with many of the problems of their lives, such as divorce, income tax, and workplace injuries. When union members have problems, the usual thing for them to do is to go to their unions for help (Pizzaferri 1994).

Although their power may derive fundamentally from their ability to shut down crucial public facilities (the harbor and airport) by striking, the trade unions of *Malta* have mainly chosen to avoid confrontation and to work cooperatively with the government. When Maltese unions do engage in conflict with the government, they rely heavily on the support of other groups in the society. In a nation that is overwhelmingly (95 percent) Catholic, they contribute a good deal of money to Catholic charities and work with the church in other ways. They regularly communicate with school children and university students. In a union-led protest march on taxes in the mid-1990s, the majority of the marchers were housewives (Calamatta 1994). Malta is an interesting case example of a labor movement that appears to be highly integrated into its national society.

Finland utilizes the "Ghent system," in which the unions help to administer the unemployment benefits system, giving employees an incentive to join unions in order to facilitate their access to these benefits (Valkonen 1989). Trade union members receive their unemployment benefits from their union funds (Ministry of Labour 1990). Approximately 85 percent of employees are unionized (Ministry of Labour 1990). Similar systems exist in *Sweden, Denmark, and Belgium* alongside very high rates of unionization (Paauwe, de Jong, and van Dijk 1990; Bratt 1996; Hammarstrom and Nilsson 1998).

As do several other European countries, *Finland* extends the results of collective bargaining to workers who are not members of a union. This builds support for unions in the society at large (Hemmer 1994). This might be expected to create a free-rider problem. However, the high rate of unionization would seem that free riding is not a significant problem in Finland.

In 1998 *Italian* unions signed a tripartite agreement with the government and employers to spur investments in the South of the country, to improve law enforcement, and to create jobs through a system of vocational training. A previous agreement was entered into in 1993 in which they agreed to wage moderation. This process of "social concertation" is also being used to deal with difficult issues involving the pension system. Two of the major labor federations have engaged in collective negotiations with the Milan city government, employers, and a Catholic organization that deals with immigrants in an attempt to help immigrants, the unemployed, and the young to emerge from the underground economy and become integrated into the economic mainstream (Pisani and Brighi 2000). Italian unions have managed to be perceived by the public as standing for fair taxation and social justice. This has lent them considerable prestige. It has helped them to maintain relatively high levels of membership (Lecher and Naumann 1994). Also, unlike many other institutions in Italian society, Italian unions have enjoyed a reputation of being free from corruption (Evans 1994).

German unions are actively involved in general adult education, a type of training that is of benefit to workers in their lives beyond the workplace. They have also become known for expressing concern about changes in work organization and technology as these phenomena affect the society at large (Furstenberg 1998).

Sweden has a long tradition of Social Democratic Unionism. In a 1995 survey of its members, the Swedish LO blue-collar union found that 58 percent of its members thought that cooperation with the Social Democratic Party (SDP) should remain unchanged or increase, 29 percent thought that it should stop or be reduced, and 13 percent either did not reply or responded that they did not know. This shows a slight increase from 1988 in the percentage favoring less cooperation with the SDP. However, contrary to expectations, young members were not more negative toward the SDP than older ones (*European Industrial Relations Review* 1995b).

Also in *Sweden*, unions have trained younger worker organizers. These organizers live and operate in tourist areas in order to prevent exploitation of summer hires in resorts. This gives these young Swedes an early introduction to the labor movement as an important part of their lives (Zellhoefer 1994).

In *Spain*, the *Basque* labor federation (ELA) provides assistance to the unemployed, including assistance in finding jobs. It performs job-search assistance for young people, along with holding conferences and colloquia for them. *German* unions have provided services and assistance to the unemployed, although this has been a source of some unhappiness on the part of the employed union members who pay for this activity without receiving any immediate benefits from it (Adamy 1994).

Belgian unions have long defended a number of "acquired benefits" that stem mainly from government. These include automatic indexing of wages to price increases, minimum wage, public-sector employee pensions, and a trade union monopoly on representation in companies. This has been in support of what they term a "socially corrected economy," an economy with a human face (van Gyes, de Witte, and van der Hallen 2000).

Training. Training is an area of activity upon which trade unions in a number of countries have focused. It can be classified under several different types of unionism. It is something traditionally done by classic craft unions, which are among the clearest examples of Pure and Simple Unionism. It can also be viewed as Cooperationist insofar as it meets the needs of employers for skilled workforces. From a Social Democratic Unionism perspective, it relates to the societal interest in having a good societal stock of human capital.

To the extent that training involves skills that are broader than those required by the particular firm for which the employee is working, it is more properly classified as relating to either Pure and Simple Unionism or Social Democratic Unionism than to Cooperationist Unionism. The examples of this strategy given here are generally considered to be expressions of Social Democratic Unionism, although some of them admittedly could be seen in terms of Pure and Simple Unionism.

In the *United Kingdom*, the peak labor federation, the Trades Union Congress (TUC), and various unions have recently engaged in a broad range of programs for worker training. Motivated in part by the generally low level of basic skills in the British workforce, the TUC has joined in the movement to make their society a "Learning Society." The TUC has developed a "Bargaining for Skills" program whereby unions negotiate for skills training for workers. The Union Learning Fund, established by the TUC and the government in 1998 with initial funding of £2 million, has lent support both to training programs and to the development of about 1,000 union trainers, known as "Union Learning Representatives." The TUC is also involved in the University for Industry, working with employer representatives to develop high-quality learning programs. The TUC has been especially active in training in basic skills such as literacy and numeracy (Trades Union Congress 2000).

Among the *Finnish* unions, at least one, Akava, has a strong interest in training for its members. Akava is the Confederation of Unions for Academic Professionals in Finland, which had around 265,000 members in 1990 (Ministry of Labour 1990). Akava has helped design and put into effect higher education programs to provide broader training for professionals (e.g., programs to provide computer training for workers trained in the humanities and business training for engineers). The purpose of this is to make these professional trade unionists more broadly employable (Hemmer 1994).

German unions have advocated training for workers who are on short time (to spread the work), and also for other workers. This training would not be limited to skills that would be useful in jobs with their present employers. The unions have expressed a willingness to share in the costs of this training (Adamy 1994).

Pure and Simple Unionism

Social Democratic strategies are what we expect to see when viewing Western European unions. Given their history and philosophy, we would not anticipate finding much in the way of Pure and Simple strategies. Yet the news (in the sense that "man bites dog" is news) from Europe is of these traditionally Social Democratic unions embracing many strategies drawn from Pure and Simple Unionism.

Pure and Simple Unionism has as its essence the operation of the union as an instrument for meeting the practical needs of its members. This involves having policies that aim to benefit members, without being particularly concerned about the effects upon the working class or society as a whole. As shown by the use of the term *Business Unionism* as another name for Pure and Simple Unionism, it also requires that the union be run as an effective business. Also, collective bargaining backed by the strike threat is the method of choice for such unions.

Two countries – the United Kingdom and the Netherlands – offer an especially broad range of examples of the use of Pure and Simple strategies. There are also some significant instances of their use in several other European countries.

Pure and Simple Unionism in the United Kingdom. There is considerable evidence of the salience of Pure and Simple strategies to British trade unions. Perhaps this is not so surprising, given that the "New Unionism" model of Pure and Simple Unionism that was adopted by Samuel Gompers and the nineteenth-century American Federation of Labor (AFL) was a British model. Yet, British unions moved rather strongly in a Social Democratic direction during the twentieth century. Although it is admittedly difficult to categorize a national style of unionism, Britain probably stands somewhere between the American Pure and Simple model and the European Social Democratic one.

Gavin Laird, then leader of the Amalgamated Engineering and Electrical Union (AEEU), said in a 1994 interview that there was a strong need to make the AEEU more businesslike, not only for reasons of efficient internal administration, but also to be more compatible with managers' ways of operating. Laird stated that his union was improving administration. This included "introducing a new word, 'budget,'" and strengthening the union financially. The AEEU reduced staff and has attempted to modernize its image by making its publications of better quality. A crucial strategy is to become, and have the image of being, more businesslike. This is part of an effort to make the union more compatible with managers' ways of doing business. Also, staff members have been upgraded in pay and training.

Also according to Gavin Laird, the AEEU has installed a variety of benefits, including legal aid, in order to persuade employees that the union has something to offer to them as individuals. According to him, "The future of unions is good if we continue to be member sensitive and provide service to our members." On the other hand, he believes that labor should "keep an arm's length relationship with the Labour Party." This last statement, combined with the emphasis on the union as a business, clearly evidences movement on the part of this one British union away from Social Democratic Unionism and toward Pure and Simple strategies (Laird 1994).

Refining collective bargaining to make it more effective is part and parcel of a Pure and Simple strategy. Along these lines, unions in Britain, as in a number of other European countries, have moved to enhance their appeal to nontraditional workers, such as part-timers, by tailoring union collective-bargaining strategy to benefit them. In the United Kingdom, the peak union federation, the TUC, has produced an "Action Checklist for Trade Union Negotiators" to help them obtain the same rights for part-time workers that are enjoyed by full-time workers (Trades Union Congress 1991). The TUC advertises trade unions as offering a variety of services to these workers (Trades Union Congress undated). One union, UNISON, the public-sector union, has moved in this direction by entering into a collective agreement with a temporary help agency (Smith 1994).

David Hunt, the U.K. Employment Secretary under the last Conservative government, has said that unions need to become more businesslike by learning lessons from successful companies. According to him, "People will always need, and value, expert advice on their employment rights and other aspects of their working lives such as training and pensions" (*The Guardian* 1994: 9). If unions provide this at the right price they will provide a "useful form of insurance." Mike Smith, Head of Press and Information for the TUC, also sees British unions moving toward providing more services to members (Smith 1994).

A strategy that U.K. unions share with corporate businesses is merger with other organizations. Union mergers have become important in the United Kingdom. The number of unions declined from 454 to 233 between 1979 and 1998 (Waddington 2000). While mergers do offer economies of scale and a rationalizing of union structures, along with increases in the membership of particular unions, they add nothing to overall union density and may create a false impression of union growth.

An important development in the United Kingdom is that both particular trade unions and the TUC have moved toward more of an arm's-length relationship with the Labour Party, arguably the world's first party of labor (Mielke, Rutters, and Tudyka 1994). Also, the Labour Party, for its part, is attempting to distance itself from the trade unions (Goodman et al. 1998).

The relationship with "New Labour" (the old Labour Party in its new clothes) is complex. It is argued by some scholars that Labour Party leaders believe that the very collective nature of unions has become obsolete, meaning that unions should move toward service to individual members. The TUC has a broader view than does the Labour Party with respect to the concept of "social partnership." Although Prime Minister Blair has embraced in principle the TUC's 1999 policy statement on social partnership, he has expressed reservations about the necessity of trade unions for workplace participation to take place (Waddington 2000). By mid-2001 the TUC was flirting with another party, the Liberal Democrats, over disagreements with Prime Minister Blair and the Labour Party involving Labour's plans to increase the private role in providing public sevices (*Guardian Weekly* 2001). This weakening of the historic ties with the political party that it created moves British labor a considerable distance in the direction of Pure and Simple Unionism, to which automatic support for any party is uncongenial.

Another Pure and Simple Unionism strategy adopted by the TUC is to move toward an organizing approach, as have many American unions. This involves getting the rank and file more involved in ongoing organizing of new members. The TUC has established an Organising Academy to facilitate this (Waddington 2000).

Pure and Simple Unionism in the Netherlands. Dutch unions have traditionally operated under a "consultation model" in which the social partners (labor and management) attempt to avoid conflict (European Trade Union Institute 1992: 53). However, in recent years both the Socialist union federation (FNV) and the Christian one (CNV) have moved strongly toward American-style Pure and Simple Unionism. In pursuit of this approach, the practical business of running a successful organization that delivers objective benefits to members has received a great deal of attention.

In 1994 interviews, representatives of both the CNV and the FNV spoke to the practical side of unionism. Jan Peter van den Toren, Research Officer of the CNV, said:

FNV and CNV are doing research together on why people join or leave trade unions. . . . We need to serve the instrumental side of employee needs. . . . For the new growth of part-time and women workers, unions have established sections on women workers, and give general information on part-time working. . . .

I am optimistic about the future because new strategies have been developed for the new groups of workers, and there have been investments in these new groups to gain members and hold them. . . . We need to offer our members more and make this visible (van den Toren 1994).

Coming from Tom Etty of the International Department of the rival FNV:

The challenge is to make unions more focused and efficient, more goal and result oriented. . . . Our unions grew [in recent years] because they provided more services, were more visible, and did more organizing. The main benefit to members is free legal aid. . . . Promising strategies include making it more visible what members get for their money. Unions must conform to their members' wishes for services. Legal aid and tax services are services that many members appreciate (Etty 1994).

Unions in the Netherlands have continued to make attempts to attract more female members. This has largely taken the forms of increasing the number of women employed in staff capacities by the unions themselves and making political demands in areas of public policy that are of special interest to women, such as equal pay and maternity leave (Valkenburg and Coenen 2000).

Dutch unions experimented with "Trade Union Shops." These provided advice and help to their members on a wide range of problems. Showing their Social Democratic Unionism side, they also made these services available to nonmembers. This eventually collapsed because it was too expensive and the returns from it were judged to be insufficient (Etty 1994).

Netherlands unions have adopted the practice (copied from the German peak federation, DGB) of taking monthly opinion polls, called "trade union thermometers," in order to keep track of what their members want (Etty 1994). They have also used sophisticated polling of members and nonmembers by academic researchers to determine what Dutch workers want from their unions (Paauwe, de Jong, and van Dijk 1990; Visser 1998). The principal change of direction of the Dutch labor movement in the 1980s was toward expanding member services. In the mid-1980s the CNV considered such benefits as inexpensive holidays, travel, insurance, pensions, and partial refunding of dues, as well as marketing these and other services (Paauwe, de Jong, and van Dijk 1990). This was part of a movement toward considering members as "Clients who wanted to be served in a professional way and with services which fulfilled their own specific needs" (Paauwe, de Jong, and van Dijk 1990: 20).

The CNV Services Union has developed specific "branch unions" and "branch union committees" to correspond to different professional categories. There is, for example, a banking sector branch and a retail outlet branch. Each branch publishes its own magazine and has its own identity. This provides a union entity that is tailor-made for each group of workers served by the union. Precise targeting of groups of workers by specialized organizational units is a tactic that has been used by a number of Dutch unions (Paauwe, de Jong, and van Dijk 1990).

Although not moving toward union mergers, as have the British, the FNV has worked to have more cooperation among individual unions. The FNV has formed two companies, one for the private sector and one for the public sector, to provide services to individual members (*European Industrial Relations Review* 1995a). However, the two largest FNV unions, the Industriebond industrial workers' union and the AbvaKabo civil service union, have opposed restructuring FNV to coordinate finances and other matters across unions. Both of these unions focus tightly upon the Pure and Simple goal of serving the interests of their own members. They are reluctant to coordinate too closely with unions that are more Social Democratic in their approach (*European Industrial Relations Review* 1994b).

The CNV has established several "clusters" of unions to act cooperatively (*European Industrial Relations Review* 1994b, 1995a). Apart from the "clusters," it planned to set up two separate unions that would represent, respectively, young workers and women (*European Industrial Relations Review* 1994b).

An interesting collective-bargaining innovation by the FNV union representing Unilever employees is the establishment of what have been called
a la carte terms and conditions of employment. In the contract entered into
in 1999, workers are allowed to exchange pay for extra leave days, determine
their own weekly working time, and decide whether they prefer payment or
compensatory time for overtime worked. They may also trade off pay for a
better company car, child care, or an improved pension (*European Industrial
Relations Review* 1999k).

Pure and Simple Unionism in Other European Countries. In addition to the
United Kingdom and the Netherlands, one finds other interesting Pure and
Simple strategic activity in Finland, Italy, the Basque region of Spain,
Germany, and in some other European countries.

Mergers. One businesslike Pure and Simple strategy that is common in
Europe is reorganizations and mergers of unions. These have taken place in
a number of Western European countries in the last few years. In *Belgium*,
the FGTB/ABVV trade union confederation has amalgamated district offices
and formed a new branch (*European Industrial Relations Review* 1999c).
There has been reorganizing or merger activity in *Denmark* (*European
Industrial Relations Review* 1999f; European Foundation for the Improvement of Living and Working Conditions 2001), *Greece* (*European Industrial
Relations Review* 1998d; European Foundation for the Improvement of
Living and Working Conditions 2001), *Ireland* (*European Industrial Relations
Review* 1994a, 1994c), and *Sweden* (*European Industrial Relations Review*
1995c; Kjelberg 2000). In *Norway*, four cartels of unions have been established, two in the private sector and two in the public sector. These act mainly
in the areas of collective bargaining and economic policy (*European Industrial Relations Review* 1996). *Danish* unions have also created cartels for
collective-bargaining purposes, the most successful of which has been for
manufacturing workers (Lind 2000). *Spain* has also seen a number of union
mergers in recent years, accompanied by a "unity of action" strategy pursued
by the two major labor federations (Lobo 2000).

Unions in *Finland* have moved in the direction of interunion cooperation
and merger. Two unions in the municipality sector have reached an agreement to cooperate with one another. Four service-sector unions – the commercial workers; the hotel and restaurant workers; technical and special
trades; and caretakers – merged in 1999 *(European Industrial Relations
Review* 1999d). The declared purposes of the merger were to improve organizing and lobbying effectiveness, as well as to eliminate jurisdictional disputes. In 2000, there was continuing merger activity in Finland, including a
movement toward forming a super union in services (European Foundation
for the Improvement of Living and Working Conditions 2001).

Driven mainly by rising costs of operation and falling memberships, several *German* unions merged or announced merger plans in 1997. This included the merger of a union that represented 191,000 textile workers with IG Metall, the metalworking union. A 160,000-member wood and plastics workers' union also merged with IG Metall. The union representing mineworkers and leatherworkers merged with IG Chemie, the chemical and energy workers' union. Other mergers were also in the works in the late 1990s (*European Industrial Relations Review* 1997g). In 2001 a super union, "ver.di," was formed in the services sector. This merger of five unions into a single union creates what is now Germany's largest union with nearly 3 million members (*European Industrial Relations Review* 2001b).

The outcomes of mergers have not always been positive. They may have the effect of weakening national union federations. They cause a move away from the industrial form of organization and toward much more heterogeneous unions (Waddington and Hoffmann 2000). This runs the risk of lessening the responsiveness of the more general union organization to the special needs of workers in particular occupations and industries.

Other Pure and Simple Strategies. An interesting phenomenon in *Italian* labor is the formation of independent (of the national federations) worker groups. This includes autonomous unions set up for the purpose of representing the interests of highly skilled public-sector employees such as doctors and teachers. Organizations have arisen to represent supervisors, technicians, and middle-level managers. In addition, there are the "Cobas" which are "grass-roots organisations in public undertakings such as railways and aviation" (Mielke, Rutters, and Tudyka 1994: 204). These independent worker groups focus on the bread-and-butter needs of their members. The Italian labor federations have formed new unions for the purpose of organizing young workers who are in "atypical" insecure jobs (Pisani and Brighi 2000). They have organized pensioners and negotiate for them on the levels of their pensions (Zellhoefer 1994).

The ELA, a *Basque* nationalist labor federation in *Spain* with about 100,000 members, has engaged in a number of rather innovative Pure and Simple style activities. In 1994 it was alone among Spanish unions in having a strike fund. In 1989, with help from the AFL-CIO, it established a trade union school. It has a policy of aggressively bargaining on issues of special interest to women. The ELA provides free legal help to its members (Betelu 1994).

One of the chief goals of *German* unions in recent years has been the reduction of working hours (Furstenberg 1998). This has been pursued primarily through the Pure and Simple strategy of collective bargaining.

In *France*, where the trade union movement is in crisis with a union density of under 10 percent of the workforce, one union federation has managed to be successful. This is the Confederation Francaise Democratique du Travail

(CFDT). This success, reflected in a substantial (42.3 percent) increase in membership in the nine years leading up to 1997, has been achieved largely through use of Pure and Simple strategies. These have included forming an association within the union labeled "Turbulences" to work for young workers, and a general re-unionization effort aimed at adopting different activities for different categories of workers. Some CFDT unions have conducted surveys of their members to learn what their members want (Boulin 2000).

Belgian unions have professionalized their staff to a high degree. It is now common to have union staff members who have university degrees. They appear to be increasingly more like officials of a business and less like participants in a social movement (van Gyes, de Witte, and van der Hallen 2000).

Danish unions terminated their formal relationship with the Socialist Party in 1996, making it appear that they were moving away from Social Democratic Unionism, and toward Pure and Simple Unionism. However, they have in fact maintained a close relationship with the party.

One *Danish* union, the white-collar HK, has experimented with "24-hour membership." This is a strategy of providing services for union members outside of work. It includes their leisure, holiday, and general insurance needs. However, the 24-hour idea has not gained wide support among HK's members (Lind 2000).

Actions by two groups of *French* workers in 2000 fall somewhere between Pure and Simple Unionism and another of Hoxie's (1921) categories, "Guerilla Unionism." In one instance workers threatened to blow up their factory and in fact dumped 5,000 litres of sulphuric acid into a river in support of their demands for severance pay when the plant was closed. In another, workers threatened to explode gas canisters in the plant and in fact spilled 31,000 litres of beer into the street in order to obtain severance pay in a plant-closing situation. Both of these instances of what were termed "workplace terrorism" by the employers' association were successful (*European Industrial Relations Review* 2000d).

Cooperationist Unionism

At least at first glance, it appears that Cooperationist Unionism has not developed to a large extent in Europe. However, in at least three countries, the United Kingdom, the Netherlands, and Denmark, there is evidence of some movement to Cooperationism.

In the *United Kingdom*, one finds in the documents of some unions, such as the AEEU, official statements favoring Cooperationist strategies. In their 1993 Annual Report (Amalgamated Engineering and Electrical Union 1993), this union says,

Harmony, co-operation and team working rather than competitive individualism is the way ahead, and this has already led to 115 single union agreements negotiated by the AEEU plus a more positive approach to training, communication and harmonised conditions of service (p. 11).

The willingness to enter into single union agreements (one agreement for all workers at a single location) has been a source of friction between the AEEU and other British unions. This issue led to the expulsion of the Electrical Workers union from the TUC. The Electrical Workers' members regained membership in the TUC only after their union merged with the Engineers union to form the AEEU.

U.K. Conservative government Employment Secretary David Hunt argued that employers will be pleased to deal with unions if the unions can "demonstrate genuine advantages," in the form of contributions to higher productivity, keeping costs down, and providing training through apprenticeships (*The Guardian* 1994: 19).

The ideas of "social partnership" and "partnership at work," taken up in 1997 by the Labour government and the TUC respectively as exemplifying "social partnership," sound more Cooperationist than Social Democratic. The Labour government and the TUC may, however, have very different things in mind. As previously mentioned, the government envisions this as being possible in the absence of unions. The TUC's position likely includes the union as an independent voice for employee interests, which would make for a partnership along the lines contemplated by American unions (see Hurt 1997; Hyman 2001).

In *the Netherlands*, the leader of the Christian labor federation (CNV) has maintained that the Dutch view of the work relationship is one of employees and employers being jointly responsible for what occurs at the workplace. The relationship is not seen as antagonistic. According to Jan Peter van den Toren of the CNV, "The idea of 'shared responsibility' is strongly entrenched in Dutch society. This comes out of the Christian background of the labor movement. It is based on the idea of sovereignty in one's own domain" (1994). CNV is said to favor a "coalition" model instead of a "confrontation" model. Among other things, this means that it uses the strike only as a weapon of last resort (Paauwe, de Jong, and van Dijk 1990). Flowing very naturally from this idea is the conclusion that workers should be allowed to participate in company policy decisions. It does seem that where, as may be the case in the Netherlands, employers recognize as a basic social value the human right of workers to have some degree of control over their own lives, a basis for true cooperation may exist. This is a situation that is usually absent in the American setting.

In *Denmark*, primarily in order to avoid numerical flexibility (layoffs) the unions have actively supported management efforts to achieve functional flexibility in the workforce. That is, workers are to be able to perform a variety of tasks. This has led management and unions to develop a concept of "developing work" – work being interesting and leading to the development of skills and qualification for higher-level tasks (Lind 2000).

Reformist Unionism

Reformist Unionism is not often spoken of in Europe, although unions in *Spain* have long been engaged in setting up and administering cooperatives (Zellhoefer 1994). As noted in Chapter 6, several European countries have strong traditions favoring producer cooperatives. The most famous example of this is the Basque region's Mondragon.

Although generally at the initiative of management, share ownership schemes have become much more widespread in Europe since the 1980s. Perhaps because of employer sponsorship, unions have tended to be skeptical of these programs. In *France*, however, worker-share ownership is regulated by legislation that permits unions to have influence over these schemes (Waddington and Hoffman 2000). A new French law extending share ownership plans to smaller employers, and otherwise facilitating employee ownership, was passed in 2001 (*European Industrial Relations Review* 2001a). In *Denmark* capital funds were begun in 1991. These have the potential to become very large aggregations of capital over which trade unions would have significant influence (Lind 2000). Politically controversial Workers Funds in *Sweden* (Hammarstrom and Nilsson 1998) provide an indirect form of worker ownership. In *Italy*, one labor federation, the CSIL, has declared itself in favor of employee-share ownership, but this idea is opposed by the largest Italian federation, the CGIL (Hyman 2001).

Spanish unions have developed relationships with the "new movements" such as those with agendas of advocating ecology, feminism, pacifism, and antiracism (Lobo 2000: 524). This may be caused in part by the relative weakness of the unions. However, it can be seen as a step in the development of a new "civil society" in Spain. Unions are among the strongest of the organizations making up this new movement (Lobo 2000).

EUROPEAN-LEVEL STRATEGIES

The need to act at the level of Europe has long been recognized by European trade unionists. There are several reasons for this. First, there is the belief that having a united Europe is the only way to solve problems such as the historic tendency toward war, as well as problems of unemployment and the environment that "do not stop at national borders" (Adamy 1994). Second, it is believed that it is no longer possible to make social policy on a purely national basis. It must instead be Europe-wide (Adamy 1994). Third, there is the view, even among national labor movements that do not stand to gain much from it (e.g., Belgian unions) that it is a practical necessity for unions to operate at the European level (Wyckmans 1994).

European trade unions have at their disposal a variety of strategic approaches at the European level. Clearly, *European collective bargaining* is a goal toward which they are attempting to move (Foden and Coldrick 1994). They are actively organizing themselves for greater coordination of collective-bargaining positions and tactics, and are seizing targets of opportunity in order to make this come about. Another strategy – one that has produced more concrete results – is the pursuit of a *Social Dialogue* with their social partners, the employers. Yet another strategy is the establishment and uti-lization of *European Works Councils* (EWCs) in multinational corporations operating in more than one European Union country, which is now backed by European Union law.

At least as early as the pivotal year 1889, when many European national trade unions were formed, there have been union efforts to act internation-ally. These include setting May 1 as a worldwide day of protest, and attempts to establish the rights to strike and bargain collectively. With the establish-ment of the European Single Market the European level became an obvious one at which to pursue these rights (Rath 1994).

As a practical matter, any effective trade union policy at the European level should include having an effective system of cross-border employee rep-resentation, having cross-border cooperation among unions, creating recog-nition of Europe as a single labor market, offering European opportunities for training, developing "social dialogue," including (eventually) cross-border collective bargaining, and emphasizing the advantages to workers of having an international (as opposed to a solely national) labor movement (Rath 1994). The logic driving such policy is the recognition of the reality that, at present, business is international while labor is largely limited by national boundaries. Within the EC the fear is that "social dumping" will occur, with powerful multinational corporations benefiting from a "race to the bottom," where European nations and their workers compete with one another as to who can offer the cheapest labor costs and the least constraining legal system (Campbell 1989). The principal limiting factor for trade unions acting inter-nationally is probably the difficulty in persuading workers to act meaning-fully in cross-national solidarity by withdrawing their labor to benefit workers in other countries.

European Collective Bargaining

The ultimate aim of European trade union policy is European-level collec-tive bargaining. Yet, it has been long recognized that there are many imped-iments to this coming about. Historically, these include the absence of either a framework or a forum in which this can take place, the lack of representa-tives who can speak for employers (and also labor) at the cross-national level, the absence of any incentive for employers to agree to bargain at this level, and, as previously noted, limited international labor solidarity among workers. Added to this are the very considerable differences among national industrial relations systems (Rojot 1978; Campbell 1989; Rojot and Bremond 1998).

In spite of the difficulties, encouraged by recent developments in EC rules, some positive steps have been taken toward European collective bargaining. First, on the labor side, there is the maturation of the European Trade Union Confederation (ETUC), which has become an effective voice for labor at the European level. Although the ETUC has generally confined its activities to the political sphere, it is potentially a spokesperson for European labor in collective bargaining as well.

Second, some interesting new international trade union structures are being created. The General Municipal and Boilermakers Union (GMB) of the United Kingdom and the German chemical workers union (IG Chemie) have signed an agreement granting reciprocal membership to members of both unions (*European Industrial Relations Review* 1997b). Member unions of the European Metalworkers Federation (EMF) have signed a solidarity pact providing members of a national union in one European country with rights of information, advice, and trade union protection while working in another European country (*European Industrial Relations Review* 1999e). A cooperation agreement has been reached between the German chemical workers union IB BCE and the chemicals division of a French union, the CFDT. This agreement provides for cooperation between these unions in exchanging information, developing closer coordination with respect to European works councils, harmonization of pay demands, and training (*European Industrial Relations Review* 1999m).

Cross-national coordination of collective bargaining strategy is taking place in two ways. First, in 1998 the peak national federations, accompanied by some national sectoral (industry-wide) unions (Germany, the Netherlands, Belgium, and Luxembourg), agreed upon a common bargaining strategy. This includes insuring that pay reflects both inflation and productivity gains. They agreed to bargain on working time (reducing hours); work sharing; and the balancing of work and family responsibilities. These trade union organizations pledge to make training a bargaining priority. They direct a call to their national governments to increase employment and preserve their social security systems. They also agree to exchange information (*European Industrial Relations Review* 1998e). Norms for wage bargaining that were agreed upon in the 1998 conference were followed reasonably well in 1999. However, in 2000 German unions undershot the agreed-upon formula by agreeing to a more moderate wage increase, creating pressure on the Belgians and others to reduce their pay demands. Nevertheless, these unions agreed to attempt to adhere to this formula in 2001 (*European Industrial Relations Review* 2000e).

The ETUC has established a bargaining committee that is comprised of the European-level federations' officials who are responsible for collective bargaining. The aim is to achieve some consistency across national boundaries in collective bargaining (R. Hoffmann 2000). In 1999 two European-level federations held bargaining conferences. In 2000 the European Federation of Public Service Employees (EPSU) agreed that public service unions engaged in strikes would notify the EPSU executive so that it could determine whether joint action was called for. This is seen by EPSU leaders as a step toward taking appropriate international action in support of a strike by a member national labor organization (*European Industrial Relations Review* 2000b).

The second way in which coordination of collective-bargaining strategies is taking place is through an industry-level agreement among metalworking unions throughout the EC. This occurred in 1998. It is especially important because this industry is "seen as a pace-setter in terms of collective bargaining in many countries" (*European Industrial Relations Review* 1999b: 20). Although expressing its support for the European Economic and Monetary Union (EMU), this agreement states its concern that this will encourage a "beggar-thy-neighbor" policy of social dumping, which can only be avoided by a "strongly-coordinated collective bargaining strategy which is able to support an autonomous, European-wide union wage and collective bargaining policy geared to the interests of the workforce" (*European Industrial Relations Review* 1999b: 20).

Last, there have been a few instances of true Europe-wide collective bargaining. A 1997 framework agreement in agriculture is the result of something resembling European-level collective bargaining. In it the European-level representatives of employers and labor agree to a reduction of the working week to 39 hours and to workforce flexibility (*European Industrial Relations Review* 1997e). There is also a handful of company-level agreements (Rojot and Bremond 1998).

Social Dialogue

The concept of "Social Dialogue" between the "social partners" was initiated by Jacques Delors in 1985 while he was President of the European Commission. His idea was for labor and employer representatives to negotiate agreements that would take the place of mandates of the commission (Addison 1999). The Single European Act, effective in 1987, included a provision that the EC had the goal of "strengthening of economic and social cohesion" (Title I, Art. 2, *Consolidated Version of the Treaty on European Union*).

Since 1987, two events have given strong impetus to the social dialogue. The first was the Agreement on Social Policy that was made part of the Protocol on Social Policy annexed to the 1991 Maastricht Treaty on European

Union. Although limited at the time by its exclusion of the United Kingdom, it made possible the adoption of social legislation on some subjects on a less than unanimous basis ("qualified majority" voting). This treaty broadened the legislative authority of the EC, not only by providing for adoption of some measures by qualified majority voting, but also by setting out five areas that could be the subject of such voting. However, under the principle of "subsidiarity," the Community may act only when the Community's objectives either cannot be achieved by the Member States individually, or can be achieved better by community action than by national-level action. The Protocol provided that, "Should management and labor so desire, the dialogue between them at Community level may lead to contractual relations, including agreements" (Title XI, Art. 139, *Consolidated Version of the Treaty on European Union*). Furthermore, if the social partners jointly request it, their agreement may become law through a Commission Directive (Rojot and Bremond 1998).

The second development was the Treaty of Amsterdam, signed in 1997. In this treaty the Agreement on Social Policy is made a part of the treaties establishing the EC, thereby giving it a higher profile. The Treaty also has an "employment chapter" through which the Member States agree to develop a "coordinated strategy for employment and particularly for promoting a skilled, trained and adaptable labor force and labor markets responsive to economic change" (Addison 1999). Also, the United Kingdom is placed under the coverage of EC social policy for the first time.

The most important result of these events is the decline, beginning as early as 1991, of employer resistance to social policy being made on a Europe-wide basis. According to Addison (1999):

Confronted by the slew of actual and prospective social charter legislation, and the likelihood of a major extension in Community competence as a result of the 1991 deliberations of the intergovernmental conference reviewing the Community constitution, there was a sea-change in the attitude of the employer side. The conventional interpretation of this change of heart on the part of the employers is of course that agreements reached between the social partners would be less intrusive than Commission mandates (p. 3).

For its part, European labor, represented by the ETUC and the various industry-level European labor organizations such as the EMF, have understandably been enthusiastic advocates of Social Dialogue. Not surprisingly, they have been more than willing to engage in this dialogue.

Social Dialogue operates to give European-level labor and employer representatives a "formal consultative role in the development of new social legislation, and the possibility of concluding European-level agreements" (*European Industrial Relations Review* 1997a: 24). The European-level agreements can be initiated by the social partners or put together in reaction to, and as a substitute for, legislation proposed by the European Commission.

In either case a Commission Directive can lead to an agreement having the force of law.

At least from an American perspective, the results of Social Dialogue are impressive. Several major issues have been dealt with in ways that significantly improve worker rights. Because these are matters that would be commonly dealt with through collective bargaining in the American system, they no doubt look more like European-level bargaining to an American than to a European.

Social Dialogue has taken place in two ways. Most importantly, it has operated at the general across-industry level. Secondly, it has worked at the industry-by-industry (sectoral) level.

The earliest general across-industry agreement to make its way into EC law by this route was a 1995 agreement on parental leave *(European Industrial Relations Review* 1997a). In 1997 the social partners entered into an agreement on part-time working providing that, among other things, permanent part-time employees would be treated as well as comparable full-timers *(European Industrial Relations Review* 1997d). These agreements were entered into by ETUC, UNICE (private-sector employers), and CEEP (public-sector employers). UEAPME, a European-level organization representing small employers, objected to being excluded from this process and unsuccessfully challenged its exclusion in court. Subsequently, UEAPME signed an agreement with UNICE providing for cooperation between the two employer organizations in engaging in European-level Social Dialogue *(European Industrial Relations Review* 1999d).

In 1999, the social partners reached agreement on fixed-term contracts of employment that, in the view of employers, "takes full account of [the] fact" that this type of work "is a necessary form of work in flexible labour markets" *(European Industrial Relations Review* 1999e: 3). Fixed-term contracts are considered to be one of the most difficult topics to be taken up in Social Dialogue *(European Industrial Relations Review* 1999g).

Since 1986 there have been a number of "joint opinions" on training, technology, and other matters, as well as "joint texts" on such matters as the future of Social Dialogue *(European Industrial Relations Review* 1997a). The social partners have engaged in discussions about national-level procedures for management providing information to and consulting with workers. This came about only after the commission raised the threat of a directive on this subject, thereby causing private-sector employers to change their position of refusing to take part in these discussions *(European Industrial Relations Review* 1998a, 1998c). These discussions have now ended without agreement being reached. However, pressure by the trade unions has continued, with German, Irish, Spanish, and U.K. trade unions calling upon their governments to cease opposing the directive (European Foundation for the Improvement of Living and Working Conditions 2001).

At the European-wide industry-by-industry (sectoral) level there has also been a great deal of activity – but only limited achievements. In the textile industry a code of conduct was agreed upon. This included adoption of the International Labor Organization (ILO) Core Labor Standards – ban on forced labor, freedom of association/right to bargain collectively, ban on child labor, and ban on discrimination (*European Industrial Relations Review* 1997f). Agreements on working time have been reached in the maritime and rail industries. In the construction industry there has been no dialogue because of employer resistance, but a directive was made effective in 1999 requiring minimum standards to be applied to workers who are assigned a posting in one Member State from another (*European Industrial Relations Review* 1999f). Also in 1999, the social partners in the sugar industry signed a joint declaration on training and apprenticeships. Among other things, the sugar accord promises to, as much as possible, make apprenticeships and training opportunities available to young people (*European Industrial Relations Review* 1999a).

There has also been some progress at the national and company levels. In Germany, a national tripartite jobs alliance forum has agreed on compensation for overtime. This is to be done by issuing credit notes for overtime worked that are transferable between jobs and can be used to build retirement funds to make early retirement possible. In Spain a social dialogue is going on with respect to reform of the pension system and labor market reforms to encourage the use of open-ended, full-time contracts of employment (*European Industrial Relations Review* 2000c).

In an April 1999 meeting of the social partners – ETUC, UNICE, CEEP – they discussed the EC's proposal for a European pact on employment. The social partners agreed to have further meetings to discuss the economic implications of this proposal and to arrive at a common position on it. The ETUC announced a list of subjects that it saw as having priority in Social Dialogue. These subjects include temporary work, teleworking, access to lifelong learning, and the transferability of "acquired" (vested) rights across national boundaries (*European Industrial Relations Review* 1999h).

In 2000 employers and unions agreed to begin a social dialogue on temporary work. Also, the European Commission has begun consulting with the social partners on modernization of work. This covers a very broad area. To start with, discussions will relate to teleworking and "economically dependent workers." Economically dependent workers are those who, though legally independent, in fact rely on a single source of work (*European Industrial Relations Review* 2000c).

All told, the European Social Dialogue appears to be a powerful mechanism for the collective assertion of worker rights and interests. Although it does not look like collective bargaining, its methods are similar and its purposes are the same. The chief difference is that the employer's cost of disagreement is not a strike, but a Commission Directive that might be more intrusive. It is clear that this is the dynamic that makes these negotiations possible. This process bears some similarity to the American experience in public-sector employee collective bargaining where the dispute-resolving mechanism is arbitration rather than the strike. It may be particularly close to the "med-arb" model where an arbitrator mediates prior to arbitration, thereby having an opportunity to indicate what he or she might do in the event of impasse.

European Works Councils

Of all the forms of worker influence on management decisions, it has been employee participation that has been the subject of greatest debate in the EC. Many of the Member States have provisions at the national level that require at least some employers to have plant-level works councils, representation on corporate boards of directors, or both. Nevertheless, when it has come to having even the weakest form of participation – disclosure of information – at the European level, employer opposition has been fierce. This opposition long stymied efforts to require European bodies for worker participation. The "Vredling" initiative of 1980 (which proposed information and consultative rights on a European basis), as well as attempts to achieve this in the European Company Statute and the Fifth Company Law Directive, were bogged down, and then stopped, by employers. It is reasonably clear that the chief problem for employers was the potential for European works councils to lead to European collective bargaining (Addison 1999).

The breakthrough on employee participation at the European level was achieved in 1994 when the European Commission adopted Council Directive 94/45/EC. This directive required the setting up of transnational European Works Councils in firms with a minimum of 1,000 employees in the Member States and 150 employees in each of two Member States. This was extended to the United Kingdom in 1997 (Addison 1999).

Under the 1994 directive, European Works Councils are for the purpose of "consultation" with employees. This is defined as "an exchange of views and the establishment of a dialogue between workers' representatives and central management or its representative or any other more appropriate level of management." This is a weaker form of participation than works councils have in several of the Member States, including France and Germany (Rojot and Bremond 1998). Firms were given until the implementation date of September 22, 1996 (December 1999 for the United Kingdom), to create their own European Works Councils. These needed only to be along the general lines indicated by the directive. Those firms that failed to do so by the deadline are required to set up European Works Councils that meet the more detailed provisions of the directive. Therefore, there was an incentive for firms to set up European Works Councils of their own design to avoid having the European Commission's form imposed upon them.

Nearly 400 firms met the deadline for establishing European Works Councils "voluntarily" in time to avoid having to establish a council in accordance with the strict guidelines mandated by the directive. The countries with the highest "strike rates" (proportion of their eligible multinationals signing European Works Council agreements) were Belgium (80 percent); Ireland (60 percent); and Finland, Japan, Norway, Sweden and the United Kingdom (all over 40 percent) (*European Industrial Relations Review* 1998b). Out of approximately 1,400 companies that are required to have European Works Councils, it is estimated that, by early 2000, a total of 600 companies had adopted them, with another 150 agreements being in process (*European Industrial Relations Review* 2000a).

Trade unions, although not required by the directive to be involved, have in fact been very active in negotiating agreements for these European Works Councils, particularly in larger firms. Trade union organizations, mainly European-level industry federations, were signatories to nearly half of the agreements setting up these "voluntary" councils. In addition, trade union officials are frequent participants in council meetings. Two-thirds of these councils are joint worker-management bodies. This differs markedly from the directive's requirements for nonvoluntary bodies that are to be comprised only of employees (*European Industrial Relations Review* 1998d).

Subsequent to the expiration of the directive's deadline, and at least into mid-1998, employers were rather slow in moving to set up councils. In the first place, several Member States had not complied with the directive by enacting national legislation. By June 1998, nearly two years after the implementation date of the directive, only about 45 additional firms out of an estimated 700 to 800 covered firms had complied (*European Industrial Relations Review* 1998b). By mid-1999 this number had reached approximately 100. The bureaucratic nature of the process of setting them up is among the reasons given for this slow take-up of legally mandated councils. It also appears that the remaining noncomplying firms are those that are smaller and less likely to have a strong union presence. Also, they may have managers who are less sympathetic to the idea of a European Works Council (*European Industrial Relations Review* 1999i). There do, however, continue to be reports of firms, such as Franco-Italian STMicroelectronics, who are setting up European Works Councils (*European Industrial Relations Review* 1999g).

There is an ongoing debate as to whether European Works Councils add value to the firm. This is related to the broader literature on the effects of works councils generally, which appears to be inconclusive (Addison 1999). Value added by European Works Councils was the subject of some debate at a 1999 conference organized by the European social partners (ETUC, UNICE, CEEP). As might be expected, representatives of workers were more favorably disposed toward councils than employer representatives. Employer objections included the cost of the councils, increased bureaucracy, and possible delays in management decisions. Employers did see some positive aspects, including improved communication with workers (*European Industrial Relations Review* 1999h). Based upon a small number of case studies, a book commissioned by a Dutch employers association has reached generally positive conclusions, at least where restructuring is going on (*European Industrial Relations Review* 1999j).

An interesting phenomenon observed in a few cases is that a European Works Council, once established, may in fact engage in a broader set of activities than just receiving information and being consulted in a limited way. For example, an agreement was signed by the chair of the European Works Council of a French utilities group, the Compagnie Generale des Eaux, in which the firm agreed to prohibit child, forced, and prison labor, and to guarantee freedom of association (*European Industrial Relations Review* 1997g). Also, the European Works Council at Danone, a French multinational food group, signed a framework agreement with the company on information and consultation in the event of corporate restructuring. This covers the 30,000 Danone employees in countries outside of Europe as well as 60,000 in Europe. It includes provisions on training, with priority being given to holders of permanent jobs, and the right of worker representatives to have time off from work to deal with restructuring-related problems (*European Industrial Relations Review* 1997a).

In 2000, European Works Councils concluded worldwide agreements on compliance with basic social standards with several European multinational corporations. They also engaged in bargaining with respect to the restructuring of General Motors and Ford Motor Company (European Foundation for the Improvement of Living and Working Conditions 2001).

European Works Councils are significant for several reasons. First, the manner of their coming into being is quite interesting. They were put in motion by a European Commission Directive that was issued only after negotiations between the social partners failed. So, the Commission's tactic of threatening to impose a Directive in the event of the failure of negotiations was demonstrated to have real teeth. The Commission took this a step further by setting up a procedure that allowed time and flexibility for negotiations between individual employers and representatives of their workers to develop structures that they preferred to the one set up in the directive. This "voluntary" process was made effective by holding over the heads of employers the threat of a mandated European Works Council if the negotiations for a voluntary one failed.

A second reason that the European Works Councils are interesting is that their establishment in individual firms required something closely approximating European-level collective bargaining. In three-fourths of the voluntary agreements, union officials signed off on the agreements constituting the European Works Councils. This in itself is an example of representation of the rights and interests of groups of workers at the European level – something that is very hard to distinguish from collective bargaining. As in the case of the more general Social Dialogue, the only significant difference between this and traditional collective bargaining would seem to be the substitution of the threat of a legislated solution for the threat of a strike.

Finally, it would appear that these councils do have some potential for developing into instruments for collective bargaining at the European level. There are already some reports of European Works Councils stepping beyond consultation and into more powerful and broader participation. We do not yet see these councils dealing with issues of pay and working conditions but, as feared by employers, this may be in the future.

Conclusions on European-Level Strategies

From a North American perspective, the European version of workers and their representatives dealing with the power of multinational corporations at the European level is not greatly different from the traditional Social Democratic unionist strategy at the national level. The historic distinction between American and European trade unions is that the American Pure and Simple unions relied on economic action in the private sphere – a strike against the employer – whereas European Social Democratic unions pursued the same goals chiefly by political means. Here European trade unions have utilized the rapidly increasing power of the government of the EC to move in the direction of more rights for workers. This is true both in the case of Social Dialogue and of European Works Councils. European-level collective bargaining is admittedly in its infancy, but it has been born. The result is a glass that is half-full, not half-empty.

EUROPEAN TRADE UNION STRATEGIES AND THE ENABLING CONDITIONS

It is rather complicated to apply the enabling conditions set out in Chapter 1 to the extraordinarily diverse set of strategies pursued by Western European labor movements. However, a number of these strategies can readily be grouped into the particular enabling conditions to which they contribute.

Many of the actions that we have identified in this chapter can be seen as affecting the attitude of government toward trade unions. The trade union thermometers used by Dutch and German unions are aimed at giving the unions credibility when they speak on behalf of workers. Aiming to contribute to economic growth, as do the Dutch unions, surely also aims to gain public support, which can translate into the support of government. The idea of representing *all* workers, not just union members, is also instrumental for gaining public support and therefore support, or at least tolerance, by government. Being among the few institutions in their society free from corruption serves a similar purpose for Italian unions. Organizing pensioners, which is done by several European unions, is also useful for gaining political power through labor influence on the votes of these citizens. Some of the other strategies, such as use of Social Dialogue and European Works Councils, are obviously facilitated by having the support of governments.

The Pure and Simple strategies and tactics would seem to serve the function of increasing the benefits of unions to their members. Striving for equal rights for part-time employees, which is a union policy in the United Kingdom and elsewhere, clearly is an attempt to make it so that part-time employees will benefit from supporting or joining a union. Specialized divisions of unions to serve special constituencies (young workers, women, etc.) can also be seen in this light. Bargaining for *a la carte* benefits, as done by a Dutch union, provides the benefit of individual choice backed by collective power. The provision of benefits such as legal aid have perhaps the most direct effects on this. The idea seems clearly established among national trade union movements in Europe that it is necessary to provide valuable practical benefits to members, and not simply rely on working-class sentiments and ideology to deliver workers to their ranks.

Several strategies aim at gaining acceptance, or at least limiting opposition, from management. Becoming more businesslike in their practices, as has the AEEU in the United Kingdom, is an example of this. Offering to share the costs of broad programs in worker training, as have German unions, appears to be calculated to ameliorate employer resistance to these programs. In addition, management resistance can be dealt with very powerfully through the support of government (that of the EC) in Social Dialogue and the development of European Works Councils.

CONCLUSIONS ON EUROPEAN LABOR MOVEMENT STRATEGIES

It is interesting that, at a time when American unionists are increasingly disenchanted with their own model of unionism – Pure and Simple Unionism – European unions are adopting aspects of it. They are making innovations in this strategic approach that American unions might do well to emulate. While hardly turning away from Social Democratic strategies overall, they have clearly been picking up parts of the American model. This is, however, all being done in a setting where the trade unions can still count on the friendly intervention of government on their behalf.

It is at the European level that some of the most interesting things are happening. Here an amalgam of Pure and Simple and Social Democratic strategies seems to be at work. Representing all workers in the various national systems, the ETUC has negotiated with European employer representatives with respect to such things as participation, parental leave, part-time work, and fixed-term contracts. Its bargaining power is based on its ability to impose a cost of disagreement upon the employers by persuading the European Commission to issue a directive that will be made into law. Given a choice of a legally mandated rule and one that they negotiate themselves, employers quite rationally choose the latter. While one could argue that something similar to this has long happened at the national level both in Europe and the United States, it has never had the trappings of collective negotiations to the same degree.

What the European experience would seem to teach is that we should think in broad terms about collective negotiations. It is not really important whether workers have collective bargaining in the style developed in the United States. What is important is that representatives of workers are able to negotiate with employers about practical matters that are of consequence to workers. This negotiation can serve a useful purpose so long as it is, in the lingo of American public-sector employment relations, collective bargaining instead of "collective begging." That is, it must be based upon power, not upon appeals to the generosity of managers with other people's (i.e., shareholders') money. This condition appears to be met not just in traditional collective bargaining backed by a strike threat, but also by Social Dialogue backed by the threat of a directive.

Another lesson of the European experience is the importance of the state to trade union power. Only truly popular movements can capture the political support necessary to survive as a contestant in the economic war between labor and capital. Labor, which by itself is usually outmatched by the power of capital, has a chance of success when backed by government.

Looking at the European-level experience through the lens of international relations and international law, something very extraordinary appears to be going on. Cross-national structures with real teeth are aborning. This is a rarity. Would it be possible to create similar structures in other regions, such as the North American region that is covered by the North American Free Trade Agreement (NAFTA)? It may be that a region-by-region approach offers the best road to a global industrial relations system in which there is something similar to a rule of law rather than a rule of the market jungle.

EIGHT

A New Twist and TURN on Social Democratic Unionism: Unions and Regional Economic Development

We want to finance an industrial investment strategy in the U.S. that respects the aspirations of its beneficiaries – our union members and working people in general – and that creates good jobs.

Leo Gerard, Secretary-Treasurer (subsequently International President), United Steelworkers of America, 1999

Union support for regional and local economic development is a contemporary Social Democratic Unionist strategy that deserves special attention. One of the interesting things about the current actions in this direction in both Western Europe and the United States is the importance of worker training as an instrument for economic development. Grassroots union involvement in economic development has become important in the European Community (EC), largely through the efforts of the Trade Union Regional Network (TURN). It is aborning in the United States, based partly on experience in Canada with Labor Sponsored Investment Funds (LSIFs).

This chapter will first discuss the origins and nature of Europe's TURN, an organization that engages in a variety of initiatives related to regional economic development. We will then look at union involvement in regional economic development in both Western Europe and North America. Training and its role in development will then be considered. An interesting special aspect of TURN, its nature as a network of local unions in different countries, will be described. Then, some conclusions on the meaning of all of this for the future of American unions will be drawn.

TURN

In its search for new directions, the American labor movement might profitably turn its attention to the Western European experience with TURN. TURN is an organization of grassroots labor organizations that is distinctive in three respects. First, it has regional economic development as its chief aim. Second, it has training as a major activity. Third, it binds together *local* union groups across countries without the intervention of national or regional labor organizations.

Why is the TURN example promising for an embattled labor movement? As one would expect of a form of Social Democratic Unionism, it has a strong potential for building support within the broader community because of its contributions to the general welfare. In addition, it has an attraction that is offered to workers by Pure and Simple Unionism – it can deliver practical results in the workplace and has the capacity to look out for worker interests when they conflict with those of employers.

TURN is a Western European network of local union organizations involved in projects and programs for job creation, vocational education, and assistance to the unemployed. It has affiliated organizations in Austria, Belgium, Denmark, Finland, France, Germany, Greece, Ireland, Italy, Luxembourg, the Netherlands, Northern Ireland, Portugal, Scotland, Spain, Sweden, and Wales. Its 1998 president was Bill Spiers, who was also president of the Scottish Trades Union Congress (STUC). It has a Secretariat that is located in England and staffed by Joe Mitchell, a consultant, who serves as Executive Secretary.

TURN had its beginnings in informal contacts between local union organizations in three countries – Spain, Denmark, and the United Kingdom. In 1987, UGT-Granada (Spain), HK Aarhus (Denmark), and the Wales Cooperative Development Centre (United Kingdom) met in Granada, Spain, for the purpose of providing technical support to a Spanish project. In 1989, these three groups, along with other "social partners" (i.e., employer and government representatives) from their regions, met in Aarhus, Denmark. This meeting was hosted by HK, the Danish white-collar trade union. From this gathering came the concept of the TURN. These early meetings were supported financially by the Trade Union Information Division of DG X of the EC. Late in 1989 a successful bid for funding to finance the network was made to DG V of the EC (*Social Affairs*).

In 1990 a workshop hosted by the UGT was held in Granada. This meeting, which included the three founding organizations (UGT-Granada, HK Aarhus, and Wales Cooperative Development Centre), created the underlying philosophy and action program for TURN. The fundamental goals were to build local economic development initiative expertise in trade unions across the member nations of the EC, and to help set up partnerships with employers and other local actors. Membership was to be open to local trade union groups who were active in local economic development. According to TURN documents, the founders reached the conclusion that "trade unions were not likely to develop a significant role in local economic development unless a network of demonstrations of 'good practice' existed, which would challenge the essentially reactive, traditional perception and role of trade unions." They also concluded that reliance on isolated local experiences was ineffective, with trade unions needing advice and technical assistance in order to move into a "proactive partnership role." In addition, they believed that ongoing transnational relationships among trade union groups engaging in these practices were necessary for the practices to be effectively exchanged.

The result is an unusual organization. According to Joe Mitchell, the Executive Secretary, "The TURN Network represents the untypical, where trade unions have played a direct animatory role in the establishment of projects and programmes of employment creation in the local economy" (1998).

UNIONS AND ECONOMIC DEVELOPMENT

In Western Europe

It would seem that the involvement of unions in regional and local economic development would flow naturally from their being organizations that "have an interest in creating, securing and improving employment" (Burns 1998). However, this has not generally been the case in Western Europe. While they have been active at the level of the firm in collective bargaining, and at the national and sectoral levels in many countries, unions have generally not been stimulators of, or influential participants in, programs for intervention in labor markets at the regional and local levels (Burns 1998).

According to Joe Mitchell, there are a number of reasons why European trade unions have been reluctant to fully support local employment development schemes. One reason is that this involves "action outside the workplace and within a complex local environment," which is difficult for unions. Another is that these schemes generally assist small firms, which have traditionally been resistant to unions. Also, union experience with these initiatives has often been unfavorable because union representatives felt that their views were ignored. Sometimes there are ideological barriers to be overcome. The new jobs are sometimes of dubious quality. In addition, national union structures are not always inclined to favor local- and regional-level initiatives (Mitchell 1998).

On the other hand, it would seem that there are some significant advantages to be gained by unions from their being active participants in programs for regional and local economic development. Joe Mitchell makes several rather convincing arguments for this. First, he maintains that other trade union strategies to cope with increased globalization of business have generally failed. "Where their strategy was reliant on outright resistance they were overwhelmed by the economic and political forces ringed against them. Where they accommodated they suffered significant falls in membership. Where they searched for an alternative path . . . their influence and membership declined." Second, he believes there to be significant advantages to unions in being full partners in local economic development. These include:

(1) unions having the opportunity to demonstrate that they are "an organic part of the community"; (2) partnerships in preparatory vocational training offering opportunities for recruitment of members in small- and medium-size enterprises (SMEs); (3) union staff development being subsidized in crucial areas; and (4) a strengthening of services to members and nonmembers. According to him, these advantages only obtain where unions have "active responsibilities" in development, and are not merely approvers of programs developed by others (Mitchell 1998).

The notion that unions have an important role to play in local economic development is one that has considerable appeal. As TURN documents argue, this is an area of activity that shows labor to be a positive force that benefits the community in general. One of the chief problems of the labor movement in the modern global economy is that it is often seen as an impediment to attracting the capital necessary for the creation of jobs. By assisting in development it moves from being an impediment to being a facilitator of job creation.

In the EC unions have served as members of various regional development bodies. In France, trade unions have been involved in regional economic and social committees. In Spain and Germany unions have been quite active in this way. In the United Kingdom unions have often been involved in reactive attempts to move to worker ownership, or to make into cooperatives, firms that are failing. Examples also include coal mines and bus companies in Scotland (Burns 1998). In Sweden and Denmark local trades unions have participated in running both job centers for the unemployed and training programs.

The TURN idea, according to Joe Mitchell, is for union participation to be more proactive, with unions performing an "animatory," rather than a passive, role. In Europe, Italian unions have been involved (in Ravenna) in establishing an economic development agency to encourage the formation of new firms and the diversification of the economy. In Sweden and Denmark, unions have been part of the process for conversions of existing firms into new businesses. In Southwest France, unions have initiated the establishment of funds to finance new firms. In Hamburg, Germany, the metalworkers union set up a center to encourage innovation in SMEs. A center in Tilburg, the Netherlands, established by the trade unions, includes the creation of new enterprises among its goals. The Italian CGIL, working with the universities, has a center for technology and training for high-tech industries. In central Sweden, a working group assembled by the TCO white-collar union federation has developed proposals for development that include new company startups.

The TURN experience further illustrates the wide variety of activities that unions can engage in for regional and local development. Among other things, these include vocational training, job creation programs, and assistance to cooperatives. In addition to initiation of training programs, the TURN affiliates in Spain and Wales have put into place programs to promote and support cooperatives. In Wales they have established a credit union and initiated a program to assist rural communities to maintain the amenities necessary to keep and attract industry.

In North America

An interesting instance of American union action in the area of regional development is the Heartland Labor Capital Project. Led by the United Steelworkers, this project, according to its journal, aims to "address the economic, financial, legal and regulatory barriers to high-road investment strategies," and "develop a regional economic development-oriented investment strategy in seven U. S. cities" (*The Heartland Journal* 1998: 1).

A major initiative of the Heartland project is the creation of a regional labor investment fund. This would have the objectives of (1) investing in regional businesses and providing services to them to create, maintain, and protect jobs; (2) promoting "economic awareness," as well as training of workers and unions and raising the level of their influence on economic development; (3) "stimulat[ing] regional economies"; (4) encouraging "the development of regional business enterprises" by involving both labor and its allies to support this through institutional investments and direct investment; (5) providing capital to employee-owned enterprises and enterprises "where unions have created more democratic and sustainable practices"; and (6) providing "prudent returns" to investors (Croft et al. 1999).

In 2000 Heartland was engaged in assembling a fund of between $50 and $75 million ($100 million eventually) to provide capital to worker-friendly SMEs. Its plan is to utilize the benefit funds of three unions, Union of Needletrades, Industrial and Textile Employees (UNITE); International Union of Electronic, Electrical, Salaried, Machine and Furniture Workers (IUE); and the Steelworkers. The original idea was to provide venture capital or assistance in setting up Employee State Ownership Plans (ESOPs), with capital infusions in the range of $50,000 to $100,000 per ESOP (Siegfried 1999). A 2000 announcement (*Heartland Journal, Special Edition* 2000) says that investments can range from $1 to $50 million. The money would be managed centrally with a single fund manager. It would assist not just unionized firms, but firms with good wages and a clear record with respect to labor relations laws. The fund will "target high performance work practices," including "positive labor-management relations," "good health and safety, environment, and employment-practice records," and "commitment to employment, training, education and workforce involvement" (*Heartland Journal, Special Edition* 2000: 1). This fund has been labeled the "Landmark Growth Capital Partners Fund." It is managed by a private investment firm.

The Heartland project has also led to the formation of the Industrial Valleys Investment Corporation for the Pittsburgh area. This organization has the same general purposes as the Heartland Fund. It was put together by the

Steelworkers and the Steel Valley Authority, an organization that manages "industrial retention" in the region. A proposal for another such fund, the Northwest Labor Investment Fund, is under development in the Seattle area (Croft et al. 1999).

In Canada, several provinces have adopted legislation providing for LSIFs. These funds are encouraged by favorable tax treatment. The money comes from employees investing their Individual Retirement Account (IRA) money in these funds (Hebb and Mackenzie 2001).

The Canadian LSIFs began in 1983 with the establishment of Quebec's Solidarity Fund. By 1998 it had grown to over $2 billion in assets. It remains the largest of these funds, and is Canada's largest venture capital fund of any kind (Falconer 1998). Under the Province of Manitoba's Employee Ownership Fund Corporation Act, the Manitoba Crocus Fund grew from nothing in 1993 to $130 million in assets in 1999. Half of its investments involve establishing employee ownership. Its socially responsible, labor-friendly, investment strategy has been highly successful in terms of return on investment (*Owners at Work* 1999; Croft et al. 1999).

All of these funds are part of a broader labor strategy to utilize labor's capital, most of which is in pension funds. Leo W. Gerard, President of the Steelworkers, has been one of the most energetic leaders of this movement. According to him:

The use of workers' capital is one of the key challenges facing the labor movement today. Our deferred wages underpin capital markets in the United States and around the world. Although we have paper ownership of $7 trillion of deferred wages in the form of U.S. pension fund assets, this fact has not altered financial market operations in any significant way. All too often, investments made with our savings yield short-term gains at the expense of working Americans and their families. . . . The challenge for labor its to find ways that align workers' savings with workers' values. We need to invest our deferred wages in companies that provide good jobs in stable, strong communities. We want to reward companies that value all the stake-holders in the enterprise, not just their shareholders. Our capital is patient and long term and our challenge is to develop a capital strategy that moves our savings beyond the quick saccharine highs of destructive corporate behavior (Gerard 2000: vii).

The AFL-CIO has founded a Center for Working Capital for the purpose of giving workers control over their own capital resources. It will encourage high-road practices and economic development through education of, and influence upon, union trustees of joint union/employer pension funds. The Heartland Fund is one possible place to invest pension monies. A strategy encouraged by the AFL-CIO is investing in something called Economically Targeted Investments (ETIs) which are legally permissible investments that target a geographic area, group of people, or industry. Unionized employers may be an appropriate target, assuming an acceptable rate of return (AFL-CIO Human Resources Development Institute undated).

There has developed a broad movement for worker and union power through the use of the capital in union pension funds (see Fung, Hebb, and Rogers 2001). At a value of $7 trillion in 1998, these funds have been described as the "primary drivers of today's financial markets in the United States and around the world" (Hebb 2001: 1). These assets may be largely managed in a short-term manner that is inconsistent with the interests of the worker beneficiaries (Hebb 2001). In addition, they hold the potential for producing not only better investment returns, but also collateral advantages such as job creation.

There is a long history in the United States of successful funds that limit their investing to companies that have social purposes that match those of the investors (Becker and McVeigh 2001). Union-friendly investment funds have proven themselves to be capable of producing "very competitive returns to their investors" as well as solid collateral benefits (Calabrese 2001: 93). There is also evidence that through the power of these funds labor can have a positive role in the current "shareholder revolution" (O'Connor 2001: 67). It is argued that "corporate governance will trump labor laws in importance, and shareholder rights will constitute a new focal point for labor relations in the United States in the twenty-first century" (O'Connor 2001: 67).

A union that has been extraordinarily creative with regard to workers' capital is the International Association of Machinists (IAM). It has established a fund that permits its members to invest in IAM-organized companies. It has also been a leader of shareholder activism (Sleigh 2001).

In all of these examples, trade unions have been proactive in serving the needs of the general community for job creation. This is a new and promising role for unions.

UNIONS AND TRAINING

Training of workers does at least four things: (1) it is a contribution to local economic development; (2) it benefits the workers who receive the training; (3) it benefits the society at large in multiple ways; and (4) it is an area in which unions can perform a function for which they may be uniquely suited.

The strategy of developing a trained workforce as a means of attracting capital is an important part of the TURN approach. Given the high mobility of voracious international capital, it makes sense to use bait that it might find appetizing. A workforce capable of being highly productive is a valuable set of available human capital. Indeed, under modern market conditions this may be the crucial determinant of the ability of a firm to compete globally. It is not just how cheaply labor can be bought that is important to many firms. It is, instead, the price of labor relative to its productiveness.

Appropriate training is of obvious benefit to the worker receiving it. The possession of marketable skills is the chief determinant of a lifetime's earnings. Skills that are useable within the employing firm will lead to a good internal job market for the worker. Skills that are more broadly applicable have the potential for leading to a good job market for the employee outside the firm. In a modern economy it may be that the only employment security that a worker has lies in having marketable skills or the ability to acquire them.

Society at large benefits from having a valuable stock of human capital. Workers with marketable skills are less likely to be among the ranks of the long-term unemployed. The productivity of a national employment relations system is highly dependent on having skilled, and therefore productive, workers. The general welfare of the society is improved by having a workforce that is well paid, is doing fulfilling work, and copes with the demands of our unstable, globalized, economy. Also, to the extent that democracy depends upon having a body of voters who are capable of making informed and rational choices, a population of skilled workers is better able to do this. Furthermore, it is an aid to democracy to have a relatively even distribution of wealth and power across the society. This will be present to the degree that ordinary workers possess valuable skills as well as the feelings of self-worth and economic muscle that go along with being skilled workers. At present, this may be the only way to truly empower and accord dignity to workers. The possession of valuable human capital not only enhances individual bargaining power. It also increases the ability of workers to band together for the assertion of collective-bargaining power.

In Western Europe

TURN affiliates have been involved in instituting numerous training programs. In Belgium, a TURN affiliate has established vocational training programs in computers, and in administrative and management skills. A Danish affiliate has put together training materials, done consulting, and taught classes having to do with ecological management. Also, there is a major program for vocational training of unemployed members of the HK (white-collar union) as export assistants. In Germany, programs for integration of immigrants into the German culture, foreign-language courses, and training in environmental protection have all been put in place. Also, there are training programs for female sales workers who want to return to the workforce and environmental training for retail workers.

In Greece, there is a project to combat racism and xenophobia and a center for vocational training, as well as programs to assist in the integration of immigrants. In Ireland, the Irish Trade Union Trust has a program to assist workers with disabilities. There is also a program to assist workers affected by mass layoffs. An interesting project of the Irish Services, Professional, and Technical Union (SIPTU) draws young people from both religious communities in Northern Ireland for a training program in the hotel catering industry. This includes, through the cooperation of the American hotel employees union (Hotel Employees and Restaurant Employees [HERE]), work experience in the United States. In Spain, there are programs to train workers in environmental care and safety. There are courses for unemployed workers from the agrarian sector and in business-management techniques.

In Northern Ireland, unions have initiated programs for training for the long-term unemployed, and courses in computers and office administration. There is also an interesting training program for ecological retail assistants.

In the United States

In the United States it is clear that increasing both the quantity and quality of training is in the public interest. It has been persuasively argued (Osterman 1990) that this country has serious failings with respect to training its workforce at a time when training has become increasingly important. The reasons for the current importance of training include:

Modern production processes shift skill from manual dexterity to data manipulation and pattern recognition. Employees need to have a broader view of the production process than required in the past, and they need to be able to respond to events that are recorded in data, not necessarily through the senses. In addition, computer-based systems lead to a tighter integration of production and more rapid speeds, and both of these characteristics place a premium on error-free operation. In new systems errors can propagate and have large-scale consequences. The role of workers is increasingly exception-handling, and this requires ability to understand and respond to unexpected and atypical situations. These reasons, taken together with the size of capital investment, are leading firms to seek a higher skilled labor force (Osterman 1990: 260).

Also, it is not only new technology, but also employer desires for more flexible production systems, that create a need to have a better trained workforce.

What should be the union role in training systems? Is this an area where unions can add value? Does it make sense for a worker advocacy organization to be involved in training? It is the view of this writer that this is a major field of opportunity for unions. There are a number of reasons for this.

The fundamental logic of union involvement in training has been compellingly argued. According to German sociologist Wolfgang Streeck (1992), suggestions that unions should move from a conflict-oriented, adversarial, distributionist position to a productive, cooperationist position, and see training as part of this new strategy, are only partly true. He contends that, rather than conflict and cooperation precluding one another, they "presuppose each other." Streeck argues:

... one can fully agree with the proposition that unions should embrace skill formation as the centrepiece of a new, cooperative, and productivistic strategy, *and at the same time insist* on unions' need for a strong independent power base giving them, just as in the past, a capacity to impose rules and obligations on employers that these would not voluntarily obey or accept. I will argue that the latter no less than the former is in fact an indispensable condition for a successful joint union-management strategy of industrial upskilling, *even from the perspective of governments and employers* (Streeck 1992: 252).

According to Streeck, it is in the interests of employers and governments to have union influence over training because this is "competitively superior." This is because the supply of labor in a modern economy is a "kingdom of the bourgeoisie only on the surface." It is "a *magic kingdom* full of paradoxes and contradictions." One paradox is that the ruler of this kingdom (the employer) can only rule effectively if his power is "constrained by a powerful citizenry" (the workers). Without being forced to do so by the workers, the employer is incapable of achieving his desired results. This is because employers are "confronted with vexing dilemmas between their collective long-term and their individual short-term interests." The first horn of the principal dilemma is that a "rich supply of skills" is an "important source of competitive advantage for firms," and the firm is the best place to acquire these skills. The second horn is that, because it is impossible to ascertain the expected returns on investment in skill building and because workers have the ability to leave and take their skills with them, it will be the rare employer that will invest adequately in skill formation for its workers.

The long-run result is that employers in general find themselves lacking workers who have the necessary skills. This also works to the detriment of society. This is the case in many industries in the United States at present. An obvious solution is for unions to exert pressure on employers to train more broadly than they would be willing to do if left to their own devices. This encourages employers to do what is in their collective long-term interests and the interests of society. Through the exertion of their bargaining power, unions are capable of imposing short-term costs upon employers for failing to train broadly. This can change the calculus of short-term costs and benefits to favor broader training.

Streeck sees the unions' making it possible for needed training to take place as being the modern equivalent of unions in the old mass-production system negotiating for the high wages necessary to support it. Unions provided a necessary condition for the survival of the Fordist mass-production system by demanding higher wages than employers were individually willing to pay on their own. The result was a level of general demand that absorbed the enormous supply of mass-produced goods. Now, it is the supply side on which the unions can have a decisive influence. They can do so by demanding broader training than employers are individually willing to provide on their own. Because they represent a worker interest in training that is broader than the needs of the immediate job and company, and this is consistent with long-run societal interests, they can perform in their traditional adversarial manner and produce a result that is for the benefit of the society in general, including employers.

There is a good deal of experience in the United States with joint union management-training programs. Joint programs exist widely in the automotive, communications, steel, and construction industries, and in public-sector employment. In some cases there has been a division of labor between unions and management, with the unions doing recruiting and outreach, and the employers dealing with the technical side of the training. A crucial difference between these programs and those that are run by the employer alone is that joint programs are based in part upon the "expressed needs" of the workers, not simply on the employers' wishes (Ferman et al. 1990).

In the United States construction industry there is a history of unions providing training in apprenticeship programs. According to Bill Luddy (1997), then Administrative Assistant to the President, United Brotherhood of Carpenters and Joiners (Carpenters), with the rise of nonunion construction companies over the last three decades has come a de-skilling of the industry that is now loudly bemoaned by employers. Luddy argues that the nonunion construction industry lived for years off of the workers who had been trained by the Carpenters. As a consequence, the industry never developed an infrastructure for recruitment and training of carpenters. In the absence of a union, wages were driven down as contractors competed with one another by cutting wages, rather than by simply managing better. Workers have left the industry as these jobs have become less desirable. There have been efforts by employers to establish industry training funds and to encourage individual contractors to engage in training. However, contractors have, not surprisingly, been unwilling to absorb the costs of training workers who are likely to move on to other employers. According to Luddy:

The union is the answer. We train the workers and put them to work for [the contractor]. We distribute the costs across the industry. The role of the trade union in construction is as the supplier of a commodity – it gets you the best unit of production for the lowest cost. When carpenters are dispatched from a hiring hall, that's their organization, the way their career works. There are different incentives. They earn a good wage based on their skills. . . . There is a different spirit. When he [the union carpenter] works, he works hard (Luddy 1997).

The Carpenters' experience is a good example of the phenomenon described by Streeck. It is especially true in the construction industry, where workers are employed on a project-by-project basis, that it is not rational for an employer to provide training for workers. However, in the long term, all employers in the industry suffer from the low productivity of unskilled workers that is a consequence of individual employers' short-term rational policy. As Streeck argues, the union can perform a highly valuable role in insisting that workers receive the training that their employers, in the long run, need them to have.

The need for union influence on training is not limited to the construction industry. According to Frank Hurt, President of the Bakery, Confectionery,

Tobacco Workers and Grain Millers International Union (BCTGM), advanced training for employees is an essential part of the path to popular schemes of workplace reengineering, teams, and similar ideas, that can actually result in improvements in efficiency, product quality, and employee satisfaction. For him, "The key to this path is for the workers to have an independent voice in the process, which is only guaranteed by a union" (Hurt 1997). Here again we see a blending of cooperation with an insistence upon the workers' distinctive interests being forwarded.

Training of considerable breadth is needed. Yet, employers will not do this without being pressured to do so. The union role as an advocate of employee interests fits this situation like a glove. The union is ideally situated to advocate and assist in training programs that not only meet the immediate needs of an employer, but also meet the long-term needs of the industry and the nation, while at the same time serving the needs of union members in a very practical way.

NETWORKS OF LOCAL UNIONS

Perhaps the most unusual characteristic of TURN is that it links local union organizations with one another across national boundaries without the intervention of national or regional union bodies. This, of course, challenges the control of these high-level organizations. It also can create real problems of coordination. Nevertheless, local-to-local interchanges do have some real advantages. In the United States, this might apply across regions within a union, or across national unions.

What Does TURN Do As a Network?

TURN has a rather complex role with regard to the regional and local economic development activities of unions. It facilitates the development of transnational projects and the formation of subnetworks, and helps with the creation of partnerships with employers and local authorities. It disseminates information on practices used in, and the lessons learned from, the various national and international experiences. TURN organizes regional workshops. It assists in the development of a manual of good practices for trade union local economic initiatives.

Through the TURN network, a training program for export assistants, developed in Denmark, has been transferred to Germany, Spain, and the United Kingdom. An annual exchange program for young workers has been set up between Germany, Spain, Italy, Denmark, and Turkey. A development agent training program established in Wales and Northern Ireland has been extended to Denmark and Italy. An initiative to study the feasibility of cultural tourism in rural areas was begun in Spain and now involves Ireland, Scotland, and Denmark. A program (MEHKON) for training needs analysis of employees in SMEs was developed in Denmark and adopted in Ireland, the United Kingdom, Spain, Belgium, and Germany. Subnetworks have been set up by trade unions in Ireland, Belgium, Italy, Germany, and Spain. A joint project of women from TURN and ILE-Women developed a manual of best practices as to entrepreneurial activities by women. Descriptions of projects have been published in five languages. An electronic mail system and Web page, http://www.ecu-notes.org/, have been set up to facilitate the sharing of information.

In reading the TURN literature, and in listening to Joe Mitchell, one finds a rather powerful rationale for the usefulness of a network of local organizations. This network developed out of the practical experience of the founder organizations (UGT-Granada, HK Aarhus, and Wales Cooperative Development Centre). From their own experience they came to believe that trade unions are not at all likely to engage in these nontraditional activities on their own. They will not do this unless they have available to them some information on successful examples that provide a set of "best practices." Only if they have these will they have some degree of confidence that this sort of thing will work.

Joe Mitchell speaks of the "power of the example." According to him, once people have seen someone else ride a bicycle, they cannot be convinced that it is impossible for this to be done. Similarly, once workers see that a nontraditional role can be successfully performed, they cannot be convinced that this is impossible. What the network does is to educate trade unionists as to the possibilities. In the process, those who do the teaching learn a great deal. They are subjected to searching questions, and in an ongoing relationship have to think about and learn from their failures as well as from their successes. Failures, though educational, are rarely talked about in the absence of a forum such as a network. The network facilitates the exchange of information about best practices and the development of a body of expertise as well as a group of experts. It provides opportunities for trainees in local economic development, or particular areas of worker training, to be exchanged among network members. It is a transmission belt for information and people.

EC funding for TURN ran out in 1996. Since that time it has operated on an informal basis, without general meetings or a completely active Secretariat. However, the network has a life of its own. The contacts made through TURN have enabled the various national affiliates to continue to work with one another as needed. The Web page, still maintained by Joe Mitchell, provides publicly available information on projects by the various affiliates.

CONCLUSIONS

It is necessary for unions to consider a wide range of alternative strategies in this very challenging world. It is too much to hope to find a single strategic answer to all of labor's problems. Nevertheless, there are some partial solutions suggested by the European and North American union experiences in supporting regional economic development and training, and in the European use of a network of grassroots organizations to do this. The TURN experience suggests some of the answers.

As argued in Chapter 1, in order for a movement of workers to prosper in a society, it is necessary for the following enabling conditions to be present: (1) workers perceiving that the work role is central to their lives; (2) solidarity among workers; (3) workers perceiving that there are distinctive worker interests; (4) the benefits of collective action must at least be equal to its costs; (5) employer opposition being held within tolerable boundaries; and (6) government support, or at least tolerance. Strategies that contribute to these conditions are more likely to facilitate labor movement success than those that do not.

The activities of aiding local economic development, involving unions in training, and having local unions network with each other, all can make positive contributions to the conditions necessary for the survival of the labor movement. The benefits to workers from regional and local economic development, both as union members and as citizens of the local community, would be expected to exceed the rather modest costs of local development programs to the union and its members.

Training has work as its focus. Emphasis on training helps to increase the centrality of work in the eyes of workers. The union's role in insuring that training is broader than the needs of the present employer emphasizes the reality that there is a worker interest with regard to training that is distinctive from the employer interest. Particularly since the training can often be done with someone else's (the government's or the employer's) money, the benefits of training to workers should exceed the costs to their union.

Networking among local unions is an effective way for achieving perceptions of solidarity among workers across regions, occupations, and industries. As TURN demonstrates, this can be done even across national boundaries. If it is necessary in the long run to have a truly global labor movement, this is one step on the road to the international solidarity that is a necessary condition for such a movement. The costs of networking are minimal, particularly in this day of cheap, quick, electronic communications. The benefits are quite substantial. Strategies that contribute to economic development and help in the creation of a skilled labor force should buy labor some degree of tolerance, perhaps even support, from both employers and government.

Taken together, the various aspects of the TURN approach make up a coherent strategy that effectively blends the cooperative and the adversarial. These two apparently contradictory but really complementary aspects of unionism must be combined for the labor movement to carry its special contribution to society into this century. American labor might be well advised to turn to the power of the TURN example for ideas to grow on.

With respect to regional economic development, the TURN strategy mainly uses the carrot of high-quality human capital to attract industry. One angle to this is that TURN hopes to use other people's (employer's or government's) money to produce the desired outcome of good jobs for workers in their region.

The North American approach to assisting regional economic development, as seen in the Canadian LSIFs and the Heartland project, provides a unique avenue for union influence and power. Unlike TURN's training-based strategy, but similar to employee ownership, they approach the firm from the standpoint of financial capital – the workers' own financial capital, but financial capital nonetheless. However, unlike worker ownership, the aim is not having workers control the policies of their own employers, but rather encouraging union-friendly "good" employers and giving them a competitive advantage. They are also attempting to attract other capital, and the resultant jobs, to the regions in which they operate. The carrot of this patient and socially conscious capital is used to attract employers to come to or remain in the region, and to make them better employers from a worker's perspective.

In both this chapter and the previous one, it is suggested that American unions can learn from European experience. Of course, it is not an easy thing to transfer structures and strategies from one cultural milieu to another. Probably the greatest difference between the United States and Continental Europe is the much greater political power of labor in Europe, along with a cultural receptivity to accord serious weight to the economic needs of the ordinary citizen. This clearly makes it easier for European trade unions to pursue their objectives through the political system.

What this book attempts to do is to avoid the trap of focusing only on strategies that produce immediate and direct payoffs for unions. Instead, the idea is to address the underlying enabling conditions that may lead to a more favorable environment, particularly with respect to employer and government attitudes. That is, the environment is not taken as a given, but rather as a set of variables that are amenable to union influence. For example, in providing financial capital and improved human capital for regional economic development, it is believed that the American labor movement can help to buy lowered resistance by employers and more support from local governments and perhaps even from the national government. It is by looking at both underlying enabling conditions and specific tactics that labor has a chance to move forward on several fronts at the same time.

In the next and final chapter there is an attempt to tie all of these threads together. It does appear to be true that in order to make the kind of shift in union strategies that is capable of making any significant difference, it is necessary to do two things. First, the full range of complexities must be identified and analyzed – the first eight chapters do this. Second, some broad conclusions and action recommendations must be posited. It is to this second task that we now turn.

NINE

A Labor Movement for the Twenty-First Century

And that giant wave Democracy
Breaks on the shores where Kings lay couched at ease.
Oscar Wilde, "Louis Napoleon"

The future of the American labor movement will determine to a large degree the fate of democracy in American society. Clearly, industrial democracy is at stake. More importantly, the fate of American political democracy may also hang in the balance. A democratic political system depends on a balance of power. It is difficult to imagine it surviving without the enormous power of organized capital being offset to some degree by that of a strong, vital labor movement. The Progressive political movement in the United States includes many organizations. However, the key to this coalition in the twenty-first century, as it was in the twentieth century, is organized labor.

Does the American labor movement have a future? On balance, the answer would appear to be *yes*. The "giant wave" of democracy is irresistible in the American system. Organizations on the side of this wave are on the side of history. In addition, American trade unions are drawing upon the American tradition of pragmatism. They are trying out a bewildering array of strategies and tactics. The times are propitious for experimentation because, unlike earlier eras, trade unionists are not constrained by ideology to avoid solutions that smack of socialism.

What is the form that the American labor movement will take in the twenty-first century? As pragmatism is American labor's guiding principle, it is the forms that work that are likely to be adopted. This will be determined by trial and error, as practical trade unionists and intellectuals experiment and evaluate again and again. The behavior of unions in recent years reveals that they are more than willing to try out a wide variety of new approaches. The current crop of leaders, both in the AFL-CIO and the national unions, is mainly comprised of persons who are more interested in experimenting than were past generations of labor leaders. This is probably driven by the fact that the severity of labor's problems has grown to the point where it is too great to ignore. This book is an effort to report and analyze some of these experiments. Let us briefly review what such an analysis teaches us.

UNION STRATEGIES AND THE ENABLING CONDITIONS

In addition to considering the obvious direct effects of union tactics such as organizing upon the labor movement's strength, it is useful to view the indirect effects of union strategies and tactics by examining their impact on the conditions that enable the existence of a strong labor movement. These are the enabling conditions set out in Chapter 1. These conditions are: (1) workers perceiving that the work role is important to their lives; (2) solidarity among workers; (3) workers perceiving that there are distinctive worker interests; (4) the benefits of collective action at least equaling the costs; (5) employer opposition being held within tolerable boundaries; and (6) government support, or at least tolerance. Table 1 provides a graphic summary of the effects of some of the more interesting potential strategies and tactics. The balance of this section discusses the effects on particular enabling conditions of these and other strategies, tactics, and approaches.

Importance of Work Role

Of the American union strategies and tactics outlined in Chapter 3, Pure and Simple Unionism strategies probably emphasize the importance of the work role most clearly. This is especially strong in craft and occupational unions that organize around a particular work role – a craft or an occupation. Industrial unions perform the same function, but focus on jobs in a particular industry or at a work site rather than in a craft.

The recently adopted Pure and Simple strategies of European unions, such as aiming to serve the special needs of groups of workers (i.e., women and youths) contribute to this enabling condition. The emphasis on training that is part of efforts by the Trade Union Regional Network (TURN) to assist regional economic development reinforces the centrality of work to workers' lives.

The old Reformist Knights of Labor spoke clearly to the importance of being a worker. They held that a person is a "producer" first, and only secondly a member of a particular political party, craft, or religion.

Cooperationist Unionism adopts a broad view of the work role and sees work as being something that is part of human self-expression. In a way, this may emphasize the importance of work, but at the same time it de-emphasizes the difference between work and other social roles.

Table 1. *Effects of Union Strategies And Tactics*

Strategies and Tactics	Enabling Conditions						
	Centrality of Work	Intensive Solidarity	Extensive Solidarity	Distinctive Worker Interest	Benefits versus Costs	Lowering Employer Opposition	Raising Government Support
Craft Unionism	+	+	–	+	+	–	–
Occupational Unionism	+	+	–	+	+	–	+
Industrial Unionism	+	–	+	+	+	–	+
Union Reform	0	0	0	0	+	0	+
Associational Unionism	+	+	–	0	+	0	+
Social Unionism	0	–	+	+	+	–	+
Worker Rights Organizations	+	–	+	+	+	–	+
Cooperationist Unionism	+	–	–	+	+	+	+
Intrafirm Networks	+	+	+	–	+	0	0
Organizing	+	+	+	+	+	–	0
Strike	+	+	+	+	0	–	–
Unions Absent a Majority	+	+	0	+	0	0	0
Corporate Campaign	+	+	+	+	+	+	0
Training	+	0	0	+	+	+	+
International Trade	+	+	+	+	+	–	–
International Pressures	+	+	+	+	+	–	–
Knights of Labor	+	–	–	+	+	–	+
CAFE	0	+	+	+	+	–	+
Employee Ownership	–	–	–	–	+	+	+
Union Networks	0	+	+	+	+	+	+
Labor Capital Funds	0	0	0	–	+	+	+

+ = Positive effect on enabling condition; – = Negative effect on enabling condition; 0 = No effect or unpredictable effect on enabling condition

On the other hand, with its emphasis on ties to the community, modern social unionism does not appear to contribute to this condition. The modern Reformist Carolina Alliance for Fair Employment (CAFE) does not have a philosophical focus on work.

Social Democratic labor movements of Western Europe historically focused not so much on work and the workplace experience as on the broad social needs of members of the working class. Centrality of work, which was an early article of faith for Karl Marx (Struik 1964), does not seem to be crucial to modern Social Democratic Unionism.

Solidarity

Among the strategies of American unions discussed in Chapter 3, the approaches of craft and occupational unionism are probably best calculated to build intensive solidarity among the members of the craft or occupation. The flip side of this, of course, is a failure to build extensive solidarity. Reforming unions to make them more democratic and honest should remove barriers to solidarity. Workers are more likely to identify with their fellow workers if they are not being robbed or manipulated. Associational unionism may build solidarity among persons such as white-collar workers who could not be brought together by more traditional forms of unions.

Organizing and bargaining that is aimed at the needs of special groups of workers such as women, minorities, youths, professionals, and temporary employees can build solidarity between these particular groups and the rest of a union's membership. Organizing these groups is an attempt to persuade them that their interests can be served by acting in common with other workers. Successful collective bargaining that works to benefit them demonstrates that it can be effective.

International tactics of American unions are a positive step in the direction of building solidarity on an international basis. Building solidarity across national boundaries is extraordinarily difficult. Strong tendencies toward nationalism and xenophobia stand in the way. Yet, it is reasonably clear that an international labor movement is necessary to deal with multinational corporations. And without solidarity there is no labor movement. Imaginative and determined efforts are required to achieve solidarity that crosses national boundaries.

The Knights of Labor's motto, "An injury to one is an injury to all," is a classic statement of worker solidarity. However, although the Knights' vision of extensive solidarity that includes all producers is a compelling one, the very breadth of this vision causes problems for intensive solidarity. This is one of the principal points of contrast between the Reformist Knights and the Pure and Simple American Federation of Labor (AFL) craft unions. The craft unions had intensive but narrow solidarity while the Knights had extensive but shallow solidarity. The same weakness exists for the modern Reformist organization, CAFE. The lack of a basis for intensive solidarity may be a problem that is endemic to this type of unionism.

In Europe, the development of "branch unions" to correspond with different professional categories, as is done by the Dutch CNV, has real potential for building intensive solidarity among unionists in these categories. This would seem to be an especially useful idea for industrial or "general" unions, given their weakness in this respect. The CNV's separate unions set up to represent youths and women serve this purpose as well. Action by unions to be twenty-four-hour unions that assist members with the problems of their lives outside of work (e.g., divorce and income taxes), such as is done in Luxembourg, builds feelings of affiliation with the trade unions and solidarity among their members. The involvement of German unions in adult education has a tendency to build ties among workers. Providing assistance to the unemployed, as do Basque and German unions, provides grounds for feelings of solidarity between the unemployed and employed unionists.

Successful use of European-level strategies such as European-level collective bargaining, Social Dialogue, and European Works Councils presuppose some degree of solidarity across national boundaries. The importance of such victories as rules on part-time employment being achieved through Social Dialogue, or the beginnings of international collective bargaining in Europe, is that they demonstrate that it is possible to take collective action across national boundaries. This demonstration effect is more powerful than any arguments of trade union leaders or tomes written by academics. As Joe Mitchell of TURN says, once you have seen someone ride a bicycle you cannot be persuaded that it is impossible. What we have seen in Europe is proof that international collective action by workers through their representatives is in fact feasible. This provides a basis for workers to recognize the commonality of their interests with those of workers in other countries. This plants the seeds of international solidarity.

Solidarity is not only a feeling of affiliation with fellow workers, but also a feeling of dissaffiliation with managers. This distinction is blurred by Cooperationist notions of compatibility of worker and management interests. Cooperationist Unionism would be expected to have deleterious effects on the negative side of solidarity by identifying management as "us" instead of as "them." Traditional Social Democratic Unionism in Western Europe, similar to Reformist Unionism, takes a broad approach to solidarity. In its general philosophy, it embraces the entire working class.

PERCEPTIONS OF DISTINCT WORKER INTERESTS

American Pure and Simple Unionism in all its forms emphasizes the distinctiveness of the worker interest and the need to represent this interest in an aggressive, adversarial manner. Even where it takes on the special twist that is associational unionism, it is clear that its goal is to serve a distinctive worker interest.

The Knights of Labor held as a central belief that the interests of "producers" were different from those of the social parasites who prevented them from receiving the full fruits of their labor. The interests identified by the Knights, however, were not "worker" or "employee" interests. They were based not on distinguishing between employer and employee, but rather on distinguishing between those members of society who are productive and those who are not. Their distinction between those who earn their bread by the sweat of their brow (i.e., their own efforts) rather than the work of others, is translatable into something very similar to the employee/supervisor distinction contained in Section 2 (11) of the National Labor Relations Act (NLRA).

On the other hand, Reformism in the modern form of CAFE does not utilize the concept of "producer" or any other particular definition of a worker interest. In practice it ends up representing low-wage workers and a lower level working-class interest. Whereas the Knights were distinguished by their inclusiveness in including unskilled as well as skilled workers, CAFE has included only unskilled workers. What CAFE does, therefore, is not to emphasize the distinctiveness of the worker interest, but rather the social cleavage between the haves and the have nots in society.

Reformism in the modern form of worker ownership largely tends to obscure the distinctiveness of the worker interest. Therefore, it pushes in a direction contrary to this enabling condition.

Social Democratic Unionism in Europe speaks in terms of a working class that has economic interests that are distinct from those of the owners of capital. TURN works both ways because it recognizes and asserts the worker interest in training that is at once distinct from and compatible with the interests of employers and society in general. The regional development initiatives of TURN and American groups such as the Heartland Fund emphasize the commonality, not the distinctiveness, of the interests of workers and other groups in society.

Reformist Unionism in the form of modern social unionism emphasizes the common interests of workers and other groups in society. It is nevertheless rooted in the notion that there are interests of workers that need to be served. Even social unionism ultimately is based on serving these interests.

Cooperationist Unionism denies the complete separateness of the worker interest. Indeed, this is its defining characteristic. Yet, in the form of labor-management "partnership" it assumes the existence of groups with somewhat differing interests that agree to cooperate on maximizing wealth but remain independent in order to engage in legitimate conflict over how the wealth is to be distributed. Although it clearly overstates the union role by implying labor equality with management, the term *partnership* does at least imply the existence of more than one distinct entity. One does not partner with oneself.

So, even though the partnership terminology and ideology blurs the distinction between labor and management, it nevertheless recognizes that this distinction does in fact exist.

Benefits of Collective Action Versus Its Costs

Looking at the American union strategies described in Chapter 3, the Pure and Simple ones very clearly have as their aim producing practical, work-related, outcomes for union members, primarily through collective bargaining. However, under modern conditions, it has become increasingly difficult for unions to deliver the goods. This is partly because unionized employers in the United States often find themselves in competition with nonunion employers in the United States or very low-wage foreign employers.

In addition, in modern circumstances the ultimate Pure and Simple union weapon, the strike, hardly strikes fear in the hearts of employers. Even with low unemployment, jobs in unionized firms are very attractive because of the successful efforts of unions over the years to improve these jobs. This makes it relatively easy to replace strikers. Workers who know that striking may cost them their jobs are loath to strike – and employers know this.

Reform of existing unions raises the benefits of collective action because it makes unions more responsive to the needs of their members, increasing the probability that a union will pursue and achieve what its members want. It also decreases the costs of union representation by eliminating corruption and ending the mishandling of union funds.

Associational unions are an attempt to achieve workers' practical goals by a somewhat different method. The goal is the same as that of traditional unions – benefits to the members. They achieve economic benefits using a mainly political approach rather than an economic one. They may be capable of pursuing the agendas of professional and white-collar workers more effectively than other types of unions.

American social unionism, whether in the form of the Knights of Labor or other forms, aims to achieve and has considerable potential for achieving benefits for union members. Similar to associational unionism, it does this partly by pursuing their interests in the broader political context as well as in the economic one. The case for the Knights in this regard is considered extensively in Chapter 4.

Cooperationist Unionism has no doubt produced some benefits for American workers. It may have softened employer opposition. It also may have saved jobs by improving quality and efficiency. It has given workers somewhat more control over their working lives. Overall, it has probably benefited workers more than it has harmed them. The chief benefit for employees has been more individual participation in workplace decisions. The chief cost, at least potentially, is a loss of militancy.

Union pursuit of training opportunities for members is especially capable of producing benefits in the modern situation. Training is probably the best answer to workers' problems of employment insecurity in a highly insecure environment. Union involvement in training programs can assure that the aim is to benefit the worker, not just the employer.

International action by American unions has so far, except in a few unusual cases like Ravenswood Aluminum, shown little in the way of practical benefits to workers. However, the costs are not high, and in some cases payoffs and the potential for long-range benefits, particularly in the area of job security, make it worth pursuing.

The inclusive, community-wide organizational structure of the Knights of Labor would seem to be highly instrumental for purposes of collective political action, if not for collective bargaining. Something similar to a Mixed Local Assembly model consisting of labor and other groups can produce favorable political and public relations outcomes for workers. This has been demonstrated in California and elsewhere, where such structures have been developed (Meyerson 2001). In the new economy workers have become more likely to have a career path that is a multiemployer one (Herzenberg, Alic, and Wial 1998). This situation calls for labor organizations that are community-wide and occupation-wide rather than limited to employees of a particular employer. A local organization that blends the functions of a Knights of Labor Mixed Assembly and a modern city central labor council can serve this purpose. At the same time it can be an instrument of local-level political action.

As an expression of modern Reformist Unionism, CAFE has proved its ability to deliver some benefits, largely through political action. It has also facilitated unionization in some instances. This has been achieved at a very low cost. The modern Reformist idea of employee ownership is also capable of offering union members both economic benefits and the power to influence corporate policy.

European national trade unions' ventures into Pure and Simple Unionism are largely aimed at delivering additional practical benefits to their members. The businesslike methods of the British Amalgamated Engineering and Electrical Unions (AEEU) and Dutch unions are calculated to serve members more efficiently. Union mergers and interunion cooperation serve to achieve economies of scale and efficiencies that tend to lower the costs of union membership.

The provision of legal assistance and other peripheral benefits by unions in the United Kingdom and other European countries are examples of benefits to workers. Particular attention being paid to the needs of part-time and women workers is an effort to provide concrete benefits to them. Expanding such benefits as holidays, travel, and insurance have the aim of providing valued outcomes to members generally.

European-level strategies are in their infancy. So far they have produced only modest results – chiefly through Social Dialogue. Whether such policies as European-level collective bargaining and Social Dialogue continue to grow probably depends mainly upon whether they show that they can produce tangible benefits for workers. The framework is in place. Some initial steps have been taken along this path of international action. The test will be whether European-level strategies can in fact produce benefits.

One cross-national European strategy does appear to have proven itself. TURN has shown that it can provide valuable training opportunities to union members. Also, the actions of TURN and North American organizations to encourage regional economic development create increased job opportunities for union members.

Controlling Employer Opposition

Of all the enabling conditions, dealing with employer opposition is probably the most important one at the present time. This is because of the extraordinary power held by capital and its representatives in the new global economy. This will probably continue to be true in the future.

One aspect of Reformist Unionism that seems to finesse employer opposition is employee ownership. When employees become owners they have the possibility of exercising their capital power to influence managerial opposition to unions and union interests.

Cooperationist Unionism has containing management opposition as its main purpose. There is no question that this form of unionism is preferred by employers. It may be that this is the only form of unionism that can survive in the presence of the overwhelming power of capital under modern conditions. The participative mechanisms that flourish under this form of unionism do provide some power to individual workers at the same time that their collective labor power declines. The question is whether, as advocated by union leaders such as Frank Hurt of the Bakery, Confectionery, Tobacco Workers and Grain Millers International Union (BCTGM) (Hurt 1997), the union can continue to perform its function of looking out for the interests of workers where they diverge from those of capital. This would amount to truly being "partners" with management. As argued by Rubenstein (2001) this may require some major changes in the way that local unions operate.

An emphasis on training has considerable potential for lowering the level of employer opposition. As is the case in the construction industry as described by Bill Luddy (1997) of the Carpenters, it is also true that in many other industries there is the potential for unions achieving for employers that which they cannot achieve for themselves – a trained workforce. As many unions, including the occupational union of waitresses, have shown, the union can play a very constructive role in managing the labor market to the benefit of both employees and employers (Herzenberg, Alic, and Wial 1998).

Unions performing a role in regional economic development should cause employers to view them in a more positive light. From being part of the problem, they move toward being part of the solution to the challenges of economic progress.

European Social Democratic unions have generally not met with as much employer resistance as have American Pure and Simple ones. This may reflect European social norms that are more supportive, or at least more tolerant, of movements that seek to act systematically to distribute income and power to the lower ranks of society. America has generally been home to the most extreme capitalist and antiunion views (Sexton 1991; Jacobs 1999). Employers and their allies have solidly opposed "social engineering" that tinkers with the workings of the free market. The American way of dealing with problems of social class is to assume that classes do not exist. Therefore, it may be that European unions having not met with more employer opposition is attributable to the culture in which they operate rather than to the particular form of unionism that they have pursued. Cooperationist Unionism, of course, has as its major goal bringing together the interests of labor and management. To the extent that this exists in Europe, it may lead employers to be more receptive to those unions, such as the British AEEU, that espouse it.

European-level strategies – collective bargaining, Social Dialogue, works councils – are aimed more at worker power versus employers than at making unions more acceptable to employers. However, once these institutions have been in place for a while, the routine dealings between labor and management may lessen the tensions between them and establish European-wide collective relations as the accepted norm. Whatever the preferences of European managers, having learned to live with it, they may cease to oppose union action at the European level as actively as they have in the past.

Historically, Pure and Simple unionist strategies of American unions at least avoided the degree of intense employer opposition that Militant Radical or Reformist unions engendered. Moreover, employers were somewhat receptive to the argument that failure to accept moderate unions might lead to the growth of Militant Radical unions. However, with the threat of socialism having receded, this rationale no longer exists. Although it might have appeared otherwise in the 1950s and even the 1960s, it is now reasonably clear that nearly all American employers would prefer to go to bed at night and wake up in the morning finding that their union had disappeared. In addition, employers seem to be increasingly willing to work actively to support policies that would facilitate the demise of unions. This is evidenced by even large, historically union-friendly companies lending support to such radical employer groups as the Labor Policy Association (now LPA), and the transformation of what used to be the relatively pro-employee American Society for Personnel Administration (ASPA) into the Society for Human Resource

Management (SHRM), which opposes unions and even such proworker policies as increasing the legal minimum wage. As predicted long ago by leaders of the Knights of Labor, a Pure and Simple union strategy has not succeeded in holding employer opposition to a tolerable level.

American Social Unionism, both in its historic form as the Knights of Labor and its modern incarnations (e.g., CAFE), has not done any better than Pure and Simple Unionism in avoiding the strenuous opposition of employers. Furthermore, virtually all of the progressive political initiatives of unions have faced vigorous opposition from executives, employers, and employer groups.

The strike is a tactic that is especially offensive to management under the current global regime. It can have devastating effects upon competitiveness by interrupting the flow of goods to customers, who may turn to other suppliers. Just-in-time inventories render employers vulnerable to a strike. Capital-intensive industries have a lower proportion of their costs in labor. Therefore, the saving of wages during a strike is not as beneficial as it is in industries where a larger proportion of costs is associated with labor. A solution may be substituting arbitration for the strike, an alternative that has become increasingly appealing to labor as the strike has declined in effectiveness. So far, employers have shown little inclination to support this alternative. This is hardly surprising, given their advantage in the current strike-based system.

The Knights of Labor brought down upon themselves the wrath of the employer community of their day and, partly for that reason, were destroyed. Their ambition to replace capitalist institutions with worker-owned ones, plus their success in a few major strikes, was sufficient to produce this reaction on the part of employers. Oddly enough from an historical perspective, employee ownership, a fundamental idea of the Knights, is now reasonably popular with managers. Of course, this is not seen by managers as an alternative institution, but mainly as an instrument for improving productivity and quality. Perhaps capitalism is too secure in the twenty-first century to be threatened by this fundamentally radical idea. Employee ownership may be the ultimate answer to the conflict between labor and capital – labor becomes capital.

The Pure and Simple strategies of European trade unions probably will not lead to decreased employer resistance. Indeed, the contrary may be true. The one exception may be the adoption of more efficient practices by the British AEEU to become more like a business organization. This was done partly for the purpose of behaving more like business executives so as to be more acceptable to them.

Support of Government

American unions have, of course, been quite active in politics over the years. Industrial unions, with their leanings toward action that benefit workers as a class, have always been particularly concerned with issues of national policy. American union political action has served the dual purposes of attempting to create a favorable framework of laws for collective bargaining and sponsoring a broad liberal, progressive political agenda. In the 2000 American presidential elections labor's support in key industrial states was nearly enough to carry Democrat Al Gore to victory. The problem with this is that the unions brought down upon themselves the wrath of a Republican House of Representatives and President. Politics has its dangers as well as its rewards.

American social unionist strategies that emphasize politics would seem to be useful for building government support. Alliances with other community interest groups broaden labor's political base. This face of unionism is more appealing to the public than Pure and Simple Unionism because it speaks directly to the welfare of the community. Cooperationist Unionism has a less antagonistic image, and would be expected to have more appeal to the general public. Public support is necessary to political power, so this strategy could be useful for gaining the support of the politicians who run governments. The tactic of training, as previously noted, has a similar effect upon the public image, and therefore the political power, of labor.

As to Reformist Unionism gaining government support, the Knights of Labor did have some success in influencing government at the local level, but never became a force on the national political scene. The modern Reformist organization CAFE operates only at the state and local levels by its very nature. At these levels it has had some significant accomplishments. Employee ownership, at least in the form of Employee Stock Ownership Plans (ESOPs) and 401 (k) plans, has had very strong support from the national government. Of course, all of this does not necessarily translate into government support for the labor movement. However, it does suggest an ability of segments of the labor movement to achieve policy goals at different levels of government.

European Social Democratic unions have always relied upon government support to achieve benefits for workers. Historically, the chief distinction between American Pure and Simple unions and European Social Democratic ones has been European unions' greater reliance upon government action. The Europeans have considerable gains to show for this. The extensive web of legal regulations pertaining to the employment relationship, although weakened by years of employer efforts to achieve "flexibility," are evidence of their success in gaining the support of governments. Perhaps the most interesting current example of the use of government support to achieve desired outcomes for workers is the European-level Social Dialogue. Here we see European-level negotiations taking place under threat of the adoption of European Community (EC) Directives. The possibility of government action has moved the parties toward agreement on such matters as parental leave, fixed-term contracts, and European-wide works councils. Also, the Pure and Simple strategies of European unions have assisted them in gaining government support by causing union membership to increase, thereby increasing the unions' political muscle.

Union action to assist regional economic development would seem to have real potential to improve their public image. This is especially true with regard to training. One of the great problems of the American labor movement is that it is viewed as an impediment to economic development. Changing this public perception would be a considerable step toward making public opinion, and by extension government, more supportive of the labor movement.

On the other hand, American Pure and Simple Unionism has a long-standing problem of being perceived by the public as a selfish and self-serving interest group. This problem has been exacerbated by widely publicized problems of corruption and undemocratic practices. This negative image has weakened it politically. It has often been the case that unions have been able to count on the support of elected officials only when they can provide them with financial and other support. The political consensus that provided cover for the establishment of public policy favoring unions in the 1930s is long gone. Although public-opinion polls show the public generally favoring unions, this is balanced by public fears that unions are too powerful. If the unions' only claim on public policy is that they want more money for their members, this leaves them in a very weak position politically. Yet they are in desperate need of a friendly legal environment for organizing and collective bargaining.

Conclusions on Strategies that Contribute to the Enabling Conditions

From the preceding analysis one can derive a short list of some of the strategies and approaches that show particular promise. Traditional Pure and Simple Unionism strategies such as adversarial collective bargaining are still of central importance. Organization of and collective bargaining for the special needs of professionals, white-collar workers, women, minorities, young workers, part-timers, and temps is a useful strategy. In the U.S. reform of unions is an ongoing priority.

Some interesting Pure and Simple ideas come from Europe. The Dutch practice of having branches for different types of employees is a good one. Also useful are union involvement in adult education, the twenty-four-hour union idea, and representing and providing assistance to the unemployed.

The Reformist, social unionist set of strategies revolving around politics and community action have shown themselves to be useful. This is especially true of the Knights of Labor concept of the worker as "producer." Worker ownership is a strategy that has considerable potential, as do labor capital strategies that involve ownership and funding of employee-friendly enterprises and assist in regional economic development. Organizing at the local level along the lines of the Knights' Local Assemblies is a natural extension of some recently successful grassroots efforts.

Cooperationist Unionism has its uses, but must be used very carefully to avoid co-optation and a weakening of the union. It can be a useful strategy if it is a true "partnership" with an independent union presence.

Internationally oriented strategies have considerable long-run potential. There is a compelling need for building an international labor movement based on cross-national solidarity and international action. The example set in Europe by the European Trade Union Confederation (ETUC) and European trade unions in building Social Dialogue, works councils, and collective bargaining on a regional basis is worth following. Another European strategy worth following is having a network of local unions along the lines of TURN.

Even our short list of useful approaches and strategies is complex, stretching across nearly all of the ideal types of unions. While at first blush it may seem impossible to pursue all of these strategies simultaneously, it is clear that this is exactly what must be done. To accomplish this task requires two things – a clear vision of what the labor movement is about, and the articulation of who should do what, and how this is to be structured. Therefore, we move to an inquiry as to (1) what the core ideas of the American labor movement should be and (2) who should be responsible for achieving the enabling conditions and building such a movement. The latter point means not only identifying the various actors, but also working out how the relations among them should be structured. It is to these subjects that we now turn.

A VISION FOR A RENEWED AMERICAN LABOR MOVEMENT

In order for a new labor movement to be born out of the ashes of the old one, at least two things have to happen. First, there *needs to be some central unifying idea* upon which most of the individuals and institutions in the labor movement can agree. Second, it is *necessary to think in terms of a complex and multifaceted movement* – not just labor unions. Once we have reoriented our thinking in this way, it becomes possible to have a new perspective.

Agreeing on a central idea involves abandoning the old war between the nineteenth-century worldviews of socialist and business unionism. This allows us to select strategies on the basis of what works out best in practice instead of on a priori ideological grounds. It then becomes a matter not so much of choosing among mutually exclusive approaches as of mixing and matching specific strategies to suit particular situations.

We can readily see from the analysis in this book that all of the ideal union types have both strengths and weaknesses. Some of these are more salient under modern conditions than others. This is also true of various strategies and tactics. What is needed is a sound understanding of how these strengths and weaknesses interact with aspects of the environment, and choosing strategies and tactics accordingly.

Seeing the *goal as the creation and maintenance of a strong labor movement* makes for thinking in broad terms that include persons and organizations in addition to labor unions. Also, it leads us to thinking systematically about what should be the role of each of the components of this movement.

A Central Idea

A good candidate for a central idea of the American labor movement is *democracy*. This includes the proposition that *human beings should have some influence over matters that affect them* in important aspects of their lives. It includes the ideal of *human dignity*. This involves individuals being free from being treated as things to be "employed" (i.e., used) arbitrarily. It further involves expressing our full humanity by being *free to act in concert* with our fellows. It includes the idea of *equitable and reasonably equal distribution of wealth* in society, without which meaningful democracy is impossible.

Human dignity requires that individual human rights such as those of free expression, life, and privacy be respected. The same is true of collective rights such as those of free association and collective bargaining (see Ogle and Wheeler 2001). It is not sufficient to guarantee these rights only against interference by government, as does the United States Constitution, but also from oppression by private sources of power (Ewing 1989; Wheeler 1994a).

The Western experience with democracy is that it works best when it is representative rather than when it is direct. Political democracy is inconceivable in the absence of political parties and organized interest groups. Similarly, industrial democracy is inconceivable without the worker interest being organized and speaking through its representatives. Capital is organized in the corporate form and represented by management. Representative organizations provide a path to real empowerment. This is not a path to mere "voice." It is a path to power.

It is also the case that political democracy is significantly aided by the presence of vital instruments of industrial democracy. Trade unions can serve to balance, at least to some degree, the enormous power of capital in the modern world.

A Structure

As Jack Barbash was fond of saying in his lectures about trade union structure, form should follow function. The form that the labor movement adopts should be one that maximizes the many functions that it must perform. Figure 3 depicts a possible form.

Figure 3 should look at least somewhat familiar to students of labor history. It resembles the "Wheel of Fortune" created soon after the turn of the twentieth century by Father Thomas J. Hagerty to describe the organization of the Industrial Workers of the World (IWW). Like that of the radical Wobbly priest, this too envisions "one big labor alliance" (Foner 1965: 38).

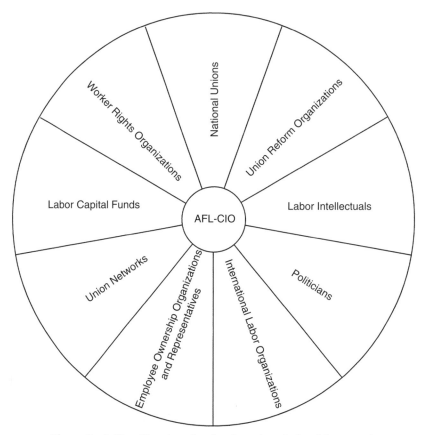

Figure 3. A New Structure for the American Labor Movement.

The AFL-CIO. The AFL-CIO should serve as the hub of a new labor movement. It is the best candidate for coordinating the activities of both the
national unions and the other components of the movement. Its confederal
structure lends itself well to coordinating the activities of independent or
semiindependent organizations. Groups other than national unions would not
be expected to have the same relationship to the AFL-CIO that the unions
do. The details of these relations would be complex, and constitute a matter
that would require skillful and creative negotiation. However, the general
idea of a loose confederation is one that makes sense for a movement comprised of such diverse groups and persons. At both the national and state/local
levels, the AFL-CIO could serve as the umbrella organization.

At the local level, the AFL-CIO should continue to lead the combining
of central labor bodies with other progressive groups such as environmental
and women's rights organizations. Worker rights organizations should be

included. The Mixed Assemblies of the Knights of Labor are an historic model for this. This could be a mechanism for acting powerfully with other organizations in what has been called the "civil society" (Hyman 2001: 176), both with respect to government and the forces of free-market capitalism.

It is to the local level that much of the energy of the AFL-CIO has been directed in recent years. There are examples of extremely effective action by local central labor councils, as by the Atlanta Central Labor Council in causing construction work at the 1996 Olympics to be done by union workers (Acuff 1999). The AFL-CIO's Union Cities program is an attempt to revitalize the local central bodies. There have been numerous efforts to link these bodies to other community groups. "Seven days in June," discussed in Chapter 3, an annual campaign for worker rights that mobilizes support for workers from religious and civic groups as well as from a cross section of unions in local communities, is a harbinger of the structure suggested here (see Voice@Work 2001).

Such a structure makes a great deal of sense for political action. The function of collective bargaining in traditional bargaining units is best left to the national unions and their locals. However, a broad local coalition, or some division of it, could serve as an instrument for multiemployer collective bargaining. It could also facilitate, or even conduct, worker training programs.

Representing the labor movement in the realm of public policy – politics – has long been among the functions of the AFL-CIO (Barbash 1967). Although, since the 1930s it has largely failed to achieve needed changes in national labor laws, it has nevertheless been a strong voice for the Progressive political agenda, both nationally and locally. The AFL-CIO has been a crucial player in the enactment and defense of civil rights laws. It has fought with some success for legislation, such as minimum wage and health and safety laws, that has benefited workers beyond the labor movement. Most recently, in the 2000 elections, it delivered crucial political support to the nearly successful presidential campaign of Democrat Al Gore. Approximately 26 percent of the voters were members of union families (up from 23 percent in 1996), and they voted for Gore over George W. Bush by a margin of 63 percent to 32 percent (Amber 2000). This was facilitated by the United Auto Workers (UAW) having negotiated into their collective-bargaining agreements an election day holiday, which freed their members to engage in political action on that crucial day.

Building on its successes in the 2000 election, the AFL-CIO has set up a political/organizing network to facilitate political action on a national basis. As previously noted in this book, it made use of this network to reach some 6,000 local unions to encourage them to oppose fast-track authority for President Bush on matters of international trade (Bureau of National Affairs 2001c).

Taken together, the national AFL-CIO, the state AFL-CIOs, and the central labor bodies in local communities constitute a powerful political force.

This seems especially encouraging given their recent success in doing what they do best, and what employers cannot match, which is supplying foot soldiers to political campaigns.

The AFL-CIO occupies a crucial position in the effort to leverage the capital power inherent in pension funds into worker and union control of corporate governance. Its Center for Working Capital, which sponsors research and holds conferences, is one vehicle for this. The Capital Stewardship Program, launched in 1997, has encouraged active ownership strategies by unions, and has identified and publicized worker-friendly investments (Silvers, Patterson, and Mason 2001). It has published guidelines to let plan managers know its views on shareholder proposals and conducted surveys to determine whether these guidelines are being followed. The voting records of investment managers are tracked and published (O'Connor 2001).

At the George Meany Center/National Labor College, the college and the Center for Working Capital have joined in an effort to educate fund trustees. The center has set up four panels to provide advice to trustees, establish working groups on particular issues, and provide technical assistance. It has been suggested that it would be useful for the AFL-CIO to set up a center for Economically Targeted Investments (ETIs). This would provide a database and support a national network of experts to assist ETIs (Zanglein 2001). In this and other ways the AFL-CIO can be a focal point for the worker capital movement.

Functioning as the "hub" of the labor movement's organizational wheel is admittedly fraught with difficulties for the AFL-CIO. This requires coordinating the activities of some highly diverse groups. Progressive political groups often take positions that are unpopular with what is sometimes a very conservative rank and file. Time and effort spent on broader issues and in support of policies of other organizations may lead to protests that the federation is being diverted away from its core function of serving the interests of the members of its affiliated unions. Yet, it seems that the federation is in a better position to do this than the individual national unions. So long as national union leaders support its performing this role, it has a chance to be successful.

National Unions. The most important spoke of this organizational wheel consists of the national unions (Steelworkers, Autoworkers, Teamsters, Service Employees, Teachers, etc.). They perform the core functions of a labor movement – organizing, bargaining, administering collective agreements, and providing a variety of services for members.

Legal assistance to workers by unions has traditionally included help in filing workers' and unemployment compensation claims, fighting discrimination, and insuring a safe workplace. It could also have a broader reach, as it does with several European unions, by providing legal aid for problems outside of work such as divorce, bankruptcy, or criminal charges.

Placing the unions in the keystone position is consistent with traditional American Pure and Simple Unionism. Whatever else a labor movement does, it will fail if its heart is weak. Unions constitute the heart of the American labor movement. Unless they are strong, and their natural functions are performed well, there is little hope for the labor movement in this country.

Worker Rights Organizations. Worker rights organizations would be more powerful than they are now if they were more tightly allied with the rest of the labor movement. They act effectively on behalf of the poorest and most oppressed of workers, and in those regions that are most resistant to unionization. Worker rights organizations perform a unique function. Their continuing to do this is clearly in the interests of the labor movement as a whole. They should be viewed by the balance of the labor movement as what they are – effective mechanisms for the pursuit of worker rights and industrial democracy.

For a modest amount of money supporting these organizations the national unions and the AFL-CIO could encourage both extensive preunion activity and effective state and local political action on behalf of workers. As argued by one of the founders of CAFE, Steve Henry, this could increase the probability of the unionization of large numbers of workers. These organizations, such as CAFE, are deserving of the unstinting support of the rest of the labor movement.

Labor Capital Funds. Another unconventional part of the labor movement consists of Labor Capital Funds. While they are just aborning in the United States, they could hold one key to achieving the crucial enabling condition of dampening managerial resistance to unions. They also have potential for improving the public image of labor by helping with industrial development. It is very harmful to the labor movement to be seen as an impediment to prosperity and development. As is the case with support of worker rights organizations, this offers substantial rewards for a relatively small investment. As argued above, the AFL-CIO is an appropriate vehicle for encouraging and coordinating their activities.

Union Networks. A regional network of local unions is a type of organization that does not currently exist in the United States. It could offer advantages similar to those of Labor Capital Funds. Such a network could be similar to Western Europe's TURN. TURN has demonstrated the workability of the coordination of grassroots trade union organizations to encourage regional economic development. Such a network can cut across national union memberships and even national boundaries. Just like Labor Capital Funds, this strategy makes the unions a part of the solution to the problems of prosperity. TURN's emphasis on training is especially useful in that it strikes at a crucial intersection of worker, management, and public interests.

Employee Ownership Organizations and Representatives. Unionized employee-owned firms, ESOPs, and the trustees of employee-owned stock in unionized firms and of labor-management pension plans, constitute another component of a broadly defined American labor movement. To the extent that the policies of corporations are influenced by unionized worker-owners, or on their behalf, this can lead to a moderation of union-adverse policies of these firms. Here, capital power in a particular firm, aggregated into collective power by a union, has the potential to be turned to the general advantage of the labor movement as a whole. This power can be used to ensure the taking into account of worker interests (including job security) by corporate policy makers. It can also encourage the withdrawal of support from antiworker and antiunion organizations and politicians.

International Labor Organizations. International labor organizations must be seen as part of the *American* labor movement. In this globalized world it makes little sense to see international institutions as being outside of the boundaries of a national labor movement. Although it should probably remain chiefly the job of the AFL-CIO to serve as the international voice of the American labor movement (Barbash 1967), the other components (unions, worker rights organizations, Labor Capital Funds, union networks) should also build stronger links to the international labor movement.

Relevant international organizations include the International Confederation of Free Trade Unions (ICFTU), the various International Trade Secretariats (ITSs), and the U.S. Labor Delegation to the International Labor Organization (ILO). One function for these bodies is the coordination of international action against global corporations. Another is support for regulation of these corporations as well as national industries to insure that international labor standards are respected. Yet another is the development of international solidarity among workers – a crucial factor in the building of a truly international labor movement.

Following the example of the ETUC, the American labor movement could begin to build a regional organization competent to act at the level of the North American Free Trade Agreement (NAFTA). As we have seen in Europe, the internationalization of the labor movement may progress best by beginning at the regional level. As unhappy as American unions are with NAFTA, it is probably here to stay. Instead of continuing to actively oppose NAFTA, the American labor movement should try to build upon it. A North American Federation of Labor would be a first step in this direction. AFL-CIO president John Sweeney has shown himself to be something of an advocate of the idea of close coordination with Canadian and Mexican labor leaders. In the interview set out in the Appendix (Sweeney 2001), he tells of his reaction to seeing a newspaper photo of a demonstration of solidarity among the *political* leaders of Canada, Mexico, and the United States. He contacted *labor* leaders in these countries with the suggestion that they should follow this example. In Europe, labor followed the lead of national leaders who unified the European economic and political systems. Perhaps the same thing can happen in North America.

Eventually, it may be possible to develop a European-style Social Dialogue, negotiating for common standards and benefits for North American workers. This could be supported by the threat of directives or rules made by a regional international governmental body. Although this is admittedly very long-term thinking, it is necessary for the American labor movement to plan for the future at the same time that it is surviving in the present.

Politicians. Politicians and political parties are necessary to any successful labor movement. Instead of viewing them as external allies – the traditional approach of American Pure and Simple Unionism – sympathetic politicians should be taken into what John L. Lewis called the "House of Labor." This could be done by means of supporting the current Labor Party. More likely, it could be achieved by building strong and lasting relationships with members of the liberal wing of the Democratic Party, as well as those few Republicans who are progressive in their views. The idea here is to treat these politicians as both being entitled to firm and predictable support from labor, and obligated to broadly support the goals of the labor movement. The so-called "New Democrats" of Bill Clinton are formally organized. Why not have a formally organized Progressive coalition that is at least loosely affiliated with labor and supported by it? Even in conservative South Carolina, there is an active Progressive Network that includes labor. The aim, of course, is to facilitate the enabling condition of having the support of government.

The AFL-CIO Executive Council made a step in this direction at its meeting in the summer of 2001 when it adopted a statement calling for candidates for political office to declare themselves in favor of the right of employees to choose a union. This statement also urges that politicians be encouraged to make public statements, attend rallies, and sponsor public forums in which, among other things, they would urge employers to remain neutral in organizing campaigns (Bureau of National Affairs 2001c). This is a move in the direction of the kind of regularized, established relationship with politicians suggested in this book. Implicit in it is the understanding that labor will support these politicians. This understanding should be made quite clear.

Labor Intellectuals. Labor intellectuals include those denizens of academia, journalists, and writers who have an affinity for the labor movement and are interested in its success. In the academic world, this includes labor educators, and scholars and teachers of industrial relations, human resources, sociology, history, law, political science, and economics. Outside of the universities, writers such as David Moberg, Thomas Geoheagan, and Robert Kuttner come to mind. Within the labor movement, there is a long history of union officers and staff members who think and write broadly and critically about issues involving the labor movement.

The suggestion made here is to bring these supporters of the labor movement more closely into the fold. In past years there have been some rather successful efforts to build bridges to academia. Many of these have been led by intellectuals within the labor movement such as Rudy Oswald, formerly Research Director of the AFL-CIO. Leadership of the Industrial Relations Research Association by Oswald, Lynn Williams, Joyce Miller, and most recently Sheldon Friedman, has been highly useful. Friedman has been instrumental in setting up a network of academics around the Voice@Work campaign of the AFL-CIO, aiming at both research and public-policy advice and support. It is vital that, with the demise of the AFL-CIO's Research Department, which was the natural connection to academia, new structures such as Voice@Work be put in place to systematically support and receive help from the intellectual community.

This writer realizes full well the resistance to intellectuals that has long been part of the traditions of American Pure and Simple Unionism (see Perlman 1949). This has stemmed in part from the traditionally leftist leanings of many academics and others interested in ideas about labor. Surely, with the demise of Communism as a threat to American power abroad and the leadership of American unions at home, this basis for being intellectually averse is no longer present. What does remain is the natural resistance of those in the trenches to taking advice, sometimes imperiously rendered, from those of us who have not earned the right to speak by fighting the good fight as trade unionists. Hopefully we academics will learn to be more humble in the manner in which we give advice and have a proper sense of our limitations. Nevertheless, it is (no doubt predictably) the view of this writer that much can be gained by labor tapping the ideas of those whose job or avocation it is to produce and debate ideas. Producing this book is a statement of this view.

Labor Union Reform Organizations. Finally, there are the intraunion and interunion organizations that are often at odds with those who hold power in the national unions. While it may be too much to expect that these be included in any formal way under the umbrella of the labor movement, it is clear that they do make a contribution to it. Organizations such as the intraunion Teamsters for a Democratic Union (TDU) and the Autoworkers' New Directions should be recognized as valuable gadflies that help unions to be more democratic and better at serving their members. The same thing can be said for the interunion Association for Union Democracy (AUD). Tolerance, or even support, of these organizations by the rest of the labor movement would give continuing proof of the movement's honesty and legitimacy as a credible voice of workers.

It is believed that the fact that some of these groups have been at odds with each other in the past does not mean that they cannot work together now. The need is great, given the weak situation of American labor. Old ideological battles belong to another century. There is really no reason that the American labor movement cannot be comprised of a diverse set of actors who can pursue a number of diverse strategies at the same time.

This book began with the assertion that we are in a time of dramatic change, creating a new environment for the labor movement. As we near the end of this analysis it may be useful to review what that environment looks like and what this means for union strategy.

Strategies that Fit the New Economy

The twenty-first–century American industrial relations system consists of two parts. First, there is the portion that is affected by globalization. Second, there is the part that is essentially, if not entirely, domestic. The future of the American labor movement depends upon its ability to function successfully in both areas.

In the parts of the system that are affected by globalization, capital crosses national boundaries easily and moves the production of goods from where labor is expensive to where it is cheap. According to Lester Thurow, "There is an iron law of wages in a modern global economy. The only wage differentials that can survive in the long run are those justified by the skills that produce higher productivity" (1996: 168).

Under these circumstances it seems that labor's strategic options are extremely limited. However, there are two strategies that seem especially appropriate. These are training and employee ownership. Whatever the global system, a worker's skills provide some employment security, providing that they are the right skills and are at a sufficiently high level. A labor movement that offers workers access to improved skills, whether through craft union-style apprenticeship programs or TURN-style regional training programs, is bound to have some degree of success.

Employee ownership is perhaps the ultimate answer to the problems of global and other forms of competition. It finesses the powerful reality of the supremacy of capital by placing this source of power in the hands of workers. It is the equivalent of the chess strategy of converting a pawn into a more powerful piece by slipping by an opponent's defenses to occupy their home territory. A powerless worker then becomes a member of the powerful royalty. If capital is too powerful to defeat, the logical thing to do is to get some of it.

If the labor movement can become truly international it does have some chance of operating in its traditional manner in a global economy. Demands not only for the barest core rights – prohibition of slave and child labor and discrimination, and freedom of association and collective bargaining – are probably not enough. It is necessary to also insist upon the rights to a living wage and a safe workplace. It is not at all unreasonable for the United States or Europe to deny access to their home markets to producers of goods who fail to meet these standards. This, of course, will not protect the wage levels in these countries to any great degree, but it will at least put trade on a somewhat fairer basis.

American labor should be encouraged by what is going on in Europe. Although some European scholars would disagree (see Hyman 2001), it appears that what is going on in Social Dialogue, and in the efforts toward Europe-wide collective bargaining, may be quite significant. International structures are always slow to develop in the absence of an all-powerful imperial power imposing its will on others. The idea of regional cross-national structures for collective bargaining, broadly defined, is one that has real promise. A North American Federation of Labor, similar to the ETUC, might be a good place to start.

In the part of the American economy that is relatively protected from the pressures of globalization, the situation is quite different. Here the problems are similar to what the American trade union movement has faced over the last century. Vigorously antiunion employers use both the carrot and the stick to convince workers that they are better off without a union. Unionized workers still make more money and have greater guarantees against arbitrary treatment than do nonunionized workers. It is in their objective interest to be unionized. Among government workers the labor movement is still prospering.

It is pretty clear that American labor is responding reasonably well to the challenges of organizing the domestic sector. A new emphasis on organizing, a rediscovery of the power of their people to influence political outcomes, innovations in developing occupational-geographical unionism, and a number of other current strategies have shown themselves to be useful. In the non-globalized sector of the American economy, and in politics, labor would seem to be headed in the right direction.

Unions' effectiveness in the domestic sector is evidenced by their relatively higher degree of success in recent National Labor Relations Board (NLRB) representation elections in industries that appear to be generally less affected by globalization. In 2000 unions won 71.4 percent of elections in finance, insurance, and real estate, 67.1 percent in services, 64.5 percent in retail, 64 percent in health care, 58.8 percent in wholesale, 54.7 percent in construction, and 52.6 percent in transportation, communications, and utilities. This compares to only 33.3 percent in manufacturing (Bureau of National Affairs 2001a).

Recent shifts in public opinion give some ground for hope. A Peter Hart survey conducted in 2001 showed 41 percent of respondents exhibiting positive feelings toward unions, as compared with 35 percent in 1993. Only 24 percent expressed negative feelings, compared to 35 percent in 1993. The proportion with neutral feelings increased from 31 to 35 percent during this period. Among nonmanagerial employees, 50 percent stated that they would either definitely or probably vote for a union, with 43 percent stating that they would definitely or probably vote against a union. Fifty-six percent disapproved of employer antiunion campaigns (Bureau of National Affairs 2001b). When one compares the 50 percent of workers who say that they would vote for a union to the 13.5 percent who are actually union members, it is very apparent that there is a substantial gap between what workers want and what they have.

The chief immediate problem with making anything of the representation gap comes from the labor laws currently prevailing in the United States. Of course, to change this requires government support. A discussion of this issue can provide a concrete example of the importance of meeting this crucial enabling condition. It can also demonstrate both the importance of the problem and the practical steps that could be taken if government support were present.

Changes in Public Policy

As Lynn Williams argues in his introduction to this book, a crucial factor in the revival of the American labor movement is changing the law to make it more friendly to union organizing. The need for this is given new emphasis by a Human Rights Watch report (Human Rights Watch 2000) declaring that the American legal system violates the fundamental human rights of workers to freely associate in unions and engage in collective bargaining.

The situation under American law was described by this writer to the Dunlop Commission in the following terms.

The Fable of the Enigmatic Elections

Once upon a time, in a kingdom between the seas, a wise king named Pepin the Long decided to permit those of his subjects who labored for hire – servants – to decide whether they wished to replace the absolute rule of their masters with a system known as "collective bargaining," whereby the rules of their workplace would be determined jointly between their chosen representatives and their masters. One of King Pepin's counselors proposed the novel idea of having something that he called an "election" in each workplace to decide this. This sounded like a capital idea to the king, because it would allow the servants themselves to make a reasoned choice of what would be best for them. Elections were ordered to be held in five years (the king believing that change should not be too rapid). When they were held, to the king's amazement, none of the workplaces opted for this form of workplace rule. Surprised by this turn of events, King Pepin appointed a royal commission to determine what had occurred. The commission made the following report.

212 The Future of the American Labor Movement

Report of the Royal Commission to His Most Royal Majesty, Pepin the Long. We, your counselors, find that the "election" results have the following causes:

I. The masters universally opposed collective bargaining. As the servants of each master, by long habit, are accustomed to obey and respect the master and desire his approval, they are reluctant to oppose his wishes. Also, because the masters have by long custom and law had the unrestricted authority to impose punishment upon servants, the servants seem to have had the impression that they might be punished for opposing the master's will (we note that masters did sometimes tend to encourage this impression). Furthermore, the masters, who occupy positions of authority in the local communities as well as at work, advised the servants that the "unions" – the groups that formed to engage in collective bargaining – were foreigners to their region, corrupt, anarchistic, and a threat to all that honest people hold sacred. Similar views were expounded by newspapers, teachers, and religious leaders.

II. Upon our announcement that there would be elections five years hence, masters immediately set out to determine the employment-related wishes of their servants by means of "opinion surveys" designed by itinerant magicians, both to give the impression that they cared about servants' desires, and to make changes that would lead the servants to believe that problems had been corrected. Also, they began, with the help of the magicians, to choose only those new employees who were divined to be averse to collective bargaining.

III. Before each election the master made the following announcement. "Servants' choosing collective bargaining would be a useless exercise because it would accomplish nothing. After all, would I not give you what you deserve if I were able to do so? Certainly all that would happen in collective bargaining would be for the 'union' to demand more than I could afford. If I acceded to their demands, I would certainly go out of business and you would lose your jobs. If I did not accede to their demands, they would 'strike' and I would replace any workers who joined in the strike, so then too you would lose your jobs. Of course, I am under no legal obligation to do what the 'union' wants, and so am unlikely to do so."

IV. Before each election the masters, using the same magicians they used for other purposes, indoctrinated their servants by means of magic lantern shows, theatre, and other new-fangled devices, with all the propaganda that their magicians could muster. They called servants together in groups, paying them for their time, requiring attendance, and prohibiting discussion, and indoctrinated them. At the same time, the "unions" were denied knowledge of the identities, let alone addresses or other information about the servants, and were only able to communicate with servants by visiting their hovels. These union "organizers" could do even this only by dark of night, owing to the fact that the servants feared that they would be punished for listening to them. The organizers were, of course, denied any access to the masters' land, given its sacred nature under the laws. Under these conditions, the unions soon ran out of the pepin-

francs necessary to pursue their purposes and were unable to even contest many elections.

   Respectfully and humbly submitted, His Majesty's Commissioners

 Upon receipt of this report, King Pepin the Long addressed the following interrogatory to the Royal Commission: "Given the masters' strong expressed desire for 'democracy' in our political system (an idea that I find particularly reprehensible) why would they oppose it in their workplaces?"

 The Royal Commission made the following answer to King Pepin's interrogatory: The reasons for opposition appear to be of three types. First, there was a rational opposition to collective bargaining that arose from legitimate fears that it would lead to increased costs for services and decreased efficiency. As they compete with other masters in this kingdom and in the Kingdom of Oz (whose king is not as progressive as Your Highness), this could cause them to lose trade. This was reinforced by an understandable resistance on the part of masters to lose control of the workplace, given that they believe that the best possible system is one that they control. Second, masters advised their overseers that a victory for collective bargaining would indicate that they were bad overseers. Naturally, therefore, they would be fired and banished forever from the ranks of overseers if such an event occurred. For some reason this led the overseers to stop at nothing to defeat collective bargaining. Third, masters tended to view collective bargaining as an attack upon their status and authority. Given the nature of the human beast (as divined by your necromancer the great Alfred Wallace), this brought forth an inclination on the part of masters to suppress this action. They, therefore, would spare no expense, and stop at nothing, to defeat this evil known as collective bargaining. They succeeded in this.

             The End

 There are several morals to this story. First, although mythical, it is probably closer to our reality than is the view that a representation election is somehow similar to a political election in which voters choose among candidates for office in a democratic political system. Second, it is obviously inconceivable that unions could be very successful under such a system. If, therefore, we want collective bargaining to be more widespread, we must change the system fundamentally (Wheeler 1994b).

 What makes this situation particularly distressing is that, as Human Rights Watch concluded, this is a matter of fundamental human rights being denied. If workers' rights to free association and collective bargaining are truly given the weight that such rights deserve, it is relatively easy to justify a number of changes in American law. This is because in the balancing of rights and interests, moral rights such as these prevail over mere economic interests (Werhane 1985).

 In the view of this writer, the following changes should be made in American labor law: (1) employers should be required, upon demand, to provide bona fide union representatives with lists of names, addresses, and telephone numbers of all employees; (2) bona fide union organizers should be provided with access to employer premises, with proper protections against interference with the conduct of the business; (3) employer actions that are *in part* illegally motivated should be considered to be unfair labor practices; (4) relatively mild criminal penalties should be imposed upon individual managers who egregiously violate the provisions of the NLRA; (5) employer "predictions" of dire consequences of unionization should be treated as what they are – threats against workers; (6) the exclusion of "supervisors" from protection under the NLRA should be repealed; (7) the requirement for an employer to bargain in good faith should be more strictly interpreted; (8) where collective bargaining negotiations have reached an impasse, binding arbitration should be available at the request of either party; (9) permanent replacement of strikers should be prohibited as an unfair labor practice; (10) the use of antiunion labor-management consultants and attorneys to plan an antiunion campaign should be proof of antiunion animus when it is being determined whether the employer acted with improper motivation; (11) employer communications to employees should be strictly monitored to insure that no threats or promises of benefits are present; and (12) union organizers should be given the same access to employees that the employer has, including the right to make captive audience speeches, use company bulletin boards, and use company publications.

The adoption of these changes in the law would go a long way toward leveling the playing field between labor and management. If these rules were put in place, it would be possible to determine the free and uncoerced choice of employees on the question of unionization. Anything less leaves the fundamental human rights to associate in unions and bargain collectively absent from the American industrial relations system.

A FINAL WORD

What will be the response of employers and government to a renewed labor movement? This depends upon what form it takes. To the degree that the changes in approach are able to finesse the traditional grounds of managerial resistance to unions, the important enabling condition of holding their opposition within tolerable bounds has some chance of being met. Employee ownership, assistance to regional economic development, and an emphasis on training are all strategies that have this potential. They also could be helpful in building a public image for labor that builds support from government.

Labor organizations have been around since the dawn of human history. They will always be with us, as Terence Powderly once said. Contrary to conventional wisdom in labor history, unions did not start with the industrial revolution (see Leeson 1979), and will not end when it ends. This conclusion is given strong support by the penetrating analysis of John Kelly (1998), who makes a strong case on theoretical and historical grounds for a resurgence of the labor movement in capitalist societies. As Robert Hoxie (1921) said, "Unionism develops by the trial method – it is a process of adaptation to a developing environment" (p. 99). The labor movement is capable of reinventing itself, as it has over many centuries. It only needs to adopt the strategies and forms that facilitate and channel the natural energy and power that flow from the needs of workers. This book suggests some ways that this might happen.

It is always difficult to attempt new approaches to well-entrenched problems. The American labor movement has over two centuries of history. It has survived wars, depressions, and repressions. It has sometimes been strong and often weak. It is an extremely complex phenomenon that defies orderly analysis. It is also a body of ideas, organizations, and persons that is nearly impossible to approach without being influenced by the observer's own biases and hopes. All one can do is to try to be both thorough and objective.

As the ancient Latin paradox goes, *Nova ex veritas* (the new must be born out of the old). Therefore, the principal approach taken here for predicting the future has been to examine the strategies that have been attempted in the past, and reach conclusions as to how well they have worked. History provides multiple natural laboratories and conditions for observing the phenomenon of unionization and the circumstances under which it flourishes or fails. The assumption is that the pragmatic American labor movement will move in the directions that are most fruitful. Hopefully, this attempt at prediction will turn out to be of some use to those who continue the struggle for prosperity and dignity for those who produce the goods and services for society.

Appendix

Interview with John J. Sweeney, President, AFL-CIO
June 7, 2001
Washington, DC

Question: What is the current state of the labor movement in the United States, how did we get there, and what are the strategies that will work best in the future?

Answer: We're changing. In 1994 we didn't do too well in the Congressional elections. Newt Gingrich scared the hell out of us. The union leadership started talking about how to change. This led to my election. I don't blame the past leadership. I had a good record at the SEIU [Service Employees International Union] of growth from organizing activities. This wasn't about Lane Kirkland or Tom Donahue. They were great leaders who spent a lifetime in the labor movement. But we had to try new approaches, to put resources into organizing, try new methods, and take risks.

We wanted to arrest the decline, not so much in numbers, but we wanted to be more effective politically. We needed to reach out to our grass roots. Polling and focus groups showed that our members wanted to be more involved. They did not want a group in Washington to dominate. They wanted to select candidates and hold them accountable.

In 1996 we picked up House [of Representatives] seats. In 1998 we did the same. 2000 was our best year in terms of union turnout, but not enough to win the House, Senate, or White House, although we do think that Al Gore won. We did improve the perception of the labor movement as to how our members and the public felt. We started to see change in political activism and grassroots involvement.

We have become more focused on organizing. Unions have traditionally focused on service and bargaining. They tried to preserve the benefits that they had achieved in the past – not focused enough on organizing. A culture of organizing has developed. This required the national unions to educate their members. We needed to sensitize labor union people to the importance of organizing and politics. Unions are doing this. We are increasing the use of volunteer organizers. We have increased organizer training at the Federation's Organizing Institute. Financial support has grown. There are more multiunion campaigns. We have developed strategies to use in assessing campaigns and in doing them. We have to organize 1 million workers a year to hold our own as a percentage of the workforce. We are now close to 500,000 new members per year.

We have a number of new programs. These include corporate affairs programs and programs like Union Summer. Union Summer involves young people who want to be active in the labor movement in a four-week summer internship. They are not necessarily going to stay in union careers, but they get to know what unions are doing.

We have restarted our retiree program through the Alliance for Retired Americans. This addresses a potential source of strength. Workers are contacted before they retire so they can stay active after retirement. We hope to capture their enthusiasm and pride in the labor movement. We are engaging in advocacy with respect to prescription drugs and other issues of interest to retirees.

Other areas of intense focus are important on the globalization issue and its effects on manufacturing jobs in the steel industry and other industries. Labor has a very good history of international involvement. Meany and Kirkland were involved in international issues long before "globalization" was talked about.

New forms of work have an impact on workers in the United States as well as around the world. Trade is important, but our focus is on what are the rules that will govern it. How do we raise the rights of workers and achieve core labor standards for workers everywhere? The essence of our fight is to promote the Declaration of Fundamental Principles on Rights at Work – the ILO [International Labor Organization] standards that include the rights to collective bargaining, not to be discriminated against, to reject child labor, and to refuse forced labor. Our aim is not to impose our standards on other countries but to make sure that human beings are treated as having rights, and have the opportunity to join unions if they desire to.

We try to impress on government, whoever is in power, and on business leaders, that they must recognize basic rights of workers in our own country and in other countries. Worker rights have never been more threatened than they are under the present administration [of President Bush]. They moved early on ergonomics to repeal standards. This is a basic issue for all workers. Ergonomics injuries are the fastest-growing group of injuries in the United States. Unions can protect union members, but unorganized workers, for example, poultry workers in the South, have no one to protect them.

I'm really optimistic that we're going to reverse the trend in power and affect policy directions in the future.

Question: What about worker ownership as a strategy?

Answer: We are guided by the affiliates on this. There is a mixed reaction at present. On the one hand there is the United Airlines experience. On the other hand, steel has been one of the more active industries in this. It is presently going through bankruptcies, with maybe twelve companies on the verge of bankruptcy.

We do have a capital strategy with pension monies. Bill Patterson, who works under Ron Blackwell, is working on this to use the power of investments. There are campaigns in building and construction, by the United Food and Commercial Workers, and by the Bakery, Confectionery, Tobacco and Grain Millers, where they are mobilizing the power of labor's capital.

Question: What is being done to organize satisfied workers – the "winners" in the global economy?

Answer: The CWA has some experience in dealing with very satisfied workers in high-tech and other technology areas. But these gains haven't kept up with the loss of jobs. SEIU and UNITE [Union of Needletrades, Industrial and Textile Employees] have organized low-wage workers, but are also organizing nurses and professionals in health care. Even so-called winners still want and need a voice on the job.

The UAW and AFT have had real successes with college and university folks. The AFT has organized at about twelve colleges and universities, so there have been some successes among these workers. Several years ago I made a speech to the American Medical Association. I told them that I was happy to talk to the largest union in America. They all laughed. They are no longer laughing. They have come to realize that they are more like employees of hospitals. We are at the early stages of organizing doctors as we were with teachers a few years ago.

Our polling shows that with people who are highly unorganized there is a realization that they have to come together to satisfy their work life grievances. Not to say that they are necessarily ready for unionization, but high-tech workers are expressing their frustrations and grievances on the Internet. They are very unhappy. They like their independence, but they have no grievance machinery, no retirement, and no provision for training for upgrading. The challenge for the labor movement is how to reach these workers and convince them that true collective bargaining is able to address their issues.

Employer opposition is one of the most serious issues. This is the force behind global issues and having a level playing field in organizing and collective bargaining. This relates to [government] budget and tax issues as well as privatization of social security. In the case of social security, it's really the workers' money and it's the most successful social program in the history of the country.

There is a lack of understanding of what unions can do in terms of stabilization of industries, in training and apprenticeship programs, and of their importance as consumers. As Henry Ford said, if the people producing the cars can't buy them we're in trouble.

We are going to the young people with issues like the living wage and the Harvard sit-ins. There is an attitude, a spirit, that we see developing across the country, whether the issue is the living wage or child labor. Not that these young people will spend a lifetime in unions. It's the same thing as with Vista or the Peace Corps. [They learn] respect for human rights – that people should get a living wage to support themselves and their families.

Question: In Europe, some interesting things are happening with the Social Dialogue. They are developing something like collective bargaining regionally. Should there be a North American Federation of Labor as there is a European Trade Union Congress?

Answer: I saw a newspaper photo of George Bush, Vicente Fox [Mexico], and the Canadian Prime Minister clasping hands. I called Mexican and Canadian labor federation leaders and suggested that unions should do the same thing. We do work through the International Trade Secretariats. We have a slowly developing dialogue with unions in Europe. The European Union provides resources to help transatlantic dialogues among businesses, but not for labor.

On the pension issue Bill Patterson [AFL-CIO] has been working through the ICFTU [International Confederation of Free Trade Unions] pension committee to get together major players – unions that are highly involved in pension funds. This includes the Europeans, Japanese, Australians, and South Africans, as well as the Canadians.

We're also seeing increasing cooperation and collaboration among unions in some industries in the United States and Europe. There is a tremendous amount of potential for this work.

References

Foreword

Bernstein, Irving. 1960. *The Lean Years*. Baltimore: Penguin Books.

Wheeler, Hoyt N. 1999. "Should American Labor Turn to TURN?" *WorkingUSA* March/April: 77–87.

Chapter 1 – A Future for the American Labor Movement?

AFL-CIO. 1994. *The New American Workplace: A Labor Perspective*. AFL-CIO Committee on the Evolution of Work.

Appelbaum, Eileen, and Rosemary Batt. 1994. *The New American Workplace*. Ithaca, NY: ILR Press.

Barbash, Jack. 1984. *The Elements of Industrial Relations*. Madison: University of Wisconsin Press.

Bonior, David. 1997. "Unions in the Twenty-First Century." *Challenge* 40, 5: 77–94.

Broder, David. 2000. "Unions changing with times, adding to their rolls." *The State* (September 4): A 17.

Bronfenbrenner, Kate, and Tom Juravich. 1997. "It Takes More Than House Calls: Organizing to Win with a Comprehensive Union-Building Strategy." In *Organizing to Win*, Kate Bronfenbrenner, Sheldon Friedmin, Richard W. Hurd, Rudolph A. Oswald, and Ronald L. Seeber, eds., 19–36. Ithaca, NY: ILR Press.

Bureau of Labor Statistics. 2001. "Union Members Summary." http://stats.bls.gov/newsrel.htm: 1.

Bureau of National Affairs.

2000a. "Economic Expansion Leaving Behind Working Poor, Conference Board Finds." *Labor Relations Week* 14, 7: 768.

2000b. "Private Industry Compensation Costs Averaged $19.85 Per Hour, BLS Reports." *Labor Relations Week* 14, 7: 767.

2000c. "Number of Union Members Rose Slightly in 1999, but Percentage Remained Constant." *Labor Relations Week* 18, 3: 64.

2000d. "Human Rights Watch Reports Increasing Violations of Workers' Associational Rights." *Human Resources Report* 18, 35: 977.

2000e. "Win Rate in NLRB Elections Increased in First Half of 2000." *Labor Relations Week* 14, 47: 1353.

2001a. "Union Members Decline to 16.3 Million As Share of Employed Slips to 13.5 Percent." *Labor Relations Week* 15, 4: 117.

2001b. "Number of Elections Down in 2000, While Unions' Win Rate Edged Up." *Labor Relations Week* 15, 25: 760.

Cappelli, Peter, and Laurie Bassi, Harry Katz, David Knoke, Paul Osterman, and Michael Unseem. 1997. *Change at Work.* New York: Oxford University.

Commission on the Future of Labor-Management Relations. 1994. *Fact-Finding Report.* Washington: U. S. Department of Labor, U. S. Department of Commerce.

Commons, John R. 1968. *Legal Foundations of Capitalism.* Madison: University of Wisconsin Press.

Edwards, Richard. 1986. "Unions in Crisis and Beyond: Introduction." In *Unions in Crisis and Beyond*, Richard Edwards, Paolo Garonna, and Franz Todtling, eds., 1–13. Dover, MA: Auburn House Publishing Company.

Edwards, Richard, and Michael Podgursky. 1986. "The Unraveling Accord: American Unions in Crisis." In *Unions in Crisis and Beyond: Perspectives from Six Countries*, Richard Edwards, Paolo Garonna, and Franz Todtling, eds., 14–60. Dover, MA: Auburn House Publishing Company.

Ely, Richard T. 1905 (originally published 1886). *The Labor Movement in America.* New York: Macmillan Company.

Freeman, Richard B. 1988. "Contraction and Expansion: The Divergence of Private and Public Sector Unionism in the United States." *Journal of Economic Perspectives* 2 (Spring): 63–88.

Geoghegan, Thomas. 1991. *Which Side Are You On? Trying to Be for Labor When It's Flat on Its Back.* New York: Farrar, Straus & Giroux.

1994. "West of Eden." *The New Republic* (May 23): 30–1.

Goldfield, Michael. 1987. *The Decline of Organized Labor in the United States.* Chicago: University of Chicago Press.

Gompers, Samuel. 1919. *Labor and the Common Welfare.* New York: Dutton.

Gould, William B. 1993. *Agenda for Reform: The Future of Employment Relationships and the Law.* Cambridge, MA: MIT Press.

Hirsch, Barry T. 1991. *Labor Unions and the Economic Performance of Firms.* Kalamazoo, MI: W. E. Upjohn Institute.

Hoxie, Robert. 1921. *Trade Unionism in the United States.* New York: D. Appleton and Co.

Hyman, Richard. 1996. "Changing union identities in Europe." In *The Challenges to Trade Unions in Europe: Innovation or Adaptation*, Peter Leisink, Jim Van Leemput, and Jacques Vilrokx, eds., 53–73. Cheltenham, U.K.: Edward Elgar.

2001. *Understanding European Trade Unionism.* London: Sage Publications.

Kaufman, Bruce. 2000, "The Case for the Company Union." *Labor History* 41, 3: 321–50.

Kaufman, Bruce, and Daphne Gottlieb Taras. 1999. *Nonunion Employee Representation.* Armonk, NY: M. E. Sharpe.

Kelly, John. 1998. *Rethinking Industrial Relations.* London: Routledge.

Klaas, Brian S., and Joseph C. Ullman. 1995. "Sticky Wages Revisited: Organizational Responses to Declining Market Wage." *Academy of Management Review* 20: 271–310.

Leone, Richard C. 1993. "Foreword." In *Rights at Work: Employment Relations in the Post-Union Era*, Richard Edwards, ed., i–vii. Washington: Brookings Institution.

Marx, Karl, and Friedrich Engels. 1959 (1848). "Manifesto of the Communist Party." In *Marx and Engels: Basic Writings on Politics and Philosophy*, Lewis S. Feuer, ed. Garden City, NY: Anchor Books.

Masters, Marick F. 1997. *Unions at the Crossroads*. Westport, CT: Quorum Books.

McClendon, John A., Hoyt N. Wheeler, and Roger D. Weikle. 1998. "The Individual Decision to Unionize." *Labor Studies Journal* 23, 3 (Fall): 34–54.

Midgley, Mary. 1978. *Beast and Man*. Ithaca, NY: Cornell University Press.

Moberg, David. 1999. "The U. S. Labor Movement Faces the Twenty-First Century." In *Which Direction for Organized Labor?* Bruce Nissen, ed., 21–33. Detroit: Wayne State University Press.

Montgomery, David. 1980. "To Study the People: The American Working Class." *Labor History* 21, 4 (Fall): 485–512.

——— 1987. *The Fall of the House of Labor: The Workplace, the State, and American Labor Activism, 1865–1925*. Cambridge: Cambridge University Press.

Osterman, Paul. 1994. "How Common is Workplace Transformation and Who Adopts It?" *Industrial and Labor Relations Review* 47, 2 (January): 173–88.

Perlman, Selig. 1949 (originally published in 1928). *A Theory of the Labor Movement*. New York: Augustus M. Kelley.

Poole, Michael. 1981. *Theories of Trade Unionism: A Sociology of Industrial Relations*. London: Routledge and Kegan Paul.

Reich, Robert. 2000. "The Great Divide." *The American Prospect* May 8: 56.

Service Employees International Union. Undated. *Directions for a 21st Century Union*. SEIU Committee on the Future.

Shostak, Arthur B. 1991. *Robust Unionism: Innovations in the Labor Movement*. Ithaca, NY: ILR Press.

——— 1994. "Tomorrow's Work, Workers and Unions." *Dialogues* 2, 1: 3–4.

Swoboda, Frank. 1997. "A Matter of Organizations: Labor Confronts Need to Boost Numbers." *Washington Post* (September 8): D9.

Thomas, Maurice. 2000. "Laboring for Attention." *The State* (September 3): G1, G5.

Thurow, Lester C. 1996. *The Future of Capitalism*. New York: Penguin Books.

Troy, Leo. 1990. "Is the U.S. Unique in the Decline of Private Sector Unionism?" *Journal of Labor Research* XI, 2 (Spring): 111–43.

——— 1999. *Beyond Unions and Collective Bargaining*. Armonk, NY: M. E. Sharpe.

Troy, Leo, and Neil Sheflin. 1985. *Union Sourcebook: Membership, Structure, Finance Directory*. 1st ed. West Orange, NJ: Industrial Relations Data and Information Services.

Webb, Sidney, and Beatrice Webb. 1911. *Industrial Democracy*. London: Longmans Green & Co.

Weikle, Roger D., Hoyt N. Wheeler, and John A. McClendon. 1998. "A Comparative Case Study of Union Organizing Success and Failure: Implications for Practical Strategy." In *Organizing to Win*, Kate Bronfenbrenner, Sheldon Friedman, Richard W. Hurd, Rudolph A. Oswald, and Ronald L. Seeber, eds., 197–212. Ithaca, NY: ILR Press.

Wheeler, Hoyt N. 1985. *Industrial Conflict: An Integrative Theory*. Columbia: University of South Carolina Press.

Wheeler, Hoyt N., and John A. McClendon. 1991. "The Individual Decision to Unionize." In *The State of the Unions*, George Strauss, Daniel G. Gallagher, and Jack Fiorito, eds., 47–83. Madison, WI: Industrial Relations Research Association.

Wheeler, Hoyt N., John A. McClendon, and Roger D. Weikle. 1994. "Toward a Test of Wheeler's 'Integrative Theory' in Six Union Election Cases." *Relations Industrielles/Industrial Relations* 49, 3: 465–82.

Wilson Center for Public Research. 1992. *Workers' View of the Value of Unions.*

Yokich, Stephen P. 1998. "Labor Day Message." United Auto Workers, September 3.

Statutes

National Labor Relations Act, Sec. 8 (a) (2).

Law Cases

M. B. Sturgis Inc. 331 NLRB No. 173, August 25, 2000.

Chapter 2 – Industrial Relations in a Time of Change

Adam, E. E., Jr. 1991. "Quality Circle Performance." *Journal of Management* 17, 1: 25–39.

AFL-CIO. 1994. *The New American Workplace: A Labor Perspective.* Washington: AFL-CIO.

Ahlburg, Dennis A. 1993. "The Census Bureau's New Projections for the US Population." *Population and Development Review* 19, 1 (March 1993): 159–74.

Appelbaum, Eileen, and Rosemary Batt. 1994. *The New American Workplace.* Ithaca, NY: ILR Press.

Arthur, Jeffrey B., and James B. Dworkin. 1991. "Current Topics in Industrial and Labor Relations Research and Practice." *Journal of Management* 17, 3: 515–51.

Bettenhausen, Kenneth L. 1991. "Five Years of Groups Research: What We Have Learned and What Needs to Be Addressed." *Journal of Management* 17, 2: 345–81.

Boyett, Joseph H., and Henry P. Conn. 1991. *Workplace 2000.* New York: Plume.

Bureau of Labor Statistics. 2000. "Employment Relations." http://stats.bls.gov/news.release.

Bureau of National Affairs. 1993. "Downsizing Motives, Long-term Effects Could Change Face of American Labor." *Labor Relations Week* (October 27): 1025–6.

1999. "Employment in the 21st Century: Technology, Outsourcing, Contingent Work." *Human Resources Report* 17, 48: 1321–3.

2000a. "Private Industry Compensation Costs Averaged $19.85 per Hour, BLS Reports." *Labor Relations Week* 14, 27: 767–8.

2000b. "More Families Had at Least One Member Working In 1999 Than in 1998, BLS Says." *Labor Relations Week* 14, 27: 768.

2000c. "Economic Expansion Leaving Behind Working Poor, Conference Board Finds." *Labor Relations Week* 14, 27: 768.

2000d. "Contingent Workers Have Fewer Benefits, Less Coverage Under Labor Laws, GAO Finds." *Labor Relations Week* 18, 30: 826.

Cappelli, Peter, and David Neumark. 2001. "Do 'high-performance' work practices improve establishment-level outcomes?" *Industrial and Labor Relations Review* 54, 4 (July): 737–75.

Cappelli, Peter, Lauri Bassi, Harry Katz, David Knoke, Paul Osterman, and Michael Unseem. 1997. *Change at Work.* New York: Oxford University Press.

Cascio, Wayne F. 1993. "Downsizing: What do we know? What have we learned?" *Academy of Management Executive* 7, 1: 95–104.

Commission on the Future of Labor-Management Relations. 1994. *Fact Finding Report.* Washington: U.S. Department of Labor, U.S. Department of Commerce.

Cooke, P. 1993. "The experiences of German engineering firms in applying lean production methods." In *Lean Production and Beyond: Labour aspects of a new production concept,* 77–93. Geneva, Switzerland: International Institute for Labour Studies.

Cooke, William N. 1994. "Employee Participation Programs, Group-Based Incentives, and Company Performance: A Union-Nonunion Comparison." *Industrial and Labor Relations Review* 47 (July 1994): 594–609.

Cordery, John L., Walter S. Mueller, and Leigh M. Smith. 1991. "Attitudinal and Behavioral Effects of Autonomous Group Working: A Longitudinal Field Study." *Academy of Management Journal* 34, 2: 464–76.

Cotton, John L. 1993. *Employee Involvement: Methods for Improving Performance and Work Attitudes.* Newbury Park, CA: SAGE Publications, Inc.

Craver, Charles B. 1993. *Can Unions Survive? The Rejuvenation of the American Labor Movement.* New York: New York University Press.

Fisher, C. D., L. F. Schoenfeldt, and J. B. Shaw. 1991. *Human Resource Management.* New York: Houghton-Mifflin Company.

Friedman, Thomas L. 2000. *The Lexus and the Olive Tree.* Updated and expanded edition. New York: Anchor Books.

General Accounting Office. 2000. *Contingent Workers: Incomes and Benefits Lag Behind Those of Rest of Workforce.* Washington, DC: GAO.

Godard, John. 2001. "High performance *and* the transformation of work? The implications of alternative work practices for the experience and outcomes of work." *Industrial and Labor Relations Review* 54, 4 (July): 796–805.

Griffin, Ricky W. 1988. "Consequences of Quality Circles in an Industrial Setting: A Longitudinal Assessment." *Academy of Management Journal* 31, 2: 338–58.

Herzenberg, Stephen A., John A. Alic, and Howard Wial. 1998. *New Rules for a New Economy.* Ithaca, NY: Cornell University Press.

Hill, Stephen. 1991. "Why Quality Circles Failed but Total Quality Management Might Succeed." *British Journal of Industrial Relations* 29, 4: 541–68.

Johnston, William B. 1987. *Workforce 2000.* Indianapolis, IN: Hudson Institute.

Jorgensen, Helene, and Hans Riemer. 2000. "Permatemps." *The American Prospect* (August 14): 38–41.

Klaas, Brian S., and Joseph C. Ullman. 1995. "Sticky Wages Revisited: Organizational Responses to Declining Market Wage." *Academy of Management Review* 20: 281–310.

Kochan, Thomas A., Harry C. Katz, and Robert B. McKersie. 1986. *The Transformation of American Industrial Relations.* New York: Basic Books, Inc.

Lawler, Edward E., III. 1992. *The Ultimate Advantage: Creating the High-Involvement Organization*. San Francisco: Jossey-Bass Publishers.

Leonard, Jonathan S. 1989. "The Changing Face of Employees and Employment Regulation." *California Management Review* 31, 2 (Winter): 29–38.

Masters, Marick F. 1997. *Unions at the Crossroads*. Westport, CT: Quorum Books.

Mishel, Lawrence, and Paula Voos. 1992. *Unions and Economic Competitiveness*. Armonk, NY: M. E. Sharpe.

Mishel, Lawrence, Jared Bernstein, and John Schmitt. 1999. *The State of Working America 1998–99*. An Economic Policy Institute Book. Ithaca, NY: ILR Press.

Naisbitt, John, and Patricia Aburdene. 1990. *Megatrends 2000*. New York: Avon Books.

Osterman, Paul. 1994. "How Common is Workplace Transformation and Who Adopts It?" *Industrial and Labor Relations Review* 47, 2 (January): 173–88.

Rehder, Robert R. 1992. "Building Cars as if People Mattered: The Japanese Lean System vs. Volvo's Uddevalla System." *Columbia Journal of World Business* (Summer 1992): 56–70.

Ross, Peter, Greg J. Bamber, and Gillian Whitehouse. 1998. "Appendix Employment, economics and industrial relations: Comparative statistics." In *International and Comparative Employment Relations*. 3rd ed. Greg J. Bamber and Russell Lansbury, eds., 328–74. St. Leonards, Australia: Allen & Unwin.

Sengenberger, Werner. 1993. "Lean production – The way of working and producing in the future?" In *Lean Production and Beyond: Labour aspects of a new production concept*, 1–22. Geneva, Switzerland: International Institute for Labour Studies.

Shimada, Haruo. 1993. "Japanese management of auto production in the United States: An overview of 'Humanware Technology.'" In *Lean Production and Beyond: Labour aspects of a new production concept*, 23–42. Geneva, Switzerland: International Institute for Labour Studies.

Steel, Robert P., and Russell F. Lloyd. 1988. "Cognitive, Affective, and Behavioral Outcomes of Participation in Quality Circles: Conceptual and Empirical Findings." *Journal of Applied Behavioral Science* 24, 1: 1–17.

Thurow, Lester C. 1996. *The Future of Capitalism*. New York: Penguin Books.

Trist, Eric L., and K. W. Bamforth. 1951. "Some social and psychological consequences of the long wall method of goal setting." *Human Relations* 4: 3–38.

Turner, Lowell. 1991. *Democracy at Work: Changing World Markets and the Future of Labor Unions*. Ithaca, NY: Cornell University Press.

U.S. Department of Labor. 2000. *United States of America Country Labor Profile*. Washington, DC: Bureau of International Labor Affairs.

Unterweger, Peter. 1993. "Lean production: Myth and reality." In *Lean Production and Beyond: Labour aspects of a new production concept*, 51–69. Geneva, Switzerland: International Institute for Labour Studies.

Watson, Mary R. 1993. "Evaluation of Alternative Approaches to Work Force Governance." Paper presented at Southern Management Association Meeting, November 1993.

Wickens, Peter D. 1993. "Lean, people centred, mass production." In *Lean Production and Beyond: Labour aspects of a new production concept*, 43–50. Geneva, Switzerland: International Institute for Labour Studies.

Womack, James P., D. T. Jones and D. Roos. 1990. *The Machine That Changed the World*. New York: Rawson.

Chapter 3 – A Survey of American Union Strategies

Academe. 2000. "Labor Board Gives Green Light to Academic Organizing." July–August: 9.

AFL-CIO. 1985. *The Changing Situation of Workers and Their Unions*. AFL-CIO Executive Council.

Association for Union Democracy. 1994. "How to Organize for Women's Issues." *Union Democracy Review*, 98 (May): 8.

Barbash, Jack. 1984. *The Elements of Industrial Relations*. Madison: University of Wisconsin Press.

Belous, Richard S. 1987. "The Union Label." *Association Management* 39, 8 (August): 39–40, 47–51.

Bernstein, Aaron. 1987. "Move Over Boone, Carl, and Irv – Here Comes Labor." *Business Week*, 3030 (December 19): 124–5.

Bradford, Hazel. 1990. "Toning Up Union Muscles." *ENR* 224, 17 (April 26): 36–40.

Broder, David. 2000. "Unions changing with times, adding to their rolls." *The State* (September 4): A 17.

Bureau of Labor Statistics. 2000. "Major Work Stoppages, 1999." *Collective Bargaining Agreements Work Stoppages Summary*. http://stats.bls.gov/news.release/wkstp.nr0.htm.

Bureau of National Affairs. 1993. "Downsizing motives, long-term effects could change face of American labor." *Labor Relations Week* October 27: 1025–9.

2000a. "AFL-CIO's Voice@Work Campaign Is Part Of Long-Term Effort to Change Relationships." *Labor Relations Week* 14, 25: 711.

2000b. "Executive Council Oks Four-Point Plan to Organize 1 Million Members a Year." *Labor Relations Week* 14, 31: 861.

2000c. "CWA Convention Speakers Put Priority On Organizing High-Tech, Contingent Workers." *Labor Relations Week* 14, 35: 993.

2000d. "Human Rights Watch Reports Increasing Violations of Workers' Associational Rights." *Human Resources Report* 18, 35: 977.

2001a. "Federation Launches Advocacy Group To Lobby on Issues of Importance to Seniors." *Labor Relations Week* 15, 23: 699–700.

2001b. "Federation Focuses on Program to Link Politics to Organizing Efforts." *Labor Relations Week* 15, 32: 972–3.

Bynum, Peter. 1992. "Use Media to Communicate." In *The Future of Labor*, 16. New York: Labor Research Association.

Carre, Francoise, Marianne A. Ferber, Lonnie Golden, and Stephen E. Herzenberg. "Nonstandard Work: The Nature and Challenges of Changing Employment Arrangements." *Perspectives on Work* 4, 2: 52–5.

Chase, Bob. 1997. "Remarks Before the National Press Club." February 5.

Cobble, Dorothy Sue. 1991. *Dishing it Out: Waitresses and their Unions in the Twentieth Century*. Urbana: University of Illinois Press.

Craft, James A. 1990. "The Community as a Source of Union Power." *Journal of Labor Research* XI, 2 (Spring): 145–60.

Craver, Charles B. 1993. *Can Unions Survive? The Rejuvenation of the American Labor Movement.* New York: New York University Press.

Dinnocenzo, Debra A. 1989. "Labor/Management Cooperation." *Training and Development Journal* 43, 5 (May): 34–40.

Edwards, Richard, and Michael Podgursky. 1986. "The Unraveling Accord: American Unions in Crisis." In *Unions in Crisis and Beyond: Perspectives from Six Countries*, Richard Edwards, Paolo Garonna, and Franz Todtling, eds., 14–60. Dover, MA: Auburn House Publishing Company.

Edwards, Richard, Paolo Garonna, and Franz Todtling, eds. 1986. *Unions in Crisis and Beyond: Perspectives from Six Countries.* Dover, MA: Auburn House Publishing Company.

Estey, Marten. 1981. *The Unions*, 3rd ed. New York: Harcourt Brace Jovanovich.

Feingold, Danny. 1998. "Putting Faith in Labor." *Los Angeles Times* August 28, 1998: E1, E8.

Fiorito, Jack. 1987. "Political Instrumentality Perceptions and Desires for Union Representation." *Journal of Labor Research* VIII, 3 (Summer): 271–89.

Frankel, Carl B. 1993. *United Steelworkers of America New Directions Bargaining in The Basic Steel Industry.* Pittsburgh, PA: USWA.

Friedman, Raymond A. 1996. "Defining the Scope and Logic of Minority and Female Network Groups: Can Separation Enhance Integration?" In *Research in Personnel and Human Resources Management*, Gerald Ferris, ed., 307–49. London: JAI Press.

Friedman, Raymond A. 1999. "Employee Network Groups: Self-Help Strategy for Women and Minorities." *Performance Improvement Quarterly* 12, 1: 148–63.

Friedman, Raymond A., and Donna Carter. 1993. *African American Network Groups: Their Impact and Effectiveness.* Cambridge, MA: The Executive Leadership Council and Raymond A. Friedman.

Friedman, Raymond A., and Kellina M. Craig. 2000. "Predicting Activism in Minority Employee Network Groups: Frustration, Calculation, or Solidarity?" (unpublished manuscript).

Friedman, Ray, Melinda Kane, and Daniel B. Cornfield. 1998. "Social Support and Career Optimism: Examining the Effectiveness of Network Groups Among Black Managers." *Human Relations* 51, 9: 1155–77.

Goldberg, Arthur J. 1959. "A Trade Union Point of View." In *Labor in a Free Society*, Michael Harrington and Paul Jacobs, eds., 110–11. Berkeley: University of California Press.

Goldfield, Michael. 1987. *The Decline of Organized Labor in the United States.* Chicago: University of Chicago Press.

Goodman, John F. 1992. "A Union Trains for the Future." *Training and Development* 46, 10 (October): 23–9.

Gould, William B. 1993. *Agenda for Reform: The Future of Employment Relationships and the Law.* Cambridge, MA: MIT Press.

Heckscher, Charles C. 1988. *The New Unionism: Employee Involvement in the Changing Corporation.* New York: Basic Books, Inc.

Herzenberg, Stephen A., John A. Alic, and Howard Wial. 1998. *New Rules for a New Economy.* Ithaca, NY: Cornell University Press.

Higginson, Thomas, and Robert P. Waxler. 1990. "Unionism in the 1990s: Better Times Ahead?" *Industrial Management* 32, 6 (November/December): 10–13.

Holter, Darryl. 1992. "Expand the Concept of Membership." In *The Future of Labor*, 40. New York: Labor Research Association.

Hunter, Larry W. 1998. "Can Strategic Participation Be Institutionalized? Union Representation on American Corporate Boards." *Industrial and Labor Relations Review* 51, 4 (July): 557–78.

Hyman, Richard. 2001. *Understanding European Trade Unionism*. London: Sage Publications.

Jarley, Paul, and Cheryl L. Maranto. 1990. "Union Corporate Campaigns: An Assessment." *Industrial and Labor Relations Review* 43, 5 (July): 505–24.

Juravich, Tom, and Kate Bronfenbrenner. 1999. *Ravenswood: The Steelworkers' Victory and the Revival of American Labor*. Ithaca, NY: Cornell University Press.

Lazarovici, Laureen. 2000a. "Child Care and Its Limits: Innovative Union-Management Programs." *Perspectives on Work* 4, 1: 28–9.

2000b. "Negotiating the Work-Family Balance." *Perspectives on Work* 4, 1: 26–7.

Masters, Marick F. 1997. *Unions at the Crossroads*. Westport, CT: Quorum Books.

Mazur, Jay. 2000. "Labor's New Internationalism." *Foreign Affairs* 79, 1 (January/ February): 79–93.

Meyerson, Harold. 2001. "California's Progressive Mosaic." *The American Prospect* (June 18): 17–23.

Miller, Ellen S., and Micah L. Sifry. 2000. "Labor's Loss." *The American Prospect* (August 14): 8.

Moberg, David. 2000a. "Temp Slave Revolt: Contingent Workers of the World Unite." *In These Times* (July 10): 11–13.

2000b. "After Seattle." *In These Times* (January 10): 14–17.

Navarro, Vincente. 1992. "Build an Anti-Establishment Movement." In *The Future of Labor*, 57. New York: Labor Research Association.

Nichols, Don. 1988. "Unions Play Catch-Up to Today's Work Environment." *Management Review* 77, 2 (February): 28–9.

Overman, Stephanie. 1992. "Retraining Puts Workers Back on Track." *HR Magazine* 37, 8 (August): 40–3.

Perry, Charles R. 1987. *Union Corporate Campaigns*. Philadelphia: University of Pennsylvania.

Pierce, Jan. 1992. "Develop an Independent Agenda." In *The Future of Labor*, 46. New York: Labor Research Association.

Rabban, David M. 1989. "Professional Employees, Collective Bargaining, and the Law." *ILR Report* 26, 2 (Spring): 29–31.

Rodberg, Simon. 2001. "The CIO without the CIA." *The American Prospect* Summer: 27–8.

Rogers, Joel. 1992. "Support a New Political Party." In *The Future of Labor*, 63. New York: Labor Research Association.

Rose, Robert L. 1993. "Unions Hit Corporate-Campaign Trail." *Wall Street Journal* March 8: B1.

Rubenstein, Saul. 2001. "A Different Kind of Union: Balancing Co-Management and Representation." *Industrial and Labor Relations Review* 40, 2 (April): 163–203.

Shostak, Arthur B. 1991. *Robust Unionism: Innovations in the Labor Movement*. Ithaca, NY: ILR Press.

1992. "Promote Change from Within." In *The Future of Labor*, 69. New York: Labor Research Association.

1999. *Cyberunion: Empowering Labor Through Computer Technology.* Armonk, NY: M. E. Sharpe.

Smith, Frederick W. 1986. *Business Answers to the Labor Question 1900–1920.* New York: Garland Publishing Inc.

Stabile, Donald R. 1993. *Activist Unionism: The Institutional Economics of Solomon Barkin.* Armonk, NY: M. E. Sharpe.

Stepp, John R. 1988. "Labor-Management Cooperation: A Framework for Economic Development." *Economic Development Review* 6, 1 (Winter): 36–9.

Strauss, George. 1991. "Union Democracy." In *The State of the Unions*, George Strauss, Daniel G. Gallagher, and Jack Fiorito, eds., 201–36. Madison, WI: Industrial Relations Research Association.

Summers, Clyde. 1990. "Unions Without Majority – A Black Hole?" *Chicago-Kent Law Review* 66, 3: 531–48.

Tomsho, Robert. 1993. "Union 'Salts' Infiltrate Construction Industry." *Wall Street Journal* (November 18): B1, B8.

Verespej, Michael A. 1991. "The Illusion of Cooperation." *Industry Week* 240, 16 (August 19): 12–22.

Voice@Work. 2000. "Focus: Community Involvement." *Now* (February).

2001a. "Innovative Community Effort Helps Seattle Hospital Workers Win." *Now* (February).

2001b. "Seven Days in June." *Now* (June 4).

2001c. "Seven Days in June." *Now* (June 11).

2001d. "Seven Days in June." *Now* (June 12).

2001e. "Seven Days in June." *Now* (June 13).

2001f. "Seven Days in June." *Now* (June 18).

Webb, Sidney, and Beatrice Webb. 1911. *Industrial Democracy.* London: Longmans Green & Co.

Wheeler, Hoyt N. 1985. *Industrial Conflict: An Integrative Theory.* Columbia: University of South Carolina Press.

Wial, Howard. 1993. "The Emerging Organizational Structure of Unionism in Low-Wage Services." *Rutgers Law Review* 45, 4 (Summer): 671–738.

Undated. *New Bargaining Structures for New Forms of Business Organization.* Unpublished manuscript. U.S. Department of Labor.

Interviews

Hurt, Frank. 1997. International President, Bakery, Confectionery, Tobacco Workers and Grain Millers International Union. Washington.

Luddy, Bill. 1997. Administrative Assistant to the President, United Brotherhood of Carpenters and Joiners. Washington.

Mills, Nancy. 1997. Acting Director, Center for Workplace Democracy, AFL-CIO. Washington.

Murray, Roy. 1999. Director, Collective Bargaining Services Department, United Steelworkers of America. Pittsburgh.

Nichols, M. E. 1997. Vice President, Communication Workers of America. Washington.

Welsh, Bob. 1997. Executive Assistant to the President and Chief of Staff, AFL-CIO. Washington.

Sweeney, John J. 2001. President, AFL-CIO. Washington.

Chapter 4 – The Old Reformist Unionism: The Noble Order of the Knights of Labor

Appelbaum, Eileen, and Rosemary Batt. 1994. *The New American Workplace.* Ithaca, NY: ILR Press.

Cappelli, Peter; Laurie Bassi, Harry Katz, David Knoke, Paul Osterman, and Michael Useem. 1997. *Change at Work.* New York: Oxford University Press.

Commission on the Future of Labor-Management Relations. 1994. *Fact Finding Report.* Washington: U.S. Department of Labor, U.S. Department of Commerce.

Commons, John R. 1968. *Legal Foundations of Capitalism.* Madison: University of Wisconsin Press.

Commons, John R., David J. Saposs, Helen L. Sumner, E. B. Mittelman, H. E. Hoagland, John B. Andrews, and Selig Perlman. 1966 (originally published 1918). *History of Labor in the United States.* Vol. II. New York: Augustus M. Kelley.

Edwards, Richard. 1986. "Unions in Crisis and Beyond: Introduction." In *Unions in Crisis and Beyond*, Richard Edwards, Paolo Garonna, and Franz Todtling, eds., 1–13. Dover, MA: Auburn House Publishing Company.

Ely, Richard T. 1905 (originally published 1889). *The Labor Movement in America.* New York: Macmillan Company.

Falzone, Vincent J. 1978. *Terence V. Powderly: Middle Class Reformer.* Washington, DC: University Press of America.

Fink, Leon. 1983. *Workingmen's Democracy: The Knights of Labor and American Politics.* Urbana: University of Illinois Press.

Foner, Philip S. 1955. *History of the Labor Movement in the United States Volume II: From the Founding of the American Federation of Labor to the Emergence of American Imperialism.* 2nd ed. New York: International Publishers.

Freeman, Richard B. 1988. "Contraction and Expansion: The Divergence of Private and Public Sector Unionism in the United States." *Journal of Economic Perspectives* 2 (Spring): 63–88.

Goldfield, Michael. 1987. *The Decline of Organized Labor in the United States.* Chicago: University of Chicago Press.

Grob, Gerald N. 1976 (originally published 1961). *Workers and Utopia: A Study of Ideological Conflict in the American Labor Movement 1865–1900.* New York: Quadrangle.

Hoxie, Robert Franklin. 1921. *Trade Unionism in the United States.* New York: D. Appleton and Company.

Kealey, Gregory S., and Bryan D. Palmer. 1982. *Dreaming of What Might Be: The Knights of Labor in Ontario, 1880–1900.* London: Cambridge University Press.

Klaas, Brian S., and Joseph C. Ullman. 1995. "Sticky Wages Revisited: Organizational Responses to a Declining Market Wage." *Academy of Management Review* 20: 281–310.

Leonard, J. S. 1989. "The Changing Face of Employees and Employment Regulation." *California Management Review* 31, 2 (Winter): 29–38.

Marx, Karl, and Friedrich Engels. 1959 (originally published in 1848). "Manifesto of the Communist Party." In *Marx and Engels: Basic Writings on Politics and Philosophy*, Lewis S. Feuer, ed. Garden City, NY: Anchor Books.

McClendon, John A., Hoyt N. Wheeler, and Roger D. Weikle. 1998. "The Individual Decision to Unionize." *Labor Studies Journal* 23, 3 (Fall): 34–54.

McLaurin, Melton Alonzo. 1978. *The Knights of Labor in the South.* Westport, CT: Greenwood Press.

McNeil, George E. 1892. *The Labor Movement: The Problem of Today.* New York: The M. W. Hazen Co.

Montgomery, David. 1980. "To Study the People: The American Working Class." *Labor History* 21, 4: 485–512.

 1987. *The Fall of the House of Labor: The Workplace, the State, and American Labor Activism, 1865–1925.* Cambridge, U.K.: Cambridge University Press.

Osterman, Paul. 1988. *Employment Futures.* New York: Oxford University Press.

Powderly, Terence V. 1940. *The Path I Trod.* New York: Columbia University Press.

 1967 (originally published 1889). *Thirty Years of Labor 1859–1889.* New York: Augustus M. Kelley.

Troy, Leo. 1990. "Is the U. S. Unique in the Decline of Private Sector Unionism?" *Journal of Labor Research* XI, 2 (Spring): 111–43.

Ware, Norman J. 1959 (originally published 1929). *The Labor Movement in the United States 1860–1895 A Study in Democracy.* Gloucester, MA: Peter Smith.

Interview

Noonan, Rosalyn. 1994. Workers' Adviser, NZCTU National Exective, New Zealand. Geneva.

Statute

National Labor Relations Act, Sec. 2 (11).

Chapter 5 – The New Reformist Unionism: CAFE

Beacham, Frank. 1995. "Suppressing History." *Creative Loafing* February 18: 6.

Carolina Alliance for Fair Employment. 1986. "CAFE Legislative Platform." *Economic Justice Journal* 71 (December): 3.

 1994. *Basic Guide to Workers' Rights in South Carolina.*

 1997. "CAFE Wins Victory in Darlington." *Special Update for CAFE Donors*: 1.

 1998a. "Surprise, Surprise . . ." *Economic Justice Journal* 76 (May): 2.

 1998b. "Justice for Temp Workers: CAFE Helps Launch A National Organizing Campaign." *Economic Justice Journal* 76 (May): 1.

 Undated. "Fighting for Social and Economic Justice in South Carolina."

"PRRAC Grantees' Advocacy Report." 1997. *Poverty & Race* 6, 3 (May/June): 6.

Sanders, Arlene. 1986. "Worker Rights in the Heart of Dixie." *Southern Exposure* XIV, 5–6: 83–5.

Taylor, Charles. 1990. "Worker Organizing in South Carolina: A Community-Based Approach." In *Communities in Economic Crisis: Appalachia and the South*, John Gaventa, Barbara Ellen Smith, and Alex Willingham, eds., 108–19. Philadelphia: Temple University Press.

———. 1997. "Union, Community Group Take on Citadel While Fighting to Save Victory at Hilton Head." *Labor Notes* (April): 10.

Newspaper Articles

"S. C. ruling favors temp employers." 1999. *The State* (October 26): B6.

"Trouble in Paradise." 1996. *Point* 7, 78 (May): 12, 19.

Blakeney, Barney. 1997. "NLRB In Landmark Decision Impact Unionization of Citadel Workers." *The Chronicle* (May 7): 1.

Faris, Jeannie. 1990. "Western Carolina Sewer Authority Sued." *Greenville News* (February 14): 3-C.

Kelly, Lindsey. 1985. "Job Rights Campaign Informs Workers." *The Spartanburg Herald-Journal* (May 9): 1-C.

Mathews, Steve. 1983. "Chamber ready to tackle rise in union activity." *The Greenville News and Greenville Piedmont* (March 5): 1.

Nye, Doug. 1998. "S. C. ETV to air Uprising of '34." *The State* (May 8): A-1.

Ocasio, Linda. 1990. "Lawyer explains job rights at employment workshop." *Spartanburg Herald* (April 18): 1-A.

Steinle, Gregg. 1981. "Pickets object to Chamber forum on labor." *Greenville Piedmont* (November 17): C-1.

Stokes, Laura P. 1998. "Man arrested during protest." *Easley Progress* (May 13): 7-A.

Taylor, Charles. 1982. "Polygraphs Unreliable." *Greenville Piedmont* (December 13): 1.

Statute

National Labor Relations Act, Sec. 7.

Interviews

Taylor, Charles. 1999. State Coordinator, CAFE. Greenville, South Carolina.

Henry, Steven. 2000. Attorney. Greenville, South Carolina.

Chapter 6 – A New Version of an Old Reformist Strategy: Employee Ownership

Aahlstrom, Per. 2000. Communication to Capital Ownership Group Web site. http://cog.kent.edu/mgo.html (September 8).

Balinky, Alexander. 1970. *Marx's Economics*. Lexington, MA: D. C. Heath and Company.

Barbash, Jack. 1984. *The Elements of Industrial Relations*. Madison: University of Wisconsin Press.

Blasi, Joseph Raphael, and Douglas Lynn Kruse. 1991. *The New Owners.* New York: Harper Business.

Bureau of National Affairs. 1998. "A BNA Special Report: 1999 Employer Bargaining Objectives." *Labor Relations Week* 12, 50: 17.

———. 1999. "Union Vote Clears Way for Sale of Champion International Paper Mills." *Labor Relations Week* 13, 19: 507–8.

———. 2000. "Committee Approves Boehner's Bill To Expand Workplace Stock Option Plans." *Human Resources Report* 18, 25: 680–1.

Carberry, Edward J. 1996. *Corporate Governance in Employee-Ownership Companies.* Oakland, CA: National Center for Employee Ownership.

———. 1998. "ESOPs and Corporate Governance." In *The ESOP Reader*, 141–6. Oakland, CA: National Center for Employee Ownership.

Clem, Steve. 2000. Communication to Capital Ownership Group Web site. http://cog.kent.edu/mgo.html (September 19).

Durso, Gianna, and Raul Rothblatt. 1991. "Stock Ownership Plans Abroad." In *Understanding Employee Ownership*, Corey Rosen and Karen M. Young, eds., 169–96. Ithaca, NY: ILR Press.

Engels, Freidrich. 1894. "Engels to Heinz Starkenburg." In *Basic Writings on Politics and Philosophy, Karl Marx and Friedrich Engels*, Lewis S. Feuer, ed., 410–12. Garden City, NY: Anchor Books.

European Industrial Relations Review. 2001. 326 (March): 21–4.

Freeman, Richard B., and James Medoff. 1984. *What Do Unions Do?* New York: Basic Books.

Galor, Zvi. 2000. Communication to ILO Internet Discussion Group on the Future of Unions.

Gompers, Samuel. 1919. *Labor and the Common Welfare.* New York: E. P. Dutton and Company.

Hester, Stephen L. 1988. "Employee Ownership: A Union View." In *Labor Law and Business Change*, Samuel Estreicher and Daniel G. Collins, eds., 267–81. New York: Quorum Books.

Householder, Bruce, and Sharon Dolmajer. 1999. *The Worker-Ownership Institute Report.* Pittsburgh, PA.

Ivancic, Cathy. Undated. "What Happens When Employees Vote Their Shares?" *The Steelworkers' Guide to Employee Ownership.* Sec. 1: 29–30.

Kurland, Norman G., and Dawn K. Brohawn. 1999/2000. "Louis Kelso's Economic Vision for the 21st Century." *Owners at Work.* Ohio Employee Ownership Center, XI, 2 (Winter): 5–7.

Kuwahara, Yasuo. 2000. "The Future of the Labor Movement in Japan: Experiments and Possibilities." *Proceedings of the 12th World Congress, International Industrial Relations Association, Tokyo*, May 29–June 2, 3: 74–84.

Mackin, Christopher, and Fred Freundlich. 1995. "Representative Structures in Employee-Owned Firms." *Journal of Employee Ownership Law and Finance* 7, 2 (Spring): 1–25.

McLaurin, Melton Alonzo. 1978. *The Knights of Labor in the South.* Westport, CT: Greenwood Press.

National Center for Employee Ownership. 1998. "Introduction and Summary of Findings." In *Employee Ownership and Corporate Performance*, 7–12.

1999. "Why People Want Stock as Pay." *Employee Ownership Report* XIX, 4 (July/August): 15.

2000a. "Congress Exempts Stock Options From Overtime Rules." *Employee Ownership Report* XX, 4 (July/August): 1, 12.

2000b. "Companies." *Employee Ownership Report* XX, 3 (May/June): 13.

2000c. "Good Ideas from Southwest Airlines." *Employee Ownership Report* XX, 3 (May/June): 12.

2001. "America's Largest Majority Owned Companies." *Employee Ownership Report* XXI, 4 (July/August): 4–5.

RIA. 1996. *Pension and Profit Sharing 2nd* 6: 97, 501–97.

1998. *Pension and Profit Sharing 2nd* 5: 71, 742.

Rosen, Corey. 1991. "Employee Ownership: Performance, Prospects and Promise." In *Understanding Employee Ownership*, Corey Rosen and Karen M. Young, eds., 1–42. Ithaca, NY: ILR Press.

1998. "An Overview of Employee Ownership." In *The ESOP Reader*, 3–24. Oakland, CA: National Center for Employee Ownership.

Schwab, Stewart J., and Randall Thomas. 1997. "Labor Unions as Shareholders: Careful Monitors or Wildcat Strikers?" Paper prepared for New York University 50th Annual Conference on Labor.

Sinha, Pravin. 2000. Communication to ILO Internet Discussion Group on the Future of Unions.

Stern, Robert N., William Foote Whyte, Tove Hammer, and Christopher B. Meek. 1983. "The Union and the Transition to Employee Ownership." In *Worker Participation and Ownership*, William Foote Whyte, Tove Helland Hammer, Christopher B. Meek, Reed Nelson, and Robert N. Stern, eds., 81–117. Ithaca, NY: ILR Press.

United Steelworkers of America. Undated a. "Starting an Employee Owned Business." In *The Steelworkers' Guide to Employee Ownership*, Sec. 1: 25–8.

Undated b. "United Steelworkers of America, 24th Constitutional Convention Policy Resolution on ESOPs August, 1988." In *The Steelworkers' Guide to Employee Ownership*, Sec. 1: 32.

Undated c. "Case Studies." In *The Steelworkers' Guide to Employee Ownership*, Sec. 2: 9–36.

Undated d. "Union Handbook on Employee Ownership" (from *The Union Handbook*, National Center for Employee Ownership). In *The Steelworkers' Guide to Employee Ownership*, Sec. 2: 1–53.

Wheeler, Hoyt N., and Thomas A. Kochan. 1977. "Unions and Public Sector Supervisors: The Case of the Fire Fighters." *Monthly Labor Review* 100, 12, (December): 44–8.

Williams, Lynn. 2000. "Employee Ownership and the Labor Movement." *Owners at Work* XII, 1 (Summer): 15–18.

Statutes

29 U.S.C. Secs. 1001–1461.

Employee Retirement Income Security Act of 1974, Secs. 403 (a), 404.

Internal Revenue Code, Sec. 409 (e) (2) (3).

Interviews

Blackwell, Ron. 1997. Director of Corporate Affairs, AFL-CIO. Washington.
Davis, Richard. 1999. Vice President for Administration, United Steelworkers of America. Pittsburgh.

Chapter 7 – Social Democratic Unionism in Action:
Strategies of European Trade Unions

Adams, Roy J. 1995. *Industrial Relations Under Liberal Democracy.* Columbia: University of South Carolina Press.
Addison, John T. 1999. "European Works Councils and Other European Union Initiatives." Paper presented at New York University Conference, Human Resource Management in a World Without Borders. Bagshot, Surrey, U.K., June 15–16.
Amalgamated Engineering and Electrical Union. 1993. *Annual Report & Accounts 1993.* London.
Blaschke, Sabine, Andrea Kirschner, and Franz Traxler. 2000. "Austrian trade unions: between continuity and modernization." In *Trade Unions in Europe*, Jeremy Waddington and Reiner Hoffmann, eds., 81–103. Brussels: ETUI.
Boulin, Jean-Yves. 2000. "Trade unions in France: how to challenge the trend towards de-unionisation?" In *Trade Unions in Europe*, Jeremy Waddington and Reiner Hoffmann, eds., 215–48. Brussels: ETUI.
Bratt, Christian. 1996. *Labour Relations in 18 Countries.* Swedish Employers' Confederation. Stockholm.
Bridgford, Jeff, and John Stirling. 1994. *Employee Relations in Europe.* Oxford: Blackwell Business.
Campbell, Duncan. 1989. "Multinational Labor Relations in the European Community." *ILR Report* 27, 1 (Fall): 7–14.
European Foundation for the Improvement of Living and Working Conditions. 2001. "Industrial relations in Europe in 2000 – a summary." www.eiro.eurofound.ie/2000/review/summary.html.
European Industrial Relations Review. 1994a. Vol. 243 (April): 8.
    1994b. Vol. 246 (July): 24–6.
    1994c. Vol. 251 (December): 7.
    1995a. Vol. 252 (January): 9.
    1995b. Vol. 254 (March): 13.
    1995c. Vol. 257 (June): 11.
    1996. Vol. 264 (January): 11.
    1997a. Vol. 276 (January): 24.
    1997b. Vol. 279 (April): 4.
    1997c. Vol. 280 (May): 4.
    1997d. Vol. 282 (July): 3.
    1997e. Vol. 285 (October): 2.
    1997f. Vol. 286 (November): 3.
    1997g. Vol. 287 (December): 7.
    1998a. Vol. 291 (April): 3.

1998b. Vol. 294 (July): 34–6.

1998c. Vol. 297 (October): 2.

1998d. Vol. 297 (October): 7.

1998e. Vol. 297 (October): 21–2.

1998f. Vol. 299 (December): 4.

1999a. Vol. 300 (January): 3.

1999b. Vol. 300 (January): 20–1.

1999c. Vol. 301 (February): 4.

1999d. Vol. 301 (February): 5.

1999e. Vol. 302 (March): 3.

1999f. Vol. 302 (March): 22–4.

1999g. Vol. 303 (April): 3–4.

1999h. Vol. 304 (May): 3.

1999i. Vol. 305 (June): 3.

1999j. Vol. 306 (July): 3.

1999k. Vol. 306 (July): 10.

1999l. Vol. 307 (August): 2–3.

1999m. Vol. 307 (August): 3.

2000a. Vol. 316 (May): 20–2.

2000b. Vol. 318 (July): 3.

2000c. Vol. 319 (August): 1.

2000d. Vol. 320 (September): 5.

2000e. Vol. 321 (October): 3.

2001a. Vol. 326 (March): 21–4.

2001b. Vol. 327 (April): 15–18.

European Trade Union Institute. 1992. *The Trade Union Movement in the Netherlands*. Brussels.

Furstenberg, Friedrich. 1998. "Employment relations in Germany." In *International and Comparative Employment Relations*. 3rd ed. Greg J. Bamber and Russell D. Lansbury, eds., 201–23. St. Leonards, Australia: Allen & Unwin.

Goodman, John, Mick Marchington, John Berridge, Ed Snape, and Greg J. Bamber. 1998. "Employment relations in Britain." In *International and Comparative Employment Relations*. 3rd ed. Greg J. Bamber and Russell D. Lansbury, eds., 34–62. St. Leonards, Australia: Allen & Unwin.

Guardian Weekly. 2001. "Blair clashes with unions over services." (July 5–11): 10.

Hammarstrom, Olle, and Tommy Nilsson. 1998. "Employment Relations in Sweden." In *International and Comparative Employment Relations*. 3rd ed. Greg J. Bamber and Russell D. Lansbury, eds., 224–48. St. Leonards, Australia: Allen & Unwin.

Hoffmann, Jurgen. 2000. "Industrial relations and trade unions in Germany: the pressure of modernization and globalisation." In *Trade Unions in Europe*, Jeremy Waddington and Reiner Hoffmann, eds., 249–75. Brussels: ETUI.

Hoffmann, Reiner. 2000. "European trade union structures and the prospects for labour relations in Europe." In *Trade Unions in Europe*, Jeremy Waddington and Reiner Hoffmann, eds., 627–53. Brussels: ETUI.

Hoxie, Robert. 1921. *Trade Unionism in the United States*. New York: D. Appleton and Co.

Hyman, Richard. 2001. *Understanding European Trade Unionism*. London: Sage Publications.

Kjelberg, Anders. 2000. "The multitude of challenges facing Swedish trade unions." In *Trade Unions in Europe*, Jeremy Waddington and Reiner Hoffmann, eds., 529–73. Brussels: ETUI.

Lecher, Wolfgang, and Reinhard Naumann. 1994. "The Current State of Trade Unions in The EU Member States." In *Trade Unions in the European Union: A Handbook*, Wolfgang Lecher, ed., 3–126. London: Lawrence & Wishart, Ltd.

Lind, Jens. 2000. "Still the century of trade unionism." In *Trade Unions in Europe*, Jeremy Waddington and Reiner Hoffmann, eds., 143–82. Brussels: ETUI.

Lobo, Faustino Miguelez. 2000. "The modernisation of trade unions in Spain." In *Trade Unions in Europe*, Jeremy Waddington and Reiner Hoffmann, eds., 499–527. Brussels: ETUI.

Mielke, Siegfried, Peter Rutters, and Kurt P. Tudyka. 1994. "Trade Union Organisation and Employee Representation." In *Trade Unions in the European Union: A Handbook*, Wolfgang Lecher, ed., 129–233. London: Lawrence & Wishart, Ltd.

Ministry of Labour. 1990. *Labour Relations in Finland*. Helsinki.

Paauwe, J., J. A. de Jong, and J. J. van Dijk. 1990. "Dutch Trade Unions in Transition: An Organizational Development Approach." Unpublished manuscript.

Pisani, Elena, and Cecilia Brighi. 2000. "The Future of the Labor Movement in Italy." *Proceedings, 12th World Congress of the International Industrial Relations Association, Tokyo*, May 29–June 2, 3: 85–93.

Rath, Fritz. 1994. "The Co-ordinates of Trade Union Policy in Europe." In *Trade Unions In the European Union: A Handbook*, Wolfgang Lecher, ed., 237–74. London: Lawrence & Wishart.

Regini, Marino, and Ida Regalia. 2000. "The prospects for Italian trade unions in a phase of concertation." In *Trade Unions in Europe*, Jeremy Waddington and Reiner Hoffmann, eds., 365–92. Brussels: ETUI.

Rojot, Jacques. 1978. *International Collective Bargaining: An Analysis and Case Study for Europe*. Deventer, Netherlands: Kluwer.

Rojot, Jacques, and Alice Bremond. 1998. "European Collective Bargaining, New Prospects or Much Ado About Nothing?" Unpublished manuscript. Paris: University of Paris I – Sorbonne.

The Guardian. "Members offered choice through market forces." May 24, 1994: 19.

Trades Union Congress (United Kingdom). 1991. "Full Time Rights For Part-Time Workers."

2000. "The TUC and Skills and Learning." May 22. www.ilo.org.uk.

Undated. "Action for Part-Time Workers."

Valkenburg, Ben, and Harry Coenen. 2000. "Changing trade unionism in the Netherlands: A Critical Analysis." In *Trade Unions in Europe*, Jeremy Waddington and Reiner Hoffmann, eds., 393–415. Brussels: ETUI.

Valkonen, Marjaana. 1989. *The Central Organization of Finnish Trade Unions 1907–87*. Helsinki: SAK.

Van Gyes, Guy, Hans De Witte, and Peter van der Hallen. 2000. "Belgian trade unions in the 1990s: does strong today mean strong tomorrow?" In *Trade Unions in Europe*, Jeremy Waddington and Reiner Hoffmann, eds., 105–41. Brussels: ETUI.

Visser, Jelle. 1998. "The Netherlands: The Return of Responsive Corporatism." In *Changing Industrial Relations in Europe*, 2nd ed., Anthony Ferner and Richard Hyman, eds., 283–314. Oxford, U.K.: Blackwell.

Waddington, Jeremy. 2000. "United Kingdom. Recovering from the neo-liberal assault?" In *Trade Unions in Europe*, Jeremy Waddington and Reiner Hoffmann, eds., 575–626. Brussels: ETUI.

Waddington, Jeremy, and Reiner Hoffmann. 2000. "Trade unions in Europe: reform, organization and structuring." In *Trade Unions in Europe*, Jeremy Waddington and Reiner Hoffmann, eds., 27–79. Brussels: ETUI.

Statutes

Consolidated Version of the Treaty on European Union. Title I, Art. 2. http://europa.eu.int.

Consolidated Version of the Treaty on European Union. Title XI, Art. 139. http:/europa.eu.int.

Interviews

Adamy, Wilhelm. 1994. International Affairs, DGB (Germany). Geneva.

Betelu, Amaia. 1994. International Representative, ELA (Basque Region, Spain). Geneva.

Calamatta, Jack. 1994. Deputy General Secretary, General Workers' Union (Malta). Geneva.

Etty, Tom. 1994. International Department, FNV (Netherlands). Geneva.

Evans, John. 1994. General Secretary, Trade Union Advisory Council, OECD. Paris.

Foden, David. 1994. Research Officer, European Trade Union Institute, and Peter Coldrick, General Secretary, European Trade Union Confederation. Brussels.

Hurt, Frank. 1997. International President, Bakery, Confectionery, Tobacco Workers and Grain Millers International Union. Washington.

Hemmer, Mona. 1994. International Secretary, AKAVA (Finland). Geneva.

Laird, Gavin. 1994. General Secretary, AEEU (United Kingdom). London.

Pizzaferri, Rene. 1994. International Officer, CGT-L (Luxembourg). Geneva.

Smith, Mike. 1994. Head of Press and Information, Trades Union Congress (United Kingdom). London.

van den Toren, Jan Peter. 1994. Research Officer, CNV (Netherlands). Utrecht.

Wyckmans, Ferre. 1994. Adjunct General Secretary, LBC-NVK (Belgium). Antwerp.

Zellhoefer, Jerry. 1994. European Representative, AFL-CIO. Paris.

Chapter 8 – A New Twist and TURN on Social Democratic Unionism: Unions and Regional Economic Development

AFL-CIO Human Resources Development Institute. Undated. *Economic Development: A Union Guide to the High Road.*

Becker, Eric, and Patrick McVeigh. 2001. "Social Funds in the United States: Their History, Financial Performance, and Social Impacts." In *Working Capital: The*

Power of Labor's Pensions, Archon Fung, Tessa Hebb, and Joel Rogers, eds., 44–66. Ithaca, NY: Cornell University Press.

Burns, Malcolm. 1998. *Trade Unions and Local Economic Development. Final Report for the Lothian Trade Union & Community Resource Centre, Edinburgh City Council, Edinburgh & Lothians Defence Diversification Initiative Trade Union Liason Group.*

Calabrese, Michael. 2001. "Building on Success: Labor-Friendly Investment Vehicles and the Power of Private Equity." In *Working Capital: The Power of Labor's Pensions*, Arcon Fung, Tessa Hebb, and Joel Rogers, eds., 93–127. Ithaca, NY: Cornell University Press.

Croft, Thomas, Joseph Bute, Jr., and Rich Feldman. 1999. *The Regional Labor Investment Fund: The Critical Nexus for a National Investment Strategy.* http://uswa.org/heartland/9region.htm.

Falconer, Kirk. 1998. "Labor's Capital in Canada." *The Heartland Journal* Fall: 8–9.

Ferman, Louis A., Michele Hoyman, and Joel Cutcher-Gershenfeld. 1990. "Joint Union-Management Training Programs: A Synthesis in the Evolution of Jointism and Training." In *New Developments in Worker Training: A Legacy for the 1990s*, Louis A. Ferman, Michele Hoyman, Joel Cutcher-Gershenfeld, and Ernest J. Savoie, eds., 157–89. Madison, WI: Industrial Relations Research Association.

Fung, Archon, Tessa Hebb, and Joel Rogers. 2001. *Working Capital: The Power of Labor's Pensions.* Ithaca, NY: Cornell University Press.

Gerard, Leo W. 2000. "Foreword." In *Working Capital: The Power of Labor's Pensions*, Archon Fung, Tessa Hebb, and Joel Rogers, eds., vii–viii. Ithaca, NY: Cornell University Press.

Hebb, Tessa. 2001. "Introduction: The Challenge of Labor's Capital Strategy." In *Working Capital: The Power of Labor's Pensions*, Archon Fung, Tessa Hebb, and Joel Rogers, eds., 1–12. Ithaca, NY: Cornell University Press.

Hebb, Tessa, and David Mackenzie. 2001. "Canadian Labour-Sponsored Investment Funds: A Model for U. S. Economically Targeted Investments." In *Working Capital: The Power of Labor's Pensions*, Archon Fung, Tessa Hebb, and Joel Rogers, eds., 128–57. Ithaca, NY: Cornell University Press.

O'Connor, Marleen. 2001. "Labor's Role in the Shareholder Revolution." In *Working Capital: The Power of Labor's Pensions*, Archon Fung, Tessa Hebb, and Joel Rogers, eds., 67–92. Ithaca, NY: Cornell University Press.

Osterman, Paul. 1990. "Elements of a National Training Policy." In *New Developments in Worker Training: A Legacy for the 1990s*, Louis A. Ferman, Michele Hoyman, Joel Cutcher-Gershenfeld, and Ernest J. Savoie, eds., 257–81. Madison, WI: Industrial Relations Research Association.

Owners at Work. 1999. "Crocus Fund Blossoms in Manitoba." XI, 1 (Summer): 17–18.

Sleigh, Stephen R. 2001. "From Workplace to Corporate Governance: Emerging IR Issues in the Twenty-First Century." *Perspectives on Work* 5, 2: 29–31.

Streeck, Wolfgang, 1992. "Training and the New Industrial Relations: A Strategic Role for Unions?" In *The Future of Labour Movements*, Marino Regini, ed., 250–69. Thousand Oaks, CA: SAGE.

The Heartland Journal. 1998. Fall.

The Heartland Journal, Special Edition. 2000. Fall.

Interviews

Hurt, Frank. 1997. President, Bakery, Confectionery, Tobacco Workers and Grain Millers International Union. Washington.

Luddy, Bill. 1997. Administrative Assistant to the President, United Brotherhood of Carpenters and Joiners. Washington.

Mitchell, Joe. 1998. Executive Secretary, TURN. London.

Siegfried, Kim. 1999. Special Assistant to the Secretary Treasurer, United Steelworkers of America. Pittsburgh.

Chapter 9 – A Labor Movement for the Twenty-First Century

Acuff, Stewart. 1999. "Expanded Roles for the Central Labor Council: The View from Atlanta." In *Which Direction for Organized Labor?* Bruce Nissen, ed., 133–42. Detroit, MI: Wayne State University Press.

Amber, Michelle. 2000. "Turnout by Union Members Contributed to Gore Majority in a Number of States." *Labor Relations Week* 14, 5: 1290–2.

Barbash, Jack. 1967. *American Unions: Structure, Government and Politics.* New York: Random House.

Bureau of National Affairs. 2000. "Win Rate in NLRB Elections Increased in First Half of 2000." *Labor Relations Week* 14, 47: 1353.

2001a. "Number of Elections Down in 2000, While Unions' Win Rate Edged Up." *Labor Relations Week* 15, 25: 760.

2001b. "Survey Finds Americans' View of Unions Improving Across Age, Gender, Race Groups." *Labor Relations Week* 15, 9: 265.

2001c. "Federation Focuses on Program to Link Politics to Organizing Efforts." *Labor Relations Week* 15, 32: 972–3.

Ewing, David W. 1989. *Justice on the Job.* Boston: Harvard Business School Press.

Foner, Philip S. 1965. *The Industrial Workers of the World 1905–1917.* New York: International Publishers.

Herzernberg, Stephen A., John A. Alic, and Howard Wial. 1998. *New Rules for a New Economy.* Ithaca, NY: Cornell University Press.

Hoxie, Robert. 1921. *Trade Unionism in the United States.* New York: D. Appleton and Co.

Human Rights Watch. 2000. *Unfair Advantage: Workers' Freedom of Association in the United States under International Human Rights Standards.* New York: Human Rights Watch.

Hyman, Richard. 2001. *Understanding European Trade Unionism.* London: Sage Publications.

Jacobs, David C. 1999. *Business Lobbies and the Power Structure in America.* Westport, CT: Quorum Books.

Kelly, John. 1998. *Rethinking Industrial Relations.* London: Routledge.

Leeson, R. A. 1979. *Traveling Brothers.* London: George Unwin & Allen.

Meyerson, Harold. 2001. "California's Progressive Mosaic." *The American Prospect* June 18: 17–23.

O'Connor, Marleen. 2001. "Labor's Role in the Shareholder Revolution." In *Working Capital: The Power of Labor's Pensions,* Archon Fung, Tessa Hebb, and Joel Rogers, eds. 67–92. Ithaca, NY: Cornell University Press.

Ogle, George, and Hoyt N. Wheeler. 2001. "Collective Bargaining as a Human Right." *Proceedings, 53rd Annual Meeting, Industrial Relations Research Association.* (forthcoming).

Perlman, Selig. 1949 (originally published in 1928). *A Theory of the Labor Movement.* New York: Augustus M. Kelley.

Rubenstein, Saul A. 2001. "A Different Kind of Union: Balancing Co-Management and Representation." *Industrial and Labor Relations Review* 40, 2 (April): 163–203.

Sexton, Patricia Cayo. 1991. *The War on Labor and the Left.* Boulder, CO: Westview Press.

Silvers, Damon, William Patterson, and J. W. Mason. 2001. "Challenging Wall Street's Conventional Wisdom: Defining a Worker-Owner View of Value." In *Working Capital: The Power of Labor's Pensions*, Archon Fung, Tessa Hebb, and Joel Rogers, eds., 203–22. Ithaca, NY: Cornell University Press.

Struik, Dirk J., ed. 1964. *Economic and Philosophic Manuscripts of 1844 by Karl Marx.* New York: International Publishers.

Thurow, Lester C. 1996. *The Future of Capitalism.* New York: Penguin Books.

Voice@Work. 2001. "Seven Days in June." (June 15, 18, and 20).

Werhane, Patricia H. 1985. *Persons, Rights and Corporations.* Englewood Cliffs, NJ: Prentice-Hall, Inc.

Wheeler, Hoyt N. 1994a. "Employee Rights as Human Rights." *Bulletin of Comparative Labour Relations* 28: 9–18.

  1994b. "Testimony before Commission on the Future of Worker Management Relations." Atlanta, GA (January 11).

Zanglein, Jayne Elizabeth. 2001. "Overcoming Institutional Barriers on the Economically Targeted Investment Superhighway." In *Working Capital: The Power of Labor's Pensions*, Archon Fung, Tessa Hebb, and Joel Rogers, eds., 181–201. Ithaca, NY: Cornell University Press.

Interviews

Hurt, Frank. 1997. International President, Bakery, Confectionery, Tobacco Workers and Grain Millers International Union. Washington.

Luddy, Bill. 1997. Administrative Assistant to the President, United Brotherhood of Carpenters and Joiners. Washington.

Sweeney, John J. 2001. President, AFL-CIO. Washington.

Index

clusters, 154
Cobble, Sue, 50–1
collective bargaining, 51
    associate membership and, 58, 76–8
    board decisions and, 67–8
    collective action costs and, 193–5
    corporate governance and, 78–9, 127
    European trade unions and, 160–2
    Finland and, 148
    New Directions and, 67
    new economy strategies and, 209–11
    NLRA and, 73–4
    NLRB and, 52–3
    nonmajority representation and, 76, 78
    organizing and, 71–6
    Seven Days in June campaign, 61
    solidarity and, 190
    TUC and, 150
    Voice@Work and, 74
    white-collar unions and, 73–5
collective representation. *See* unions
Columbia University, 113
Committee on the Evolution of Work, 8–9
Committee on the Future, 9
Commons, John R., 88–9
Communication Workers of America (CWA), 73
community issues, 64, 111–12
Community Voices Heard, 64
Compagnie Generale des Eaux, 168
company unions, 5
Compassion House, 115
competition, 90
    globalization and, 25–7, 46–7
computers, 26
concerted action, 107–9
Confederate flag, 111
Confederation Francaise
    Democratique du Travail (CFDT), 156–7, 161
Congress of Industrial Organizations (CIO), 54
Construction Industry Labor-
    Management 1990s Committee, 81
consultation model, 153
"consultative influence," 128

contract work, 12
Contreras, Miguel, 62
Cooperationist Unionism, xv–xviii, 18, 21, 84, 145
    collective action costs and, 193
    Denmark and, 158–9
    enabling conditions and, 200
    European trade unions and, 150, 157–9
    Netherlands and, 158
    network groups and, 69–71
    strategy of, 65–8
    worker interests and, 192–3
    work role and, 188, 190
cooperatives, 121
corporate campaigns, 78–9
corporate governance, 126–31
"corporatist-style concertation," 146
costs, 12
    corporate campaigns and, 79
    globalization and, 26
    human resources model and, 33
    lean production model and, 33–6, 40–3
craft unionism, 50–1, 59, 83
Craver, Charles, 73
creative tension, 34
customer service, 26
cycle time, 42

Danone, 168
Daufuskie Island Resort, 106
Davis, Richard, 139
debt-financed corporations, 98
decertification elections, 2
Declaration of Fundamental Principles on Rights at Work, 218
deferred profit sharing, 121
Delors, Jacques, 162
Democracy, xiii–xiv, 201
Democratic Party, 3, 8
    CAFE and, 105
    future and, 207
    union, strategies and, 62
Denmark, 147, 155, 157–9
Department of Labor, 112–13, 119
    ERISA and, 125
    ESOPs and, 124–5

246 *Index*

market forces and, 27
production and, 34–5, 179–83
work conditions and, 31–3
temporary workers, 12, 28–9, 33
CAFE and, 104, 112–13
white-collar unions and, 75
Temp School, 112–13
Temp Testing Project, 112–13
Tennessee Industrial Renewal
Network, 64
Tharaldson Motels, 120
Thomas, Norman, 55
Thomas, Randall, 136–7
Trades Union Congress (TUC), 150,
152–3, 158
Trade Union Regional Network
(TURN), xviii, 146
collective action costs and, 195
description of, 172–4
economic development and, 172–4,
179, 184–6
education and, 178–9
enabling conditions and, 200
Europe and, 174–6
networks and, 183–4, 205
new economy strategies and, 209
solidarity and, 191
work role and, 188, 190, 192
Trade Union Shops, 154
trade union thermometers, 154, 169–
70
training. *See* education
transportation, 26
Treaty of Amsterdam, 163
Trist, Eric, 44
Troy, Leo, 4–6
TTC Inc., 120
TWA, 135, 140

UEAPME, 164
UNC Housekeepers, 64
unemployment compensation, 28
UNICE, 164–5, 167
Union Democracy in Action (Thomas
and Benson), 55
Union Guide (United Steelworkers of
America), 141
Union Learning Fund, The, 150

Union of Needletrades, Industrial and
Textile Employees (UNITE), 176,
219
Union Privilege Benefit Program, 77
unions, xiii
alliance structure for, 201–9
alternatives to, 14, 17, 36–7
associational, 56–8, 76–8, 83
autonomous work groups and, 36–7
Belgium and, 149
branch, 154
CAFE and, 103–17
clusters and, 154
collective bargaining and, 76–8,
193–5 (*see also* collective
bargaining)
company, 5
Cooperationist Unionism and, 65–71
corporate campaign and, 78–9
craft, 50–1, 59, 83
decline in, 2–5
dishonesty and, 54–5
education and, 80–1, 178–9 (*see also*
education)
employee ownership and, 123, 133–8
employer opposition and, 195–7
enabling conditions, 14–17, 188–91
ERISA and, 137
ESOPs and, 134–6, 138, 140–2
European strategies and, 145–6,
159–60, 169–71
Finland and, 148, 150, 155
Germany and, 149, 156
globalization and, 46–7
industrial, 53–4
international labor organizations
and, 81–3, 206–7
Italy and, 148–9
labor accord and, 5–6
Luxembourg and, 147–8
Malta and, 148
Militant Radical Unionism and, xv,
18, 20–1, 53–4, 145, 196
minority, 70–1
national, 204–5
Netherlands and, 153–5
networks and, 69–71, 183–4, 205
new economy strategies and, 209–11

real pay and, 27, 29
service sector and, 29–30
U.S., 27–8
Wagner Act, 5
waitresses, 51
Wales Cooperative Development
Centre, 173, 184
Wal-Mart, 106
Ware, Norman, 87, 89, 93
Washington Alliance of Technology
Workers (WashTech), 74–5
Webb, Beatrice, 9, 64
Webb, Sidney, 9, 64
Weirton Steel, 140
Welsh, Bob, 65
WEP Workers Organizing
Center/ACORN, 64
Which Side Are You On? Trying to Be
for Labor When It's Flat on Its
Back (Geoghegan), 8
white-collar unions, 57–8, 73–5, 83
Wial, Howard, 51–2
Wickens, Peter D., 35–6
Wildcat strikes, 20–1
Wilde, Oscar, 187

Williams, Lynn R., xiii–xix, 118, 208,
211
Wisconsin School, 87
Worker Organizing Committee, 64
Worker-Ownership Institute (WOI),
138–9
worker rights organizations, 63–5, 205.
See also unions
workers. *See* employees
Workers' Rights Project (WRP), 104,
107–8, 115
legal issues and, 113–14
politics and, 109–11
workforce diversity, 4, 12
Working Partnerships, 64
Workplace 2000 (Boyett and Conn), 26,
31, 33
Workplace Project, 64
World Bank, 122
World Trade Organization (WTO),
82
World War II, xiv
Wrongful Discharge Act, 110

Yokich, Stephen, 8